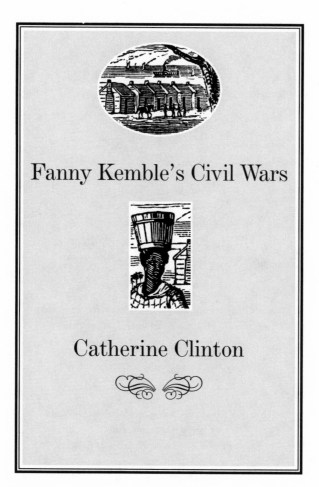

Fanny Kemble's Civil Wars

Catherine Clinton

SIMON & SCHUSTER

New York   London   Toronto   Sydney   Singapore

SIMON & SCHUSTER
Rockefeller Center
1230 Avenue of the Americas
New York, NY 10020

Simon & Schuster and colophon are registered trademarks
of Simon & Schuster, Inc.

Designed by Jeanette Olender
Manufactured in the United States of America

1   3   5   7   9   10   8   6   4   2

Library of Congress Cataloging-in-Publication Data
Clinton, Catherine, date.
Fanny Kemble's civil wars / Catherine Clinton.
p. cm.
Includes bibliographical references and index.
1. Kemble, Fanny, 1809–1893. 2. Actors—Great Britain—Biography.
3. Plantation owners' spouses—Georgia—Biography. I. Title.
PN2598.K4 C58 2000
792'.028'092—dc21
[B]   00-030097
ISBN 0-684-84414-1

FOR MICHELE GILLESPIE

noi non potemo aver perfetta vita senza amici

CONTENTS

...ible of what those see who are standing upon a pinnacle
far above the vapour that folds us in —

November 27th 1881 — My Mother began talking about poor
dear Hall — but my Mother is not the person to grasp
Hearts' being the least in the world — no oh no, 'tis not a
healthy mind — far, far from it — but yet 'tis most highly
intellectual — Hal reminds me of Hamlet very much, their
thoughts are of the same colour — there is that vague & dreaming
existence which seems aimless & objectless, that deep & earnest
& constant reflection tending to no result, the same melancholy
perception, or rather sensation of life — I feel every now & then
he is possessed of great power — but they serve to me only to add
by contrast to the morbid nothingness of all her thoughts &
feelings — I know no other way of expressing the sense of
vagueness she gives to me but by saying her mind is of no
colour, a species of gloomy neutral tint, & over this world of
colourless outlines, the Spirit of doubting in some shape or
other for ever holds mastery — She doubts herself, she doubts
others — she doubts the very life she lives, she doubts that beyond
it — she doubts that wh she sees & touches, she doubts that
wh her senses cannot perceive — she doubts as she prays,
she doubts as she fears, she doubts as she
hopes — I believe she sometimes must doubt her own identity
& 'tis the doubt that this doubting is evil that oppresses &
disturbs her — Oh she is very like Hamlet — dear dear Hall
I love her entirely & admire her much & pity her more —
no vast are her mental powers compared to my own, I
wd not possess them — they are too wide — they have no
distinct boundary — her thoughts dwell over too large
an extent, they wander beyond her jurisdiction &
bring her back but faint & fearful histories of their
explorings into forbidden land

An unpublished excerpt from Kemble's girlhood
diary, written in her own hand.

PREFACE

Henry James liked to say that his great friend Fanny Kemble was meant to be twins, for she manifested energy, talent—and personal conflict— enough for two individual women joined in spirit by an all-consuming passion for living. Her life bridged a historic expanse, from the first decade of the nineteenth century to its last. As a girl, Fanny basked in the reflected glory of the Kemble family, who were theatrical royalty in England. Following the lead of her legendary aunt Sarah Siddons, Fanny Kemble launched her celebrity on stage. But the acclaim—and, not infrequently, notoriety—that engulfed her for well over half a century rested as much on her literary talents and personal magnetism as on her acting career.

She turned to writing after marrying a wealthy American, who insisted she retire from the stage. The marriage changed more than her name; the vibrant ingenue became a morose and restless matron. The eventual divorce and her bitter estrangement from her children devastatingly marred her private life.

But these clashes pale considerably against her most courageous struggle—the fight she waged against slavery. In 1836, when she had been married for just two years, Kemble's husband, Pierce Butler, inherited the second-largest slaveowning empire in Georgia. Her eyewitness testimony of life on an antebellum plantation offered a disqui-

eting glimpse into the world the slaveholders made. Published in 1863 as *Journal of a Residence on a Georgian Plantation*, Kemble's vivid writings—replete with insights on women's rights, slavery, and race—made an indelible impact. Newsmongers claimed that the work influenced England to deny the Confederacy's plea for diplomatic recognition; abolitionists in England and America celebrated the journal for portraying, with grace and humanity, the plight of enslaved blacks. This international best-seller permanently linked Kemble's name with debates over slavery and made good on her solemn pledge that it was her "imperative duty, knowing what I know, and having seen what I have seen, to do all that lies in my power to show the dangers and the evils of this frightful institution."

Kemble's passion and vitality leap from nearly every page she wrote. When John Brown was hanged in 1859, Kemble prophesied "from his grave a root of bitterness will spring, the fruit of which at no distant day may be disunion and civil war." These words would ring as true for her adopted nation as for herself. Americans fought to the death over sectional, racial, and political ideals—conflicts tragically replicated within Kemble's own family. As a British abolitionist married to a Southern plantation owner, she was an unlikely heroine of the Union cause. She bore two daughters—one loyal to the Union, the other to the Confederacy. Her marriage foundered, much as the Union had. For the rest of her life, Kemble struggled to erase the effects of family mistrust and betrayal, to heal the wounds left by bonds rent asunder. Her quest bleakly mirrored the fraught political and social interactions that characterized the years of Reconstruction and beyond.

Henry James once predicted that Fanny Kemble's literary gifts would "make her what I call historic." What emerges most clearly from her autobiographical writings is an ardent desire to create a world where men and women, black and white, would redefine freedom of their own volition. One of the most remarkable women of her era, she boldly voiced her convictions, forging a compelling record of social action that endures to this day.

. . .

I have written more than a dozen books, but I have been studying Fanny Kemble's life for more than half of my own. I first read her Georgian journal as an undergraduate, and was instantly captivated by the drama of her life. Each time I thought I had uncovered all there was to know, I always found there was more I wanted to know, more I felt I must know. Like all biographers, I best remember the moments when I stumbled upon something precious: the piece of her china in a storage box at the Lenox Library; the portrait of her best friend pasted into a scrapbook at the Folger Library; her handwritten annotations in the margin of a journal at Columbia University's Butler Library.

Kemble published nearly a dozen volumes of memoir, creating a permanent record of her strong-mindedness and unerring resolve. She was less willing to reveal the intricacies that lay beneath her beguiling demeanor. An obscure letter, tucked away in a private collection, illuminates one such tantalizing complexity. For years after her divorce from Pierce Butler, and even after his death, Fanny Kemble preserved in her sewing basket a scrap of her wedding dress, a nostalgic reminder of the fragile love story she and her husband shared. *Fanny Kemble's Civil Wars* is a tribute to the remarkable psyche that fueled her restless energy, to the tangle of contradictions that compels us to revisit her remarkable career.

Fanny Kemble's Civil Wars

KEMBLE FAMILY TREE

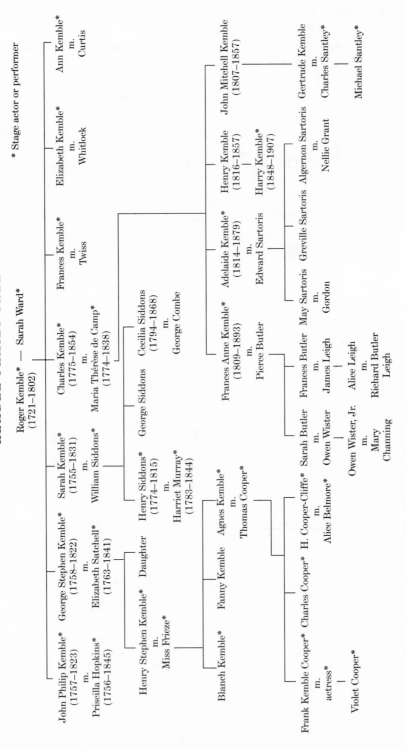

Roger Kemble* — Sarah Ward*
(1721–1802)

John Philip Kemble*
(1757–1823)
m.
Priscilla Hopkins*
(1756–1845)

George Stephen Kemble*
(1758–1822)
m.
Elizabeth Satchell*
(1763–1841)

Sarah Kemble*
(1755–1831)
m.
William Siddons*

Charles Kemble*
(1775–1854)
m.
Maria Thérèse de Camp*
(1774–1838)

Frances Kemble*
m.
Twiss

Elizabeth Kemble*
m.
Whitlock

Ann Kemble*
m.
Curtis

Henry Stephen Kemble*
m.
Miss Frieze*

Henry Siddons*
(1774–1815)
m.
Harriet Murray*
(1783–1844)

Daughter

George Siddons

Cecilia Siddons
(1794–1868)
m.
George Combe

Frances Anne Kemble*
(1809–1893)
m.
Pierce Butler

Adelaide Kemble*
(1814–1879)
m.
Edward Sartoris

Henry Kemble*
(1816–1857)

John Mitchell Kemble
(1807–1857)

Blanch Kemble*

Fanny Kemble

Agnes Kemble*
m.
Thomas Cooper*

Frank Kemble Cooper*
m.
actress*

Charles Cooper*

H. Cooper-Cliffe*
m.
Alice Belmore*

Sarah Butler
m.
Owen Wister

Frances Butler
m.
James Leigh

Alice Leigh
m.
Richard Butler Leigh

May Sartoris
m.
Gordon

Greville Sartoris

Algernon Sartoris
m.
Nellie Grant

Gertrude Kemble
m.
Charles Santley*

Harry Kemble*
(1848–1907)

Violet Cooper*

Owen Wister, Jr.
m.
Mary Channing

Michael Santley*

CHAPTER ONE

Enter Fanny Kemble

In 1809 Frances Anne Kemble was born into the most celebrated theatrical family in Europe. The decade of her birth, known among historians of the British theater as the Kemble era, marked the convergence of a powerful theatrical dynasty and the triumphant ascendancy of theater as an art form.

Led by patriarch Roger Kemble, the Kemble clan spearheaded the campaign waged by British actors throughout the eighteenth century to bring the theater into the rarefied circle of artistic esteem long accorded opera, ballet, and orchestral performances. Striving to reverse the prejudices his craft had faced for centuries, Kemble was steadfast in his efforts to help managers secure theater permits and establish permanent homes for acting companies. And he railed against the long-held stereotype that women who pursued careers on the stage were hardly a cut above the courtesans who filled the third tier of the gallery.

Roger Kemble defied that opinion in a most personal way, by taking an actress as his bride. He married Sarah Ward, the daughter of a pop-

*Roger Kemble, Fanny's paternal grandfather, the
founder of the illustrious acting clan.*

ular actor acclaimed for his 1746 benefit performance at Stratford, Shakespeare's birthplace, to raise funds for the restoration of a monument to the playwright. The Kemble affinity for Shakespeare—so evident in the superb performances of Roger's granddaughter Fanny Kemble—had its roots in the world of eighteenth-century traveling troupes.

At that time, a royal license was required to operate a theater, and London supported just two patents: Covent Garden and the Drury Lane. Further, the Act of 1737 forbade performing plays for profit outside London, forcing theatrical companies to find a way around the law by transforming their troupes into musical companies that charged admission to concerts, but offered plays "free." The authorities turned a blind eye; by the end of the century, a crude circuit had been established among Bath, Bristol, and other provincial towns. It was into this bustling milieu that the Kemble clan threw its fortunes.

Roger Kemble and Sarah Ward produced twelve children, eight of whom survived childhood. Sevenof the eight turned to the stage, but it was John, Sarah, and Charles who shone. Their father, however, prized education above celebrity, and if Roger Kemble had had his way, his children would never have achieved such fame. Hoping to achieve the distinguished status of father of a priest, he sent three of his sons to the seminary.

The oldest of the Kemble sons, John Philip, was the first to defy his father, leaving seminary in 1778 to join a reputable theatrical company in York. By 1783, he was ready to make his London debut at the Drury Lane, playing Hamlet. Just weeks before, his younger brother George had debuted at Covent Garden, as Othello. A theatrical sibling rivalry seemed imminent. But George's performances were less than memorable; John Philip went on to become the leading interpreter of Shakespeare for his generation.

John Philip Kemble's work at the Drury Lane made such an impression on its owner, the playwright Richard Brinsley Sheridan, that by 1788 he offered John Philip Kemble the opportunity to manage the playhouse. Just as Roger Kemble had done in his day, John Philip seized the opportunity to innovate. He insisted on historical accuracy in costuming and staging, perfectly re-creating Elizabethan dress and décor. When Kemble broke with his mentor in 1802, he used his earnings from the Drury Lane to buy a one-sixth share of its rival.

Kemble's arrival at Covent Garden in 1803 seemed to assure the peak of the Kemble era. Sister Sarah and brother Charles claimed spots in the repertory company, and their popularity grew alongside John Philip's reputation. But other Kemble siblings, craving successes of their own, did not meet with the same good fortune. George, after his disastrous debut in London, reestablished himself in Edinburgh. Us-

*Fanny's aunt Sarah Siddons, whose career raised the
status of female performers in the British theater.*

ing his middle name, Stephen, he was founder of a successful theater
company. Elizabeth Kemble Whitlock journeyed to America, where
she won better roles than she could have expected at home. Frances
married and retired from the stage entirely.

But it was Ann Kemble who found the most notoriety. She first married a bigamist, then embarked on a shady career as a public lecturer on
sex which culminated in her being shot in the face in an altercation in
a London bawdyhouse. The more distinguished Kembles put a stop to
these antics by granting their sister an annuity, intended to prevent her
from exploiting the family name on handbills. The payoff came at a
high price—expulsion from London.

In contrast, Sarah Siddons, born in a tavern in Wales while her parents were on tour, was destined to be John Philip Kemble's true rival. In 1773, traveling with her father's troupe, she married fellow actor William Siddons. But after an inauspicious London debut as Portia at the Drury Lane Theatre in 1775, she was banished to the provinces, where she remained for six full seasons.

It was her 1782 return to London, leading the popular tragedy *The Fatal Marriage,* that made her the most respected and awe-inspiring actress of her generation. Madame de Staël described Siddons's spellbinding performance: "At last comes the moment when Isabella, having broken free from her women, who wish to prevent her from killing herself, laughs, as she stabs herself, at the uselessness of their efforts. The effect of this laugh of despair is the most extraordinary and difficult achievement of dramatic art; it is far more moving than tears; misery finds its most heart-rending expression in its bitter irony."

A commanding presence on stage, Siddons was equally comfortable in the presence of aristocratic admirers. During her second season in London, Sir Joshua Reynolds painted her portrait as "the Tragic Muse." Edward Gibbon, Edmund Burke, and William Pitt the Elder all fawned over her, and King George III brought members of the royal family to her performances until she retired in 1812. Lord Byron exulted, "Nothing ever was or can be like her."

Despite her impeccable paternal bloodline, Fanny Kemble always believed that "whatever qualities of mind or character I inherited from my father's family, I am more strongly stamped with those I derived from my mother." A popular starlet in her own right, Maria Thérèse de Camp began performing song, dance, and theatrical roles at age six, when her Swiss mother and French father emigrated to England. Named for the archduchess of Austria because she was born in Vienna, Maria Thérèse displayed courtly manners well suited to entertaining in society parlors, including the drawing room of the prince regent's mistress, Mrs. Fitzherbert, where she would delight the future king with her dancing. When her father died, leaving her mother indigent, Maria

*Fanny's mother, Maria Thérèse, was an actress
when she married Charles Kemble.*

Thérèse—the eldest of five, though not yet in her teens—became the
family breadwinner. Two of her younger siblings, Adelaide and Vin-
cent, later followed her on stage.

After her critically acclaimed theatrical debut at the Drury Lane,
scandal struck in 1795 when a drunken theatrical manager burst in on
the twenty-one-year-old Maria Thérèse in her dressing room. She was
able to fight him off, but, like all actresses, she feared her reputation
might be tainted by sexual innuendo. She demanded a formal apology
from the offending cad, who was none other than John Philip Kemble.
His fondness for drink had no ill effects on his stage performances, but

all too often clouded his judgment offstage. Kemble apologized in the newspaper for his transgression and absolved Miss de Camp of any blame, and that seemed to be the end of the story.

But the entire family was shocked anew when Charles Kemble, after appearing with the young Maria Thérèse de Camp in several dramas, professed his love for the former object of his brother's lust. In 1800 he announced his intention to marry Maria Thérèse, who returned his affections. The Kemble family voiced strong objections, and went to great lengths to prevent the union. An even greater obstacle, however, was the wrath of John Philip Kemble, whose power in London theatrical circles was so great that defying him meant professional doom.

Charles pleaded with his brother. John Philip finally consented— on one condition: Charles must postpone the wedding until he reached the age of thirty, more than five years distant. Presumably John Philip hoped his baby brother would outgrow his infatuation. But Charles's feelings never faltered. And so it was that John Philip himself gave the bride away when his brother and Maria Thérèse were wed in 1805.

Maria Thérèse may have been a Kemble by marriage, but the family never regarded her as one of their own. That her mother was perpetually made to feel an outsider, perhaps even an outcast, was painfully clear to Fanny. Late in life she reflected: "The great actors of my family have received their due of recorded admiration; my mother has always seemed to me to have been overshadowed by their celebrity." Fanny longed for affirmation of her mother's worth.

Fanny's very birth occurred in the midst of a Kemble family crisis. In 1808 Covent Garden burned to the ground, destroying many valuable costumes and props owned by the Kembles, along with the grand old structure itself. John Philip Kemble received an outpouring of support from aristocratic patrons, which allowed him and his partners to undertake rebuilding. But the new plans called for a theater much

*Fanny's father, Charles, was a Shakespearean actor and
later became the manager of Covent Garden.*

grander and more elaborate than its predecessor, and the project was
slowed by ballooning costs and dueling egos.

In the fall of 1809 Covent Garden once again opened its doors to
the public. Theatergoers quickly discovered that this ornate replacement bore little resemblance to their old favorite. Especially offensive
was the owners' decision to increase the number of expensive private
boxes by limiting that of more reasonably priced gallery tickets. Seats
in the pit, previously affordable by patrons of even the most modest
means, had gone up in price. In effect, Roger Kemble's crusade to raise
the profile of the theater as an art form had been reborn—through
economic means.

A chorus of complaint broke out on opening night, and protests continued unabated. Audiences incessantly booed, catcalled, and chanted "Old Prices" so loudly that performers were drowned out by the din. Favorite players, trotted onstage in attempts to appease the angry mob, did little to soothe them; they waved banners and tossed orange peels at the likes of Charles Kemble as Cromwell in *Henry VIII*, Sarah Siddons as Lady Macbeth, and even Maria Thérèse Kemble—seven months pregnant—as Lucy in *The Beggar's Opera*.

But it was John Philip Kemble who bore the brunt of the public's displeasure. He was hissed off the stage nightly and he was serenaded with rude songs at his home. Theater protests were not uncommon and the vitriol of boisterous crowds was an ordinary part of doing business—but the intensity and duration of the "O.P. riots" were extraordinary. Finally, on December 15, after sixty-seven nights of

*The interior of Covent Garden, where generations of
Kembles performed and Fanny made her debut.*

John Philip Kemble, Fanny's uncle and the most
famous Shakespearean actor of his day.

protest, John Philip Kemble conceded defeat and rolled back the price of admission. Given the debt he had incurred rebuilding Covent Garden, this decision would prove financially ruinous. But after months of violence and mayhem, the show could go on only by the grace of the public.

Maria Thérèse's brush with the "Old Price" mob was enough to keep her off the Covent Garden stage indefinitely. She secluded herself at the family home on Newman Street in the Soho district, where, on November 27, 1809, as the riots raged on, she gave birth to Frances Anne Kemble. The Kembles' third child (after John Mitchell, two years her senior, and a boy who died in infancy) and their first girl, she was named Frances after her father's sister, the retired actress who became her godmother, and Anne after one of her mother's dear friends. She was always known as Fanny.

True to her dramatic roots, as a child Fanny took every opportunity to steal the show, even when she shared the scene with Aunt Sarah Siddons. One family story recalls a severe lecture delivered by the theatrical legend on the subject of rude behavior. Fanny listened solemnly to the scolding, then delivered a perfectly timed compliment of her imposing aunt's "beautiful eyes," which were indeed Sarah's most impressive feature. Siddons melted.

But while Kemble's childhood had its share of precious moments, disruption and upheaval were just as common. She learned from an early age that the wages of an artist yielded few comforts. As a mother of young children, Maria Thérèse found the clamor and squalor of London's most populous neighborhoods increasingly difficult to endure, and episodes of parental discord erupted frequently. Charles harbored thwarted ambitions of his own: "The fame of my brother John in tragedy caused me for long to avoid trespassing upon his ground."

Although the time when the Kemble family would depend on Fanny for its livelihood was not far off, her rebellious early years proved difficult for her parents. Long anxious that Charles's indulgence toward Fanny was spoiling her, Maria Thérèse believed that the only cure was discipline and training outside the household. In 1814—following the birth of Adelaide, nicknamed Totty—Fanny was sent away, the first of many exiles, to a girls' school in Bath run by her aunt Frances Twiss. But as Twiss discovered over Fanny's twelve-month stay, her niece had already developed a stubborn streak that made her indifferent to punishment.

She was sent back to London, where her family had found a larger home to accommodate two more additions—Fanny's baby brother Henry, nicknamed Harry; and Maria Thérèse's sister, Adelaide de Camp, called Dall. Dall had been a member of Stephen Kemble's Edinburgh troupe, but retired to her sister's household after a bitter disappointment in love. She never married, and devoted the remainder of her life to her sister's family, especially her nieces.

By 1816 Fanny was sent away for a second time, to a boarding school in Boulogne, France. It was not unusual for a family of means to have a daughter spend her formative years away from home, but young Fanny found the arrangement unbearable. That Boulogne was actually closer to London than Bath was didn't make the renewed separation any easier.

Fanny earned stellar marks in her lessons, and her instructors in French and Italian discovered a facility for languages. While her intellect was beyond dispute, her willfulness remained unchecked. For punishment, she was shut into an attic room, but she soon learned to climb out onto the roof. When a passerby caught sight of her, alarm ensued, and from then on Fanny's errant behavior was corrected in the escape-proof cellar. The French schoolmistress, finding Fanny incorrigible, called her "cette diable de Kemble"—dubious praise that the nine-year-old proudly repeated upon her return to England.

By this time, Maria Thérèse had relocated the household yet again, this time to the farthest edge of London: Craven Hill, in Bayswater. Although his wife's desire for fresh air and open spaces was assuaged to a degree, Charles Kemble, unable to afford a coach, was forced to walk five miles daily each way between home and work. Eventually he was able to lease a small flat in Soho, which eased his commute and allowed the family overnight city excursions.

John Philip Kemble finally retired in 1819; in early November 1820, he signed over to Charles his one-sixth share of Covent Garden and moved permanently to Switzerland.

Now Charles had a chance to truly make his mark. By the time he was able to wrest management of the theater from his partners two years later, he had waited so long in the wings that critics were intensely eager to judge his abilities.

He chose to open his first season with *The School for Scandal,* casting the popular William Macready in the lead and himself as a supporting player. The critics applauded, welcoming the "superior taste" of a "scholar, gentleman, and perfect master of his art." Charles Kemble's brilliant success ensured that even after John Philip's retirement and his death in 1823, the Kemble name would continue to thrive. The family finances were another matter.

Fanny Kemble recalled the elation the family had felt at this seeming windfall—presumably worth more than £40,000—that her uncle had granted them. She was only eleven then; years passed before she understood that her father's stake in Covent Garden made him liable for the theater's enormous debts. She later characterized Covent Garden as "a hopelessly ruined concern" and blamed it for the collapse of the Kemble family fortunes.

Under extreme financial pressure, the Kembles could ill afford to be distracted by their daughter's more and more outrageous antics. When, following minor infractions, she resorted to such drastic measures as running away from home, hiding in a neighbor's cottage, or throwing herself in a pond, they became desperate for a solution. In Paris they found a school run by a Mrs. Rowden, a pious and austere Englishwoman who brooked no interference with her rigid routine. She required her pupils to attend mass at a French convent as well as Anglican services at the British embassy. Fanny remembered an increasing appreciation of the Bible and its lessons during these four years; Mrs. Rowden also fostered in her a love of literature—French writers, Italian writers, and even Byron, in purloined copies. She was to embrace these incongruous passions—for writings both sacred and profane—throughout her lifetime.

Mrs. Rowden believed that another of her pupil's passions, the theater, was ill-suited to her. Fanny had learned to love the great dramas of Racine, even playing the lead in a school production of *Andromaque,* but Rowden pronounced her talent for the stage "nonexistent."

Throughout her lonely years in Paris, Fanny worried constantly that she might forget her mother's face. Their reunion—at the family's new home in Weybridge, a village twenty miles southwest of London—was touching. A renewed intimacy helped Fanny heal the wounds caused by their time apart. Kemble's troubled youth was filled with torments about her relationship with her distant and demanding mother.

Fanny had become aware at an early age that her mother suffered from some kind of nervous disorder. Her attacks grew increasingly debilitating over the years of Fanny's childhood. From the time of her retirement from the stage until her premature death, Maria Thérèse became more and more reclusive, and less capable of dealing with the demands of her family and household. Her family coped with her mental decline. She tried to soothe her fraying nerves with bracing fresh air, sedentary routines, and the slower pace of country life. She especially enjoyed fishing, and would invite Fanny along to while away the afternoons along a riverbank.

Yet their pastoral reunion was marred when Maria Thérèse allowed Fanny to be exposed to smallpox; a mild case of the disease would immunize her for life. However, there was no way to control the severity of the resulting infection, and Fanny suffered a serious bout. As a result, her lovely face was marked by a murky complexion ever after. Maria Thérèse protected Adelaide from exposure, and both Kemble boys were enrolled at boarding school in nearby Bury St. Edmunds, so they too escaped the virus. But the damage Fanny had already suffered was irreversible.

During her convalescence, her brothers' schoolmaster Dr. Arthur Malkin visited the Kemble home and was impressed by Fanny's lively intellect. Malkin became something of a mentor to the sixteen-year-old, providing her with reading lists, tutoring her in German, and suggesting ambitious translation projects to sharpen her already keen mind.

Maria Thérèse was well pleased with her daughter's progress, but the hours spent poring over lessons made no improvement on Fanny's adolescent slouch. This had to be corrected, for carriage was a mark of breeding. The Kembles had the novel idea of hiring a member of the

Royal Foot Guards to teach their daughter proper posture. Fanny's mother also tried to train Fanny's singing voice, but eleven-year-old Totty chimed in with perfect pitch while Fanny struggled to keep in tune, and the lessons were soon abandoned. Fanny eventually developed a strong singing voice, but she chose to use it for her own pleasure, rather than for public entertainment.

During the period from 1825 to 1826, Fanny was a frequent guest at Heath Farm, an estate owned by the Earl of Essex and currently on loan to John Philip Kemble's widow. Fanny greatly enjoyed these expeditions to Hertfordshire, especially because it was there that she met Harriet St. Leger in 1826.

Harriet St. Leger was an Anglo-Irish aristocrat, the spinster mistress of Ardgillan Castle (near Dublin), fourteen years older than Fanny and known for her eccentric tastes. St. Leger's costume always consisted of a gray riding habit embellished with cashmere collar and cuffs, handmade leather boots, and a distinctive beaver hat. Her wardrobe and her outdoorsy manner made her the frequent subject of idle gossip.

But Fanny was plainly smitten with this handsome woman, so confident in her demeanor. Throughout the time when they were both at Heath Farm, Harriet and Fanny shared a bedroom, where they talked into the night about religion, politics, and whatever caught their fancy. When St. Leger returned to Ireland, the two promised to begin a correspondence.

They kept this pledge all their lives, and through their letters a deep and lasting friendship grew. Although they rarely met over the next fifty years, Harriet St. Leger became Fanny's sounding board, her confidante, and—thanks to the shared passion for religion and theology revealed in their letters—soul mate. Kemble's attachment was permanent and lasting, although it did not have the homoerotic component that imbued many female friendships during this era. St. Leger never married and spent most of her adult years with a female companion, Dorothy Wilson, but, as with many similar arrangements, this relationship never interfered with her devotion to Kemble.

In Harriet, Fanny found the best friend she so sorely needed. Her parents were so preoccupied with Covent Garden that they had little attention to spare her. Aunt Dall was a comforting presence, but even she could not provide the stimulation seventeen-year-old Fanny craved. Fanny began to cultivate intimacies outside the family: she befriended Caroline Norton, a granddaughter of Richard Brinsley Sheridan, visited Lord and Lady Egerton (later Earl and Countess Ellesmere) at Oatlands, their nearby estate, and made the acquaintance of such famous personages as the writer Anna Jameson. On rare occasions, she explored London in the company of her father, most memorably touring the Thames Tunnel with its engineer, Sir Marc Isambard Brunel. But these diversions were not enough to satisfy her restless curiosity.

In an effort to capture her thoughts and emotions, Fanny began to keep a diary, but was frustrated by the artifice of solitary conversation and longed for company. She preferred "the sifting, examining, scrutinizing, discussing intercourse that compels one to analysis of one's own ideas and sentiments." Fanny was fond of society, especially its capacity to foster intellectual discussions. As a young woman lacking the means to make a formal social debut, she was dismayed to find herself on the sidelines. Her parents had neither the means nor the inclination to allow their daughter to mix in high society.

Fanny's relative isolation compounded her inherent lack of confidence. Throughout her adolescence she constantly measured herself against the only society available to her: her brothers and sisters. While her older brother John had won academic distinction and her sister Adelaide had musical gifts, Fanny feared she possessed no talents of her own. Deep in the throes of schoolgirl melancholy, she especially envied her younger siblings' natural buoyancy; she was certain that her mother's critical supervision had robbed her of her natural good humor. Her "exacting taste," Fanny confessed, "made in her everything most keenly alive to our faults and deficiencies. . . . The unsparing severity of the sole reply or comment . . . 'I hate a fool' has remained almost like a cut with a lash across my memory."

Whatever her mother's lacerating criticisms, Fanny was vivacious and ambitious, with a natural verbal flair. She eventually cast aside her doubts and set her sights on an exalted goal: she wanted to become a writer.

The opening decades of the nineteenth century were a grand time for British women writers; among their ranks were the likes of the Brontë sisters, Maria Edgeworth, Hannah More, and Jane Austen, whom Fanny passionately admired. Also, a long line of distinguished Kemble authors preceded her. John Philip Kemble had produced verse and essays; Sarah Siddons had published Shakespearean criticism; and Fanny's parents had published original dramas (Charles) and "stage adaptations" (Maria Thérèse). These Kemble authors had gained entrée into the publishing world through their stage reputations. But the Kemble name was well known among readers and playgoers alike, so Fanny believed that there might be a ready literary market for another Kemble scribbler.

When Fanny confessed her ambitions to Harriet St. Leger, she had her heart set on creating a novel and had gone so far as to choose a historical theme. This plan met with Harriet's approval. Halfway through her story Fanny decided to turn the project into a play, "Francis the First." When she gathered her family in the parlor for a dramatic reading from the script, her parents praised it extravagantly and her older brother John, home from school, pronounced it full of true literary merit.

Fanny accepted the compliments gracefully, but remained privately discouraged about her prospects. Her writing, she explained to Harriet St. Leger in February 1828, amounted to "a clever performance for so young a person, but nothing more." Yet she guarded her ambitions fiercely, vowing to "exercis[e] and develop the literary talent which I think I possess. This is meat, drink, and sleep to me; my world, in which I live, and have my happiness; and moreover, I hope by means of fame (the prize for which I pray)."

Like any young writer, Fanny indulged her fantasies freely, even imagining herself as a literary "lioness." But such whimsical moments were curtailed all too often by the daunting realities of money. Writing, Fanny realized, would be "to earn hard money after a very hard fashion." She identified acting as a fallback career, reasoning that "if my going on the stage would nearly double that [Charles Kemble's] income, lessen my dear father's anxieties for us all . . . would not this be 'consummation devoutly to be wished'?"

Fanny worried constantly over her family's financial situation. From an early age, she complained of suffering from "blue devils," which may have been clinical depression. Her mother's illness manifested itself in frequent outbursts of manic behavior. Fanny and her siblings never knew when they might come home to find their mother collapsed in bed, or on the other hand rearranging the furniture with plans to remodel a home for which they could barely afford the upkeep. These disruptive family scenes contributed to Fanny's bleak moods and emotional instability. She confided to Harriet in January 1828 that she had once tossed a manuscript of eight hundred pages into the fire, destroying her only copy. She immediately regretted the impulsive action, admitting that her year's work "should not have been thrown away in a foolish fit of despondency."

News of her father's ongoing struggles at Convent Garden did nothing to raise Fanny's low spirits. Charles Kemble's long and contentious dispute with Henry Harris, a business partner, dragged through Chancery Court, sadly depleting the household coffers. Kemble's offstage appearance was so threadbare and bedraggled that he joked about wearing nothing but his "Chancery suit."

Lackluster theater receipts compounded his legal woes. This situation, Charles Kemble surmised, would be easily remedied by the arrival of a promising young actress on the London scene. But none emerged, and not for lack of searching. Managers scoured provincial theaters with no success, while Maria Thérèse scouted the talent among the acting students she taught at the Kembles' Soho flat. Theatergoers, it seemed, would continue mourning the retirement of her remarkable sister-in-law, Sarah Siddons, until a replacement was offered.

Many of the Siddons clan—Fanny Kemble's distant cousins—were living in Edinburgh. Sarah's son Henry Siddons, known as Harry, had been a popular actor in his day, and his widow, Harriet, was an actress so beloved by the Scots that fans called her "our Mrs. Siddons." In 1828, eighteen-year-old Fanny accepted Harriet Siddons's invitation to make a visit. She looked forward to the change of scene and to escape from her own increasingly volatile home life.

Fanny spent a blissful year with this favorite cousin, but perhaps it was the attentions of young men that persuaded her to linger. Maria Thérèse wrote Harriet frequently, imploring her to strictly monitor Fanny's circle of friends. These came to include the physician Andrew Combe and his brother George, a lawyer whose career took a well-publicized turn toward the "science" of phrenology, the practice of reading bumps on the skull to ascertain moral character.

Both men later professed to have been half in love with Fanny Kemble. But it was Cecilia Siddons, Sarah's daughter and Fanny's favorite first cousin, whom George eventually married; Andrew, a confirmed bachelor, remained a devoted friend to Fanny over the years. Harriet Siddons's own son, Harry, made romantic overtures toward Fanny, going so far as to have her name engraved on his sword blade before he shipped out for military service in India. But these were all innocent flirtations.

As much as she enjoyed the company of friends and relations, Fanny was becoming increasingly introspective. To truly know herself, she realized, she must experience life outside her own limited sphere. She was especially drawn to the villages along the Scottish coast, where she explored the seaside shanties. Here she developed her renowned affinity for "plain folk"; for the rest of her life she devoted time and energy to those "less fortunate" than herself.

Fanny would later pronounce this year of spiritual reflection the best of her life. She drew strength and comfort from the serenity of Harriet Siddons, an antidote to her mother's erratic ways. Harriet Siddons devoted a part of each day to religious reflection, an example that inspired Fanny to imbue her own daily Bible readings with deeper meaning, pausing often to ponder the verses and their lessons. Under Harriet's gentle influence, Fanny even gave up reading Byron. Although years apart in age and vastly different in temperament, Fanny and Harriet Siddons became extremely close. Fanny tried to emulate this woman she so came to admire.

She returned to London in 1829 with her spirits lifted, to find that the Kemble house on St. James's Street had become the site of frequent gatherings of intellectuals and clever conversationalists, among them the novelist William Makepeace Thackeray. Others, like the poet Alfred Tennyson, the poet and translator Edward FitzGerald, and the future Baron Houghton, Richard Monckton Milnes, came at the invitation of Fanny's brother John. This circle of friends, classmates at Cambridge, numbered twelve; they began by calling themselves the Cambridge Conversazione Society, but abandoned this fanciful title in favor of the joking "Apostles."

Charles Kemble was displeased by his son's choice of friends, especially their religious leanings. Charles took the opposite view of his own father. Roger Kemble had wanted Charles to be a priest, a vocation Charles feared. He himself had sent his bookish son John to Cambridge intending that he should read law. But John disappointed him, taking up theology and wishing to study religion abroad. Two of the Apostles would go on to become Anglican archbishops, but according to Charles, John's Cambridge degree in theology was tantamount to "failing."

Nearly one-third of the family income went toward John's education, and Charles was determined to see a return on that investment.

His urgent desire that his son find a lucrative career was doubtless propelled by the spiraling financial difficulties at Covent Garden. Late in the summer of 1829, Charles traveled to Ireland on tour, still desperate to locate that elusive starlet whom he was counting on to rejuvenate Covent Garden. But the accolades and income won abroad could not stave off disaster.

In his absence, creditors repossessed the theater, plastering it with posters proclaiming it FOR SALE and suing Charles for the sum of its debts. Fanny Kemble came home one day to find her mother collapsed, debilitated by fits of hysterical weeping. It seemed that the situation was beyond repair. Fanny wrote to her father, proposing that she might take a position as a governess. But Maria Thérèse overcame her fears and decided that those dark days called for bolder plans. She instructed her husband to return home at once, as she plotted with Fanny to save the family from ruin.

Maria Thérèse planned to transform her dutiful daughter into a star of the stage. She began by carefully coaching Fanny in the role of Portia. When Fanny had delivered a fairly strong reading, she graduated to Juliet. This was the most coveted of Shakespeare's female roles, and a guaranteed box office draw. By the time Charles returned, Fanny was ready to give a private performance, offering up her lines while her mother spoke the other parts. In response, her parents neither praised nor scolded her, but disappeared behind closed doors to plan, while Fanny succumbed to her fears and wept. She soon dried her tears, however, when one of Charles's trusted colleagues witnessed yet another private audition, this time at Covent Garden, and confirmed that her beguiling Juliet was bound to be a success.

A few weeks shy of her twentieth birthday, Fanny became the talk of London. How dramatic that the fate of London's leading theatrical family rested on the shoulders of its teenage daughter. Fanny, beset by worries over costumes and rehearsals, wrote to Harriet St. Leger in late September 1829 that even the date of her opening had not been set: "The nearest period talked of for my debut is the first of October, at

*Fanny's debut as Shakespeare's Juliet in October 1829
launched her theatrical career.*

the opening of the theater; the furthest November; but I almost think I should prefer the nearest for it is a very serious trial to look forward to, and I wish it were over."

Maria Thérèse, who had sacrificed her own childhood for her family's sake, worried that she was forcing her daughter into the same unenviable position. She alternated between shame and despair. To show her support—and perhaps to assuage her guilt—Maria Thérèse decided to come out of retirement for one night only. Appropriately, she would play Juliet's mother. Charles Kemble, who usually cast himself as Romeo, would play Mercutio in this Kemble-studded production.

When Fanny's first performance in *Romeo and Juliet* was announced for October 5, 1829, the box office was deluged. And on the appointed night, the throng of demanding theatergoers and critics were joined by the cream of London society, who arrived at the theater in brightly painted landaus, dressed in silken finery to witness this historic occasion.

At the first sight of Fanny onstage, the crowd—from the boxes to the pits—gave a thunderous roar of approval. But as she began to perform, losing herself in the role of Juliet, the audience responded not just to her fame, but to her talent. At the end of the play, they cheered in recognition that a new queen of the stage had been crowned that night.

To Fanny, this overwhelming response felt like a dream. She was flooded with childhood memories, recalling especially the night when, five years old, she had hidden in a theater box, peeking out as her famous aunt Sarah gave a rare benefit performance. Tonight the tables were turned, as Sarah Siddons witnessed Fanny's premiere from behind the curtain of a private box. They both knew, perhaps, that on this night the torch had been passed. At the family's victory supper that night, her father gave her a gold watch. Delighted, Fanny dubbed it "Romeo" and tucked it under her pillow.

The spell continued uninterrupted for days. The London *Times* reported: "Upon the whole, we do not remember to have ever seen a more triumphant debut. That Miss Kemble has been well and carefully instructed, as, of course, she would be is clear; but it is no less clear that she possesses qualifications which instructions could not create, although it can bring them to perfection." The critic for *New Monthly Magazine* volunteered: "For our part, the illusion that she was Shakespeare's own Juliet came so speedily upon us as to suspend the power of specific criticism."

Several longtime critics volunteered that although Fanny's performance did not surpass her famous aunt's theatrical powers, perhaps Fanny was well on her way toward rivaling the Tragic Muse. Some even suggested Fanny was better than Sarah Siddons had been at the same age.

Fanny's triumph propelled her toward the goals which had lured her onstage: pleasing her parents and helping them financially. She was elated by the benefits her earnings promised her family—further studies for John in Germany, where he wanted to pursue theology, and music lessons for Totty. At the end of the first week of performances, Fanny went to the theater to collect her salary in person. Ticket sales ensured a record-breaking season. It seemed that Fanny had indeed earned that gold watch.

There being a great demand for likenesses of the actress, the portraitist John Hayter prepared a series of sketches. Another important artist, Sir Thomas Lawrence—he participated in the founding of England's National Gallery—begged to make her acquaintance. While he was unknown to Fanny, he required no introduction to her family.

Lawrence had a long and significant connection to the Kembles, especially Sarah Siddons, whose portrait he had first painted when just a youth. Rumor had it that the painter was bewitched by the much older woman, perhaps even romantically involved with her. In 1797, while still in his twenties, Lawrence completed a portrait of Siddons that later hung in the National Gallery. That same year, he courted Sarah's older daughter, Sally. But when the twenty-two-year-old Sally suddenly fell seriously ill, Lawrence transferred his affections to her eighteen-year-old sister Maria, and the two became engaged.

Belatedly realizing he still loved Sally, Lawrence broke off the engagement. By this time, his behavior had appalled the Siddonses and the Kembles alike. When Maria lay bedridden with consumption in 1798, she exacted a promise from Sally that she would never marry Lawrence, then promptly died. Sally spurned Lawrence's advances and died shortly thereafter.

It was Fanny Kemble who smoothed over the quarrel. Lawrence paid courteous attention to her, promoting her career with tender and tenacious devotion. Working closely with Maria Thérèse, he took a directorial interest in Fanny's craft, attending many performances and commenting on everything from costume to staging and delivery. Fanny valued his advice, reading his detailed critiques backstage in

Young Frances Anne Kemble, known as Fanny.

preparation for upcoming scenes. Doubtless, Fanny's physical resemblance to her departed cousins endeared her to Lawrence all the more.

Lawrence planned to immortalize Fanny on canvas, just as he had done for Sarah Siddons. His pencil sketch of Fanny, Maria Thérèse remarked, bore a striking resemblance to his portrait of Maria Siddons. Lawrence was planning a full-length portrait of Fanny as Juliet, but his sudden death—under mysterious circumstances that suggested suicide—left the work unfinished.

Just three days before his death Lawrence had written of his strong feelings for Fanny: "I have almost a Father's interest in her." He asserted that she was just as good as Sarah Siddons had been at her age;

Fanny's popularity resulted in parody,
evident in this doctored image.

he knew, he wrote, that Fanny would one day play Lady Macbeth—Siddons's signature role—beautifully. Deeply affected by Lawrence's praise, the young actress confessed that despite the difference in their ages, she feared that if he had lived she would have fallen in love with him—and perhaps let him bring even more heartache to the women of her family.

Lawrence was just one of dozens of distinguished Londoners vying for Fanny's attentions. She felt the crush of fame. "From an insignificant school-girl, I became an object of general public interest. . . . Approbation, admiration, adulation were showered upon me." This seemed to come about "by the wand of a fairy." Perhaps it was this fairy-tale quality that allowed her to float through these heady days more or less unscathed.

Fanny went from having a twenty-pound-a-year allowance to having a carriage at her disposal and purchasing fine new gowns. She needed the wardrobe and carriage for her many social engagements. She confided to Harriet the details of one busy week: "a dinner party on Monday; Tuesday, the opera; Wednesday, I act Isabella; Thursday, a dinner at Mr. Harness's; Friday I act Bianca; Saturday we have a dinner party at home; the Monday following I act Constance; Tuesday there is a dance at the Fitzhughs'; and sundry dissipations looming in the horizon."

After her success in the capital, her father booked her into lucrative engagements on the provincial circuit. From Bath to Edinburgh, from Brighton to Glasgow, Fanny became the toast of Great Britain. In Dublin, Fanny recalled, a "bodyguard of about two hundred men, shouting and hurrahing like mad," escorted her back to her hotel, where aristocratic admirers crowded into the drawing rooms to meet her.

Much was made of Kemble's onstage allure, but men and women alike commented on the fact that her offstage appearance was surprisingly plain. One male gallant who spotted her backstage demanded to know how she contrived to be so beautiful while performing. A female admirer jovially asserted: "Fanny Kemble, you are the ugliest and handsomest woman in London!" A few years later the young Robert E. Lee, a cadet at West Point, attended a performance and became completely enthralled by the actress. But when he spotted her at a ball, Lee confessed, he found her "next door to homely."

The sole dissenter was Washington Irving, then secretary at the American Embassy in London, who used his influence to make Kemble's acquaintance shortly after her debut. Irving, who became a great friend, argued that she was lovelier in person: "The nearer one gets to her face and to her mind, the more beautiful they both are."

Fanny Kemble's beauty might have been debatable, but her impact was not. Some attributed her bewitching hold over an audience to her superior stage presence; she used her remarkable voice and skilled gestures to project majesty and beauty. Admirers recalled her as having a tall, lithe form and a face without blemish. But up close, her figure appeared short, even stocky, and her skin mottled.

Kemble herself seemed indifferent to the public's bald assessment of her charms. She quipped about the burden her Romeos bore when forced to lift a weighty Juliet, and made playful reference to her "gipsy complexion." Although she took pride in her appearance, Kemble was remarkably free of the vanity common not just among actresses but among all young women of her era.

Kemble confessed that the overabundance of attention turned her head; it would have to be a "strong head not to be so," she said. Her parents, mindful of the dangers of sudden fame, kept her on a strict schedule, never allowing her to idle in the greenroom. When they were unable to accompany her to social functions, they required a chaperone. Adelaide de Camp was her niece's constant companion, especially on tours of the provinces.

As a member of theatrical royalty, Kemble had no romantic notions about a career in the theater, and so was shielded against the bedazzlement of the spotlight. Although "dramatic personation" held some appeal, she found everything else about acting "repugnant." She commented nearly a decade after her retirement that she had never gone in front of an audience "without a shrinking feeling of reluctance." She also felt that her performing talents were fueled more by nervous energy than skill, and she felt the effort of physical exertion required for performance was "unhealthy," the resultant exhibitionism "odious."

In 1830, less than a year after her debut, these strains had already begun to ravage her health and sap her creativity. She confided to Harriet St. Leger, "My life in London leaves me neither time nor opportunity for any self-culture, and it seems to me as if my best faculties [are] lying fallow."

Upon Harriet's cross-examination, Fanny admitted that celebrity afforded her "many social pleasures and privileges." She was one of fewer than twenty invited on the maiden excursion of England's first steam railway by the entrepreneur George Stephenson, for instance. (She loved the sense of "flight" her first train ride evoked.)

The upper crust found Fanny's company most engaging and she received invitations to more parties and dinners than she could possibly attend. In London, she dined at the home of the poet Samuel Rogers, where Thomas Macaulay, the great wit Sydney Smith, and the poet Thomas Campbell were known to grace the table at his famous Sunday luncheons. Lady Dacre, a talented poet and translator, took Fanny under her wing, making her a frequent guest at the Hoo, her country estate in Hertfordshire. Even the great Sir Walter Scott, Fanny's childhood hero, flattered the actress by arranging for an audience in Edinburgh.

Years later, Kemble had mixed memories of these extravagant episodes, worrying that she had developed, to her great detriment, a taste for the "luxurious refinement and elegant magnificence of a mode of life never likely to be mine." She recalled in particular her stay in Manchester at Heaton, the country estate of Lady Wilton. Her hostess was "extremely kind to me, petting me almost like a spoiled child, dressing me in her own exquisite riding habit and mounting me on her own favorite horse." While such "kindly indulgence" was "very delightful" to Fanny, these attentions and adventures among the titled nobility brought her far from her "proper sphere." And she felt responsibility weighing heavily upon her. She was ever mindful of her obligations to her family: "It is incumbent upon me to banish all selfish regrets about the surrender of my personal tastes and feelings, which must be sacrificed to real and useful results for myself and others."

Questions of propriety became pressing, too, for Fanny's celebrity dramatically improved her prospects for marriage. Her parents had wed purely for love. But the example of more well-to-do relatives, like Fanny's godmother, Frances Twiss, taught them that the combination of wealth and love made for far less strain. By the late eighteenth cen-

Theatre Royal, Covent Garden.

This present THURSDAY, May 27, 1830,

Will be acted, the Tragedy of

ISABELLA,

Or, The FATAL MARRIAGE.

With new Scenes, Dresses, and Decorations.

The New Scenery painted by Messrs. GRIEVE, T. GRIEVE, and W. GRIEVE.

Count Baldwin, Mr. EGERTON,   Biron, Mr. WARDE,
Biron's Son, Miss HUNT, Carlos, Mr. G. BENNETT, Villeroy, Mr. ABBOTT
Maurice, Mr. HENRY,   Belford, Mr. HORREBOW,
Officer, Mr. ATKINS,   Samson, Mr. MEADOWS,
Gentlemen, Mess. Irwin and Goodson
Braves & Tipstaves, Mess. Collett, Grant, Addison, F. Sutton; Pedro Mr. Fuller
Isabella   by   Miss   FANNY KEMBLE,
(Her 11th appearance in that character)
Nurse, Mrs. WESTON,   Ladies, Mesds. Parsloe, Reed, Shotter, Shultz, Vials.

In the 3d act,   **AN EPITHALAMIUM.**

The MUSIC arranged by Mr. G. STANSBURY.

From the Works of MOZART, &c. &c.

The principal Vocal Parts by Miss HUGHES, Miss PERRY, Mess. DURUSET and PURDAY, and CHORUS.

With (42d time) a NEW FARCE, in one act, called

TEDDY the TILER.

Lord Dunderford, Mr. EVANS,   Henry, Mr. HENRY,
Frederick, Mr. BAKER,   Bombardine, Mr. HORREBOW,   Mr. Scrivener, Mr. TURNOUR,
Teddy Mulowney the Tiler,   Mr. POWER,
Tim Mr. ADDISON, Stiff Mr. RANSFORD, Apewell Mr. IRWIN, Constable Mr. Fuller, Richard Mr. Heath
Lady Dunderford, Mrs. WESTON,   Oriel, Miss LAWRENCE,
Flora, Miss J. SCOTT,   Julia, Mrs. BROWN,   Ladies, Mesdames Hudson and Appleton.

To conclude with (31st time) a New MUSICAL ROMANCE, in two acts, called

Robert the Devil,
Duke of Normandy.

The OVERTURE and MUSIC, entirely new, composed by I. BARNETT.
The new Scenery painted by Messrs. GRIEVE, T. GRIEVE, W. GRIEVE, FINLEY, &c.

Robert, Duke of Normandy,   Mr. G. BENNETT,
Lindor, Mr. BAKER,   Edmond, Mr. HORREBOW,
Picolo, Mr. KEELEY, Jaques Bocage Mr. MEADOWS, Gontran Mr. Turnour
Vassals, Peasants, Soldiers, &c. Mess. G. Smith, Irwin, Beale, Fuller, Miller, May, Purday, Sbegog, Tett, &c.
Countess de Rosambert, Miss LACY,   Blanche, Miss HUGHES,
Matilda, Mrs. VINING, Lodine, Miss CAWSE, Dame Gertrude Mrs Weston.

NO ORDERS WHATEVER WILL BE ADMITTED.

The TWO LAST PERFORMANCES of
Miss FANNY KEMBLE.

To-night,   ISABELLA.
And Tomorrow, will be acted the Comedy of

THE PROVOKED HUSBAND.

Lady Townly, (First time) Miss FANNY KEMBLE,
Her Last Appearance this Season,

On this occasion, the FREE LIST, will be suspended, the Public Press excepted

---

Miss FOOTE
will perform on Tuesday, Rosalind.

The new OPERA of

CINDERELLA: or the Fairy and the Little Glass Slipper
will be repeated on MONDAY & WEDNESDAY NEXT.

Tomorrow, the Comedy of THE PROVOKED HUSBAND. Lord Townly, Mr. C. KEMBLE,
Lady Townly, Miss FANNY KEMBLE,   (being her first appearance in that character)
To which will be added, **THE MASTER'S RIVAL.**

For three seasons, Fanny Kemble's performances were the
highlight of London's theatrical offerings.

tury onward, prejudices against marriage between penniless actresses
and well-born men of wealth were crumbling. From time to time a respectable actress, snaring a baron or duke, rose to the top of London
society without a hitch. Perhaps the Kembles aspired, through Fanny,
to take their place among London's elite.

Kemble was already an object of adoration by lovesick men of all
ages. She was pursued by a bevy of "Stage Door Johnnies," among
them the Reverend Augustus FitzClarence, an illegitimate son of the
King of England. The son of actress Dorothy Jordan and the Duke of
Clarence (later crowned William IV), FitzClarence used his influence
to obtain admission to Fanny's dressing room, where his visit was
closely supervised by Charles Kemble. But when this young man made
impertinent remarks to Fanny on the dance floor at a society ball, she
threatened to return to her seat before the waltz was ended. He tried
to demonstrate his contrition, asking Fanny to write sermons for
him—as Caroline Norton had. Kemble was not tempted by this invitation; she terminated their acquaintance.

But in the late spring of 1831, during Fanny's second season on the
stage, the Kembles were unable to prevent one of their daughter's
friendships from blossoming into love. Fanny Kemble was invited by a
group of aristocrats to join in their amateur theatricals. Her professional schedule generally precluded her from granting such a favor, but
the invitation came from Lord and Lady Egerton, Fanny's former
neighbors at Weybridge. Remembering her many happy days at their
Oatlands estate, she felt beholden.

Lord Egerton had translated Victor Hugo's *Hernani* and begged
Fanny to play the lead, Dona Sol. She had no special relish for the role,
but any reservations she felt evaporated the instant she laid eyes on Augustus Craven, the handsome young nobleman who had been chosen
to play opposite her. At each successive rehearsal and performance—
culminating in a command performance for the royals—their affection grew, so that by the end of the run, the lines they spoke onstage
were genuine words of love.

Sarah Siddons, revered in London society, died in 1831.

In the 1870s, Fanny published her diaries, which recorded in detail the hours she spent with her first love. Long afternoons of horseback riding, boating, and walking through the countryside were followed by evenings of music and repartee (in French), and midnight story-telling sessions. In town, the couple appeared together often. On one especially festive evening, Charles Kemble, upon arriving to escort his daughter home, was kept waiting in his carriage until past four in the morning, while Fanny remained at the ball dancing with her beloved "Mr. C."

Fanny indulged herself with bridal fantasies. Her older confidantes, however, rushed to temper her eagerness with some plain talk on the realities of marriage. Adelaide de Camp soberly explained to her niece, "While you remain single, . . . and choose to work, your fortune is an independent and ample one; as soon as you marry, there's no such thing." And Anna Jameson, whose own unhappy marriage led her to crusade for divorce reform, held out so little hope for a woman's chance of married happiness that her words haunted Fanny ever after.

Overwrought, Fanny sought the advice of a Gypsy. But the magic arts proved powerless to keep the happy courtship from souring. "Somehow I don't think a man would have the heart to break one's heart, but to be sure, I don't know." The passages following this lament were excised from her published journal; in place of what must have been heartfelt romantic confessions stood a series of telling ellipses. Fanny's infatuation was an "ephemeral love of serious consequence," a heartbreak from which she would not soon recover.

In the second week of June 1831, Sarah Siddons died, and all of England joined the Kemble family in grief. What was intended to be a sacred mourning period, however, was unceremoniously interrupted by professional concerns. With the passing of the Tragic Muse, it was expected that Fanny would master her aunt's more memorable roles, which she had hitherto avoided. The prospect was daunting: "And so I am to act Lady Macbeth! I feel as if I were standing up by the great pyramid of Egypt to see how tall I am."

It was difficult for a young actress to offer convincing portrayals of characters twice her age, and Fanny berated herself constantly when her efforts fell short. "The house was good, but I played like a wretch—ranted, roared and acted altogether infamously." It was no comfort when, after she had an especially difficult struggle with the part of Constance in Shakespeare's *King John,* her mother said soothingly, "You have done it better than any other girl of your age."

Despite her growing self-doubt, Fanny's talents continued to be much in demand, and she vastly expanded her repertory during her third season. To her Shakespearean catalogue of Juliet, Portia, and Beatrice she added Bianca in Henry Hart Milman's now forgotten *Fazio* and Julia in James S. Knowles's *The Hunchback.* The latter became one of her most popular roles. She even tasted her first success as a playwright, selling the publication rights for *Francis the First* to John Murray for £450, then performing the female lead in its first stage production.

But as Fanny continued to win critical and popular success, her family fell into an alarming state of disarray. The lucrative bookings Fanny brought to Covent Garden proved insufficient to stave off the theater's creditors, and Charles Kemble teetered on the brink of bankruptcy. Fanny sold her horse (no longer able to afford its upkeep) and the family practiced austerity, but prospects continued bleak. Kemble's mother seemed less and less able to cope with her active household.

Meanwhile, older brother John had rushed off to Spain with his fellow Apostles, who had joined General Torrijos's ill-fated rebellion against the royal government there. His activities had to be concealed from his high-strung mother, and the family breathed a sigh of relief when he returned, barely escaping execution—the fate of several of his comrades. Meanwhile, Harry Kemble was adrift in London, "lounging about the streets . . . a mere squanderer of time." Fanny used her income from *Francis the First* to buy her younger brother a commission in the army, and in 1832 he joined his regiment in Ireland for duty in the West Indies.

By the fall of 1831 it was clear the burden of keeping the Kemble finances afloat was too great for Fanny alone to bear. She recognized that Charles lacked "any hope of support for himself and my mother but toil, and that of the severest kind." She feared her father might resort to desperate measures—and he did, proposing a solo theatrical tour of the United States. Fanny, who hated "the very thought of America," once again intervened, insisting that she accompany him. When, at Christmastime, Charles contracted a serious inflammation of the lungs, it became clear that responsibility for success would, once again, rest on Fanny's shoulders.

CHAPTER TWO

O Brave New World

By the summer of 1832, final plans for the two-year tour of the United States had been made and the Kembles had one final announcement to make: the date of Fanny's farewell performance at Covent Garden. On the night of June 22, as she stood for the final time on the stage where she had made her debut less than three years before, the crowd chanted her name in unison and waved handkerchiefs in a bittersweet gesture of farewell. Too moved by this display of genuine emotion to summon up any eloquent speech, Fanny silently tossed single flowers into the crowd, weeping inconsolably all the while.

Fanny had previously been away from Britain only on a handful of excursions to France and Ireland—little more than hops. Parting company with theatrical colleagues, especially her beloved dresser, was difficult enough. But the prospect of a two-year separation from her mother was almost more than Fanny could bear. To ease her daughter's mounting fears, Maria Thérèse enlisted Fanny's cherished aunt Dall as a traveling companion. All four of them went on a holiday to Edinburgh before Dall, Charles, and Fanny were scheduled to set sail.

Caricature of a shipboard scene from
Fanny's Journal *(1835).*

When, on July 19, the trio left for Liverpool on the first leg of their journey—having said their final good-byes to well-wishers and loved ones—both father and daughter broke down sobbing. Even a farewell visit from the Combe brothers and Harriet St. Leger did little to lessen Kemble's melancholy.

The *Pacific,* with the Kembles' twenty-one trunks full of props and

costumes on board, set sail on August 1, 1832. Fanny and her aunt settled into the vessel's best accommodations, dreaming of better days ahead. True to her lifelong habit, Kemble kept a journal. It was dedicated to a "brave new world," and its opening passages vividly convey Fanny's frank infatuation with her first taste of adventure: "I have seen the glorious sun come up and look down upon this rolling sapphire; I have seen the moon throw her silver columns along the watery waste; I have seen one lonely ship in her silent walk across this wilderness, meet another, greet her, and pass her, like a dream, in the wide deep."

But the spiritual euphoria of oceangoing travel alternated with physical misery. The roiling waves caused Fanny particular discomfort; she likened shipboard existence to a drunken reel. Eventually she gained her sea legs, and she was not as troubled by seasickness as many of her fellow passengers. Aunt Dall was laid low during the frequent squalls, which played havoc with both mealtimes and appetites.

Unwilling to succumb to the monotony of the journey, Kemble occupied herself with reading and writing. She composed dialogue for her second play, *Star of Seville,* and plotted another. She practiced German by translating verse, continued her exploration of Dante, and indulged her romantic streak with volumes of Byron. She also sought out the company of other passengers—particularly a British father and daughter, William and Harriet Hodgkinson—who enjoyed her lively company.

But after a month on shipboard, Kemble was anxious to see land again. At the sight of Manhattan, the entire ship celebrated: "We . . . sang all the old songs, laughed at all the old jokes, drank our own and each other's health, wealth, and prosperity and came to bed at two o'clock."

When they landed on September 4, she had an enthusiastic first impression of New York, which reminded her "a little of Paris." Writing from her hotel room, she marveled that the "lighted shop-windows and brilliant moonlight were like a suggestion of the boulevards. It is very gay and rather like a fair." But the conduct of New York's inhabitants bore little resemblance to that of cultivated Parisians. Kemble complained that American manners reduced her to "sulky fits." Her journal recorded a litany of offenses: "Your washerwoman sits down before you, while you are standing speaking to her; and a shop-boy bringing things for your inspection, not only sits down, but keeps his hat on in your drawing-room." But the magnifying glass with which Kemble examined American manners would soon be trained on her own behavior, highlighting her best and worst characteristics.

Kemble's reputation for erudition and wit had preceded her, and much of New York society raced to make her acquaintance. The former mayor Philip Hone recorded that "she appears deserving of her reputation—a good figure, easy manner, sprightly and intelligent, self-possessed, not very handsome but with features animated and expressive, and calculated for great stage effects." The qualities that made Kemble such a desirable commodity onstage, however, did little to endear her to Manhattan's social elite.

It had never occurred to her that the best parlors of the city would not, as a matter of course, be open to her. The American aristocracy was suspicious of theater people; few native-born stage stars came from the educated classes. So when Manhattan favored Kemble with calls, she offended by blithe indifference.

Kemble was dismayed by the constant stream of visitors and had few kind words for them or their intentions. "These democrats are as title-sick as a banker's wife in England." Fanny was especially put off by American women, whom she singled out for ridicule by calling them "decayed" and claiming they all walked as if their shoes were too tight. Seemingly incapable of masking her true feelings offstage, she made many enemies by her bluntness.

She fell into the habit of favoring those who most amused her over those with better pedigrees, thus breaking the rules of American etiquette. Following a particularly egregious gaffe—she had ignored every other guest at a dinner party so that she could catch up on "English folk and doings" with a secretary to the English legation—her host warned: "Her fault appears to be an ungracious manner of receiving the advances of those who desire to pay her attention. This may proceed from the novelty of her situation, and may soon be removed. But now is the time to make friends if she wants them."

But with her New York debut imminent, Fanny was preoccupied with the more tangible demands of drilling a new set of actors and the rigors of performing a different play each night. To her great disappointment, American theater proved inferior in every way.

Her American debut, as Bianca in *Fazio,* called for her to play opposite a Mr. Keppel, with whom she was painfully familiar. Keppel's appalling lack of talent during a British tour of *Romeo and Juliet* had incited Kemble to call him "a washed-out man." On opening night, her worst fears were realized: Keppel repeatedly forgot his lines, and Fanny had to prompt him. Fazio died at the end of Act II, which came none too soon. Nevertheless she was greeted with thunderous applause. However, the adoration that had so delighted her in England seemed in America to have the opposite effect. The applause, complained Kemble, set her teeth on edge.

Her outlook on life in Manhattan was bleak: "My days are passed in dawdling about cold dark stages, with blundering actors who have not even had the conscience to study their parts, all the morning. All the afternoon, I sort out theatrical adornments, and all the evening I enchant audiences, prompt my fellow-mimes, and wish it had pleased heaven to make me a cabbage in a corner of a Christian kitchen garden!"

By night, she enchanted the critics, who could not find enough superlatives. The New York *Evening Post* saw in Kemble an "intensity and a truth never exhibited by an actress in America, certainly never by one so young." Philip Hone confided to his diary, "I have never witnessed an audience so moved, astonished and delighted." Walt Whitman was just a lad from Brooklyn, saving his pennies for a seat in the balcony. He later recalled: "Fanny Kemble! Name to conjure up great mimic scenes withal—perhaps the greatest. . . . Nothing finer did ever stage exhibit."

Fanny Kemble's celebrity created a popular craze across America. Young ladies began to adopt "Fanny Kemble" curls and to ask for "Fanny Kemble caps" at fashionable shops. Many stores took to displaying her portrait in the window to attract customers. Many equestrians named favorite horses after her, a tribute to her popularity and her reputation as a horsewoman. And even gardeners got into the act, as prized above all was a new tulip named "Miss Fanny Kemble": one collector bought a prize specimen in the autumn of 1832 for nearly two hundred dollars.

Kemble was especially impressive as Julia in Knowles's *The Hunchback*. Since the part of the self-sacrificing daughter had been written for her by the British playwright and since Kemble was known to be helping her father to recover his financial footing, this role proved extremely compelling. The play became so popular it was quoted in pulpits and editorials. But while Kemble played the conventional formulas of womanhood, her offstage life took a different turn.

Along with heavenly accolades came the brimstone of vengeful jealousy. Some friends of two New York actresses hatched a plot, never realized, "to hiss us off the New York stage, if possible; if not, to send people in every night to create a disturbance during our best scenes."

When their New York run concluded at the end of September, the Kembles moved on to Philadelphia by boat. Fanny's lively diary entries suggest that the trip was aesthetically displeasing, what with the tobacco-chewing gentlemen who covered her in "a perfect shower of saliva," and the American coach that delivered them to the city "bumping, thumping, jumping, jolting, shaking, tossing and tumbling over the wretched road."

The moment they stepped onto solid ground, Fanny opened her arms to her new host city. "The town is perfect silence and solitude compared with New York, and there is a greater air of age about it too, which pleases me. The red houses are not so fiercely red, nor the white facings so glaringly white, in short, it has not so new and flaunting a look which is a great recommendation to me."

Fanny was charmed by a "bewitching Newfoundland puppy whom I greatly coveted." His owner bestowed the pup on her, and she named him Neptune. He was the first of the many canine companions to accompany her throughout her adult life.

Second only to New York in population during the antebellum era, Philadelphia was a city full of energy and accomplishment. In the 1820s, one observer concluded that Philadelphia society had lines of demarcation as "strongly drawn as Europe, or more so, with the enormous difference, however, that there was not the slightest perceptible shade of difference in the intellects, culture or character of the people on either side of the line."

Philadelphians took great pride in their cultural achievements. The town supported several periodicals and, by the 1830s, an important publisher, Mathew Carey. The Pennsylvania Academy of Fine Arts, established in 1805, had built a museum on the corner of Chestnut and Tenth Streets to house fine European paintings. The city fathers favored cultural and philanthropic endeavors and welcomed theatrical and musical fare.

The Philadelphia press, however, had warned the inhabitants of Kemble's lapses in etiquette; they were none too eager to return the actress's warm overtures. The Kembles remained in town for over a month but received very few social invitations. Many aristocratic Pennsylvanians viewed her as simply a "stroller," one cut above a "Gypsy."

One Philadelphian who refused to ostracize Kemble was Thomas Sully, an artist of considerable reputation. His English parents had settled in Charleston, South Carolina, shortly after Thomas's birth. Before establishing his Philadelphia studio, Sully had studied in London with Sir Thomas Lawrence, and that connection with the Kembles led him to call on them. Fanny was charmed by Sully, who, she said, had a "pleasant family to match." He later completed several portraits of her.

Kemble was susceptible to the romantic attentions showered on her by the gentlemen of Philadelphia. The three most frequent callers were Dr. Charles Mifflin, a well-connected physician, the banking heir Edward Biddle, and Pierce Butler, who stood to inherit a family fortune.

Butler was expected to wed a Miss Emily Chapman, thus merging two prominent Pennsylvania clans, but that didn't prevent him from embarking on a new round of courtship. He called on Fanny at her hotel on October 13, the day after her Philadelphia debut. Fanny's voice, strained from the rigors of performance "like a cracked bagpipe," left her feeling poorly, and anyway she found Butler the least impressive of her suitors. "He is, it seems, a great fortune; consequently, I suppose (in spite of his inches), a great man."

If Kemble was not impressed by the appearance of the "pretty-spoken, *genteel* youth" who came to tea that day, he did make one notable suggestion: He "offered to ride with me." Kemble, as Butler must have known, was a fanatic about fitness and fresh air who thought her health "one of God's best gifts." Butler's offer to find horses superior to Philadelphia's "rickety hired mounts" was most tempting. On numerous occasions during her initial stay in Philadelphia, he filled Fanny's parlor with nosegays, signing himself "A Friend"—a pun on his heritage as a native son of the city of Quakers. These tender gestures touched the Kembles.

After a successful run in Philadelphia, the Kembles returned to New York in early November, where Shakespeare's *Taming of the Shrew* brought in a phenomenal $5,000 on opening night. When they returned to Philadelphia on December 4, Butler began to pay court in earnest, riding with Kemble almost every day and lavishing her father and aunt with kindness. The Kembles remained throughout the holidays, performing in *Macbeth* on Christmas day. On New Year's Eve, when the trio left for Baltimore, Pierce Butler was with them; two weeks later, he traveled on with them to Washington, D.C.

"How they do rejoice my spirit"

"In walked that interesting youth Mr——. with a nosegay as big as himself in his hand."

Vol. 1. page. 176.

Fanny was besieged by admirers with bouquets, lampooned in this parody from her Journal *(1835).*

Kemble found that the nation's capital paled in comparison with London. Laid out over ten square miles, the city had few prominent facades and was sparsely dotted with houses. Fanny was particularly unimpressed by the White House, "a comfortless, handsome looking building, with a withered grass plot enclosed in wooden palings in front and a desolate reach of uncultivated ground down to the river behind."

As Fanny had from a very young age been familiar with political life in London, she took a lively interest in the American capital. She saw republican values at work in the breakdown of class barriers in everyday encounters. Kemble had a mixed response to this leveling atmosphere. On the one hand, her long-standing fondness for "plain folk" heightened her enjoyment of mingling with commoners of every description. But she saw these interludes as diversions, relying upon the escape hatch of privilege and celebrity as a frequent refuge from unwanted familiarity or crude behavior. She found so much of the latter on her travels that she took to keeping a list of rude expressions uttered by Americans, for example, "enough to make a Quaker kick his mother." Determined to delve further into the workings of democracy than these offhand demonstrations of "freedom of speech," she turned to the U.S. Senate. She had high hopes that a visit to the Senate—with its legendary oratory and exchange of ideas—would prove riveting, but the audience seemed strangely unresponsive to the speakers.

Even if the Senate lacked the theatrical flair Kemble prized so highly, President Andrew Jackson lived up to his fiery reputation. Jackson's heated 1832 campaign for reelection had dominated American politics during Kemble's first days in the States. A war hero who projected frontier values, Jackson has been long remembered, for better or worse, for ordering the removal of the Cherokee people to western territories, in direct defiance of John Marshall's Supreme Court.

Jackson aggressively aligned himself against the power of the federal government—embodied by the Washington bureaucracy—so the establishment had breathed a collective sigh of relief when he lost to John Quincy Adams in the presidential election of 1824. When he captured the White House in 1828, his foes knew Jackson would use the power of his office to wreak political changes. Indeed, during his first term, he took on the Second Bank of the United States, and, by extension, the bank's defender, Philadelphian Nicholas Biddle. This battle over the bank earned Jackson a reputation as a champion of the common man. His veto of the bank's recharter in 1832 secured his reelection.

Kemble arrived in Washington shortly before Jackson's second inauguration, as anxious as any American to learn what this formidable man would do next. In the midst of the election campaign, South Carolina had threatened to secede from the Union rather than obey the federal tariff. Kemble watched from the wings as the president jousted with his former vice president, John C. Calhoun, over the explosive issue of states' rights. But even amid such political upheaval, the country's power brokers were eager to be introduced to the famous young actress, and Fanny was flattered by the attention.

She was granted a private audience with Jackson and found him "very tall and thin, but erect and dignified in his carriage." Well versed in political issues on both sides of the Atlantic, Fanny gamely engaged Jackson in a dialogue about the Nullification crisis: "He talked about South Carolina and entered his protest against scribbling ladies, assuring us that the whole of the present southern disturbances had their origin in no larger a source than the nib of the pen of a lady."

Kemble's debut in Washington on January 14, 1833, was attended by prominent national figures. One box contained both Dolley Madison and John Quincy Adams. In another sat Chief Justice John Marshall and his illustrious colleague Justice Joseph Story. Story wrote to his wife: "I have never seen any female acting at all comparable. . . . she threw the whole audience into tears. The Chief Justice shed them in common with younger eyes." Senator Daniel Webster, seated nearby, also witnessed Marshall's emotional display. His presence symbolized the repayment of Kemble's professional courtesy of attending Webster's recent Senate address.

Also in attendance during her Washington run was a favorite acquaintance from her London days, Washington Irving. Irving's considerable influence ensured that the Kembles met with greater respect during their stay in the nation's capital than they had in Philadelphia. Shortly after her Washington debut, Kemble was given personal introductions to Daniel Webster and to the statesman Edward Everett. Indeed, anyone Kemble might name was happy to accommodate her with an audience, so widespread was her fame.

But Washington society proved fickle when what began innocently enough with an invitation for horseback riding turned into a scandal so volatile that it threatened to disrupt the theatrical tour. On an afternoon outing, her host, a Mr. Adams, unbeknownst to Fanny, made their date a trio by including his friend Mr. Fulton (a nephew of Robert Fulton, the developer of the steamboat). Kemble was displeased at the presence of this unexpected additional companion, but when she saw that Mr. Fulton had brought along a horse for her to ride, she brightened immediately. In jest, she bantered with Fulton that she should pay him two dollars for the hire of his horse.

But Mr. Fulton took great offense and departed in angry silence. Soon afterward, a gentleman confidentially reported to Charles Kemble that his daughter was said to have disparaged America and Americans in the presence of Mr. Fulton. Unless she apologized or explained, the visitor warned, Fanny would be hissed off the stage. To emphasize the utter seriousness of the matter, he confided that fifty members of Congress had mentioned the incident to him. The anxiety surrounding this circumstance drove Fanny to near collapse. Although no hissing erupted when she performed, she complained she passed the intervals between her scenes crying offstage.

Fanny feared that her reputation was beyond repair. But when the Kembles and Adelaide returned to Philadelphia on January 30, 1833, she was greeted by a surprising turn of events. She took the stage on the first night of the run to a spontaneous outburst of applause. Handbills detailing Mr. Fulton's charges had been circulated. But instead of joining the attack, Philadelphia fans rejected the accusations, embracing the Kembles with one of their warmest American receptions. This thawed Kemble considerably toward the City of Brotherly Love.

Slowly but surely, Fanny was finding kindred spirits in America. When the tour moved back to New York in February 1833, she befriended the novelist Catharine Sedgwick. Catharine's brother Charles was married to Elizabeth Dwight Sedgwick; Elizabeth and her daughter, Kate, later became Kemble's most intimate friends in the United States. Catharine Sedgwick wrote ahead to friends in

*The writer Catharine Sedgwick was one of several
Sedgwicks to befriend Fanny Kemble.*

Boston, telling them of Kemble's impending arrival: "She is the most captivating creature, steeped to the very lips in genius. . . . I have never seen any woman on the stage to be compared with her. . . . On the stage she is beautiful, far more than beautiful; her face is the mirror of her soul."

Sedgwick's admiration was echoed by many in Boston, including the anonymous "A.Z.," who paid tribute to the Kembles in print: "Their visit to this city I consider as a public advantage. It temporarily redeems one of the amusements of the people from its ordinary degradation and shows to those who have the direction of it and the public what the stage might be and ought to be—what it would be whenever the patronage of this opulent and enlightened metropolis is judiciously and liberally directed to the object."

In return, Kemble lavished praise on the city, "one of the pleasantest towns imaginable" because it reminded her of home: "The houses are like English houses; the Common is like Constitution Hill; Beacon Street is like a bit of Park Lane; and Summer Street, now the [horse] chestnut trees are in bloom, is perfectly beautiful." She had more good words for the dramatic players at the Tremont Theatre, "decidedly the best company I have ever played with anywhere out of London," and, moreover, all the citizens of Boston, whom Kemble praised as being "intellectual . . . abundantly good-natured and kind."

Boston's theatergoers wore their intellectualism as a badge of honor. One night, Kemble took part in a heated debate between John Quincy Adams and Daniel Webster; Webster claimed that Knowles's *Hunchback* was not as good as Shakespeare. When Fanny agreed, but replied that Shakespeares did not "grow on every bush," Adams, who claimed to worship the writer, dismissed *Othello* as "disgusting" and *Romeo and Juliet* as "childish nonsense." Finally, Kemble "remained silent—for what could I say?"

The only snag in the entire Boston run came on the second night, when the manager of the Tremont Theatre scheduled Charles and Fanny to appear together onstage. The Kembles preferred to stagger their performances, Charles Kemble first playing alone in one of his showcase roles, such as Hamlet, then Fanny Kemble performing solo in one of hers, such as Beatrice in *Much Ado About Nothing*. Excitement and momentum built toward a dual third performance.

But Boston audiences were so enthusiastic about the Kembles that the shift in schedule had no noticeable effect. Every day the box office was mobbed. Young men smeared themselves with molasses to push ahead in the crowd and fended off rivals for scarce tickets. College attendance fell off so sharply on the afternoons of Kemble's matinees that Harvard faculty threatened to cancel classes. Aristocrat Henry Lee, then a Harvard undergraduate, recalled: "I scarcely ever go by the

Tremont House without gazing once more at the windows of her room, in the superstitious hope that her radiant face may shine forth." So desperate was he to have some association with Kemble, no matter how faint, that he rented a horse named Niagara because she had once ridden it.

But the lovesick Lee could see a great rival in Pierce Butler, who was by now Kemble's constant companion. He attended most of her performances and even played the flute in the orchestra pit. Above all, the Kembles grew to rely on his ability to alleviate the discomfort and inconvenience of their extended travels. Butler's friend Henry Witkoff confessed his own "wild intoxication" with Fanny, but recognized Butler as the clear front-runner: "Pierce Butler, a man of good family and fortune, became desperately enamored of the marvelous creature, who to the sorcery of the stage added rare charms of person, brilliant accomplishments and high culture. Pierce Butler was envied, and almost detested, by a swarm of rivals for his victory over the Kembles."

Fanny Kemble's theological appetite was whetted in Boston by her acquaintance with the illustrious Reverend William Ellery Channing, a leading Unitarian theologian. Catharine Sedgwick had introduced them in New York, but Kemble was already well acquainted with Channing's work. The two struck up a correspondence, and Fanny and Pierce attended Channing's services whenever they could.

After nearly a month's run in Boston, the Kembles were reluctant to move on, but they had an engagement at the Park Theatre in Brooklyn in early June. In nine straight months of back-to-back bookings, a pattern had emerged at the box office. While Charles Kemble alone was not enough of a draw to fill the house, a bill featuring either a solo appearance by Fanny, or father and daughter together, always sold out. The Kembles were scheduled to play both Albany and Toronto in the summer season. Charles, careful to protect both his daughter's health and his future contracts, decided they must go on holiday after their New York engagement ended on June 30, 1833, before heading to Albany and Canada.

Charles Kemble had been in touch with a distant relation, Gouverneur Kemble, whose palatial estate in Cold Spring, New York, would be the first stop on their way up the Hudson, and onward to Niagara Falls. Pierce Butler was obliged to return to Philadelphia on business, but planned to join the Kembles in Utica, New York, then holiday with them at the Falls.

Fanny stepped onto the steamer in New York harbor to discover another celebrity on board, Edward John Trelawny. The forty-one-year-old Englishman, known the world over for his association with the likes of Lord Byron and Percy Bysshe Shelley, dazzled Kemble: "Mr. [Trelawny] is sun burnt enough to warm one . . . with a look."

Trelawny had acquired his exotic appearance on worldwide adventures, always dramatic—and sometimes fatal. When, in 1822, a violent storm in Italy's Gulf of Spezia carried Shelley out to sea, Trelawny and Byron discovered his drowned body. They made a funeral pyre on the seashore near Viareggio. When Shelley's heart failed to burn, Trelawny—on an impulse still celebrated—pulled it from the flame and returned it, along with Shelley's ashes, to his wife, Mary Shelley. Two years later, Trelawny discovered Byron's body in Greece, where they had both gone to help the rebels fight invading Turks. He hoped to bury Byron in Greece as the poet had wanted, but finally shipped the body back to England, as the poet's family wished.

Trelawny's closeness to the deaths of two of England's most eminent literary figures was what made his name in the world of letters, although he had done some writing of his own. In 1831, he anonymously published his *Adventures of a Younger Son,* recounting his own thrilling exploits in India and the South Seas. When the book sold well, Trelawny, finally credited with authorship, was proclaimed one of England's most intrepid explorers and daring autobiographers. In truth, he was a fabulist: most of his wild accounts were pure fiction.

On the steamer, Trelawny quickly proved his abilities as a raconteur. He "killed us with laughing," reported Kemble. But she was as drawn to his dashing physicality as to his verbal prowess:

What a savage he is in some respects. . . . A man with the pro-
portions of a giant for strength and agility, taller, straighter,
and broader than most men, yet with the most listless indo-
lent carelessness of gait . . . as if he didn't know where he was
going, and didn't much wish to. . . . His face is as dark as a
moor's with a wild, strange look about the eyes and fore-
head, and a mark like a scar upon his cheek. . . . His hands are
as brown as a laborer's: he never profanes them with gloves,
but wears two strange magical looking rings; one of them
which he showed me, is made of elephant hair.

Fanny's journal during this period reveals that she was preoccupied
with Trelawny, to the exclusion of her admirer Pierce Butler. A descendant suggests that Kemble had already accepted Butler's offer of
marriage by April 1833, but even if this was so, she and her family were
reluctant to lose Trelawny's charming company. They begged him to
wait for two days while they visited Gouverneur Kemble at Cold
Spring, and then join them on their steamboat north to Mohawk Falls,
near Cohoes and Canada.

The foursome must have made a pretty portrait of the English on
holiday. Near Albany, they boarded a skiff to tour some nearby falls.
And on their canal boat from Schenectady to Utica, Trelawny read out
loud from *Don Quixote*. By the time they reached Utica, relations between Kemble and Trelawny had become quite cozy, much to the con-
sternation of Pierce Butler.

The Kembles had written ahead to him, informing him of the addition to their party, so he arrived in Utica prepared to compete for
Fanny's affections. In a less than subtle demonstration of his wealth
and largesse, Butler brought along genuine silver for the jaunt to Niagara, so the party wouldn't have to put up with shoddy eating utensils
at the inns they visited along the way.

But despite these grand gestures, Butler knew he was outclassed by
Trelawny, who was nearly twice his age, and who towered over him in

Pierce Butler, the second largest slaveholder in Georgia
when he claimed his inheritance in 1836.

both height and accomplishment. So Butler quietly acquiesced to his rival. It must have been difficult to ignore the fact that his beloved was so captivated by another man.

Years later, Trelawny spoke glowingly of Fanny Kemble and a mutual friend proclaimed that she might have been Trelawny's one great love. However, Fanny was as aware of Trelawny's vagabond character as she was of Butler's reputation as "a man of great fortune." Besides, Trelawny had a checkered romantic career.

His first wife was an Arabian sheik's daughter named Zela, whose tragic early death brought him back to England in heavy mourning.

His second wife, a proper English lady, gave him two daughters and hope for a respectable family. But after less than five years of marriage, Trelawny discovered that his wife had taken a lover, and sordid divorce proceedings ensued. When, a few years later, his second wife died while Trelawny was with Byron in Greece, Trelawny remained abroad, leaving his children dependent upon the charity of others.

He next married a Greek chieftain's daughter, rumored to be one of a "harem" of local women he had collected. (In reality, Trelawny had bought several Greek slaves so as to set them free in their native land and thus demonstrate his opposition to slavery.) In any case, after his wife cut her hair without his permission, he divorced her and took their infant daughter, whom he had named Zella, back to Italy. Refusing to be tied down by his responsibilities, he left his children behind and set off for North America, alone, in 1833.

Trelawny was far more vibrant and worldly than Kemble's American suitors—more than Butler, especially. For the cause of Greek liberation, he had taken a bullet, whose fragments were still lodged in his body. While Butler was the scion of an old American family whose wealth was derived from slaveholding, Trelawny had opposed slavery and oppression in word and action.

But Trelawny's tangled marital history, coupled with his lack of financial resources, weighed heavily against him. Financial security was of paramount importance to Fanny; whatever Butler lacked in sophistication, he made up for with his promised income and social standing.

A decision between her two suitors loomed at the end of the holiday, but the journey to Niagara allowed Fanny to escape into the magical beauty of her surroundings. With every stop along the way her enthusiasm grew; at the "extremely beautiful" sight of Trenton Falls, Fanny proclaimed, the water "came pouring down like a great rolling heap of amber." But Trelawny, who shared her passion for the place, promised that Niagara would be even more breathtaking.

He had spoken truly. Fanny recorded that the falls embodied an "awful, terrible loveliness." "The impulse to jump down seemed all but irresistible," but Fanny restrained herself from sliding down the "huge green glassy mountain of water," instead frolicking barefoot on the rocks.

It seemed that nothing could spoil the journey, but then their coach overturned rounding a sharp curve, and the accident proved rather serious. Although Pierce escaped with only a scratch, Trelawny was knocked nearly unconscious; Charles and Fanny were thrown from the coach and landed in a heap, shaken and bruised. Dall suffered a head wound, and was carried into a nearby tavern, where a bandage was applied to stop the bleeding. After a hearty meal, the party continued to tour, but the holiday atmosphere had evaporated.

The scare jolted Charles's attention back to business concerns. He intended to stay away from England as long as possible, as he feared that any American earnings would be seized, upon his return, by voracious London creditors. Perhaps, Dall suggested, Charles might follow his older brother's example and retire to the Continent, where his family could live unencumbered by lingering English debt. Descendants have speculated that Charles might have considered a permanent exile in America, where he and Fanny drew an enthusiastic following throughout the winter of 1833–34.

Accounts of Fanny's ongoing romance with Pierce Butler and rumors of their impending nuptials circulated. Dall's melancholy romantic history and Charles's own split loyalties—his need for the steady income his daughter provided conflicted with his desire to see her settled with a husband who would provide for her handsomely—prevented them from making an objective assessment of the match. Fanny's friends, however, were quick to express concern.

The novelist Mary Russell Mitford confessed: "Butler is a gentlemanly man, with good sense and amiable disposition, infinitely her inferior. Poor girl, she makes a dangerous experiment; I have a thousand fears for the result." Fanny later wrote that William Hodgkinson, a fast friend since the voyage from England, intended "to make my aunt and father aware of Mr. Butler's character . . . but of course, Mr. Hodgkinson spoke guardedly and generally, tho' I suppose he knew much of Mr. Butler's early career of profligacy." As Fanny later admitted, she was so in love that she ignored the "cautions which reached me at second hand through my aunt."

By autumn, news of Butler's attachment to Kemble had crossed the ocean, giving Maria Thérèse Kemble great cause for alarm. Fanny's brother John wrote: "Do let me know, dearest Fan, when this terrible affair of marriage is to be . . . much righteous indignation has been excited . . . that when you have a house and a nursery to look after, you will leave off writing plays." In closing, he added: "You will be happy if your husband only knows how to value you."

Relatives in Butler's family had long indulged in elopements and disinheritances. When Butler's strong-willed mother died in 1831, his need for family approval seemed to diminish. Mere acquaintances, however, were quick to weigh in. One society belle from Philadelphia reported: "The whole world is talking. . . . we shall probably see this celebrated actress placed in one of the most elegant establishments in our country and leading the circle which now scarcely deigns to notice her."

When the Philadelphian Walter Stirling, a great friend of Sarah Siddons, was asked pointedly about Fanny's virtue by a Butler family friend, he replied: "Her character is above question . . . she is a perfect lady . . . but she is troublesome and self willed . . . despising all authority and advice. . . . Since infancy she has been the source of perpetual annoyance and anxiety—I am sure [her parents] will be glad when she is married but I pity the poor man . . . especially if he is so amiable a person as you think Mr. Butler."

In October 1833, the Kembles discovered that Dall's head injuries from the coach accident were far more serious than originally suspected. The doctor offered very little hope of full recovery. During the long winter of 1833–34, Dall's health deteriorated, and by early spring she was permanently paralyzed from the waist down.

It was at this anxious juncture that Fanny agreed to allow Carey, Lea & Blanchard, the Philadelphia publishers, to print her American journal; she hoped that the royalties would pay for Dall's care. Consumed with worry, Fanny traveled to Boston to fulfill theatrical engagements, but returned, canceling several performances, when Dall began to have convulsions.

Her nursing duties, combined with the rigors of performance, distracted Fanny from the May wedding she and Pierce were planning. Despite Dall's illness, Butler was growing impatient; however, Charles Kemble played on Fanny's feelings of filial duty to extract from her a promise not to abandon their theatrical commitments. In an attempt to appease her father, she promised to return to England with him, and he booked passage for them to sail on the *United States* at the end of June.

Believing that the wedding had been postponed, Charles Kemble wrote to a friend: "How happy Fanny's friends will be to see her once more before she is married, won't they? The legitimate drama will have another chance, I hope, of resuscitation; and we shall both at least take leave of the British stage in a manner worthy of the house of Kemble!"

While Charles savored the pension his daughter would in effect be providing, Fanny had not undertaken the commitment happily. On April 11, 1834, she reported to her old friend George Combe: "I did not expect to remain on the stage after the month of May when my marriage was appointed, and hoped to be free from a profession which has always been irksome to me, but it is otherwise. I shall return to England with my father in June and continue my labors for another twelve months either there or here."

Dall died shortly thereafter, and in the last week of April was buried in Mount Auburn Cemetery in Cambridge, Massachusetts. The loss of Fanny's beloved confidante precipitated a crisis. Nearly incapacitated by grief, Fanny wrote to Anna Jameson: "I shall not return to

England, not even to visit . . . certainly never to make my home there again . . . rejoice with me that there is a prospect of my leaving [the stage] before its pernicious excitement has been rendered necessary to me."

Fanny's bravado, however, was confined to her correspondence. Knowing that any decision on her part was guaranteed to displease one of the two men she loved most, she agonized over whether to remain in America and marry Butler, or return to England with her father. To exacerbate her indecision, Trelawny resurfaced, using a condolence letter as an entrée to explore unfinished romantic business.

He confessed that Fanny's last words—"We cannot like those who *force* themselves upon us!!!"—haunted him, and wondered if his renewal of contact was "deepening my offenses in again thrusting myself in a new shape upon your notice, when you were congratulating [yourself] that you had shaken me off forever." Fanny was unmoved, so he departed for the West via the Gulf of Mexico to spend his final weeks in America alone.

By May 31, Kemble had made up her mind. That day, she wrote to her friend Sarah (Saadi) Perkins: "I will now tell you a piece of news which may perhaps be of some interest to you. I am going to be married next Saturday, and after then you are not to imagine me in your mind's eye as Fanny Kemble racing along (Chekie) beach or dipping her feet into Jamaica Pond, but sober Mrs. Pierce Butler with a ring on her finger (bells on her toes, I suppose)."

In a letter of the same date to Kate Sedgwick, Kemble revealed her relief at finally having done right by all: "I must tell you how bright a ray of sunshine is parting my stormy sky. Pierce has behaved *most* nobly, and my Father most kindly." For Fanny's sake, the two men had called a truce: Pierce and Fanny would wed, and then Fanny would return with her father to England, where she would give her final theatrical tour before coming back to America. (However, Pierce never did feel warmly toward his future father-in-law, whom he believed had "committed an injustice" toward him in urging Fanny to return to England.)

> Pierce has promised me that this [the wedding] shall not interfere with my departure or the discharge of my duties to my father, and relying implicitly as I do on his word, I could not resist his earnest entreaties to be his wife before I gave myself up to those chances which perhaps might never have suffered him to call me by that name. I think now that it will be better that he should feel I am his, fast for life, tho' at a distance and I shall have reason without appeal for resisting any further claim which might hereafter have been made upon me. . . . I think seventeen happy days snatched on the very brink of bitterness and parting not to be denied to one who has followed my footsteps for a whole year with a hope which he now beholds defeated.

Kemble and Butler were married by an Anglican bishop in an Episcopalian ceremony at Christ Church in Philadelphia on Saturday, June 7, 1834. That night, a crowd gathered outside their hotel for a wedding serenade. Postponing a honeymoon, Kemble and her new husband traveled to New York, where Fanny and Charles finished their final American engagement.

And now Butler broke his word. According to the Philadelphia socialite Rebecca Gratz, he "could not consent to the separation or to her continuing in the stage—her father was angry at losing the aid of her professional talents, considered himself wronged and deceived."

Butler reasoned that, according to marital law, any money his wife earned was rightfully his. As a reverse dowry, intended to placate Charles Kemble and compensate for lost future earnings, Fanny signed over to her father the income on her American savings. After two years, she had amassed a considerable sum, over $35,000, which was on deposit in a New Orleans bank. The interest would provide Charles with a handsome annuity.

But Charles Kemble sailed home to England uneasy about his daughter's future. He dreaded what Fanny herself had suspected: perhaps she was not destined for marital bliss.

When she was just nineteen, she had confessed doubts about her romantic fate: "I do not think I am fit to marry, to make an obedient wife or affectionate mother, my imagination is paramount with me, and would disqualify me, I think, for the everyday matter of fact cares and duties of the mistress of a household and the head of a family. I think I would be unhappy and the cause of unhappiness to others if I were to marry. I cannot swear I shall never fall in love, but if I do I will fall out of it again, for I do not think I shall ever so far lose sight of my best interest and happiness as to enter into a relation for which I feel so unfitted." Despite her teenage prophecy, at the age of twenty-four Fanny Kemble surrendered her liberty, giving up the stage to play the role of wife.

CHAPTER THREE

Not So Somber Airs

Before her marriage, Fanny knew she possessed "fortune and fame (such as it is)—positive real advantages, which I cease to own when I give myself away, which certainly makes my marrying anyone or anyone marrying me rather a solemn consideration for I lose everything and my marryee gains nothing in a worldly point of view—and it is incontrovertible and not pleasant." These words, written in 1832, precisely described the reversal of fortune she experienced as a new bride in 1834.

Accustomed to depending on the largesse of his family, Pierce lacked independent wealth, vocation, or even direction for his life. His brother, John, was also "a mere idler . . . totally without education or intellect," but he had married an heiress, Gabriella Morris, and was comfortably fixed "in dress, house & equipment."

The brothers' maternal grandfather, Major Pierce Butler, had died in 1822, leaving them second in line (behind their aunt Frances Butler, the major's executrix) to inherit his vast holdings of rice and cotton plantations in Georgia's Sea Islands. This promise of wealth

*Thomas Sully's portrait of Fanny Kemble during
the early years of her marriage.*

condemned the Butler-Kemble union, from its earliest days, to strife
and misery.

With the brothers' financial interests inextricably linked, it seemed
only fitting that John and Gabriella accompany Pierce and Fanny on
their honeymoon to Newport. Upon their return, the Pierce Butlers
were to set up housekeeping under the aegis of the aged Frances. She
had promised them Butler Place, the family's three-hundred-acre
property in Branchtown, some six miles beyond the outskirts of
Philadelphia. But the house was in such disrepair that it was uninhab-
itable, and remained so well after the couple's return from Rhode Island.

As Butler had no means to provide for himself and his bride—and Fanny no longer had an income of her own—the couple had no choice but to seek refuge with Pierce's brother and sister-in-law, who lived in a fine Philadelphia mansion. John and Gabriella had every reason to be favorably disposed toward Pierce, although neither was very fond of Fanny.

Rather, in keeping with the tastes of the entire Butler family, John and Gabriella valued their social connections above all. They regarded Fanny's flamboyant ways as an embarrassment people of their position could ill afford, and they demanded from her a seamless transition from belle to matron. For her part, Fanny was unwilling to abandon her distinctive appearance and social flair. When she insisted on dressing for horseback riding in Turkish trousers and on decorating her rooms in garish fabrics, her new family ridiculed her mercilessly.

Instead of using his influence to help, Butler joined his family in criticizing and correcting his new bride. Throughout their two-year courtship, Pierce had treated Fanny like a princess. But once they were wed, he felt neither the necessity nor the inclination to continue his tender solicitude; he simply expected her to accede to his wishes. Any differences of opinion between them should cease.

Believing the first few months of wedlock to be a trial period, Butler set out to implement this literal interpretation of the vow to "honor and obey." Citing his wife's "great energy of will," he complained that her preference for her own views gave rise to "a sense of imagined oppression." Fanny could best demonstrate her loyalty, Butler maintained, by agreeing with him in every regard.

Butler's attitude toward marriage, perhaps excessively severe to the modern sensibility, reflected prevailing views. Within the Southern antebellum household, the white male patriarch ruled unchallenged, and prescriptive literature supported his position completely. Caroline Gilman, in *Recollections of a Southern Matron*, advised young brides: "The three golden threads with which domestic happiness is woven: . . . to repress a harsh answer, to confess a fault, and to stop (right or wrong) in the midst of self-defense, in gentle submission." A wife's greatest fault, short of impurity, was disobedience in thought or deed.

Surrounded by disapproving Butlers at every waking moment, Fanny longed for contact with friends and acquaintances from her old life. A visit with the English writer Harriet Martineau was respectable enough, and Fanny was even granted permission to receive her former suitor Edward Trelawny when he passed through Philadelphia. But when she wished to invite to dinner a Mr. and Mrs. Charles Mathews, English actors who were great friends of her parents, the Butlers refused. Pierce icily pointed out to his wife that the elevated social status she enjoyed through him barred any future association with those from a lower station, which included theater people. Fanny was dumbfounded at this—and appalled to find that she had no say.

With a lifetime of isolation and discontent stretching before her, Fanny turned against her husband in a most dramatic way. The simmering conflict erupted when Fanny's plans to publish her American journal proceeded despite Butler's wishes. Rightly suspecting that the journal contained information that might embarrass him or his family, Pierce demanded that Fanny break her publishing contract. Fanny pointed out that the royalties were already promised to Dall's heir, Victoire de Camp (Fanny's spinster aunt, who was eking out a living as a governess). She felt compelled to fulfill this obligation.

When demands and threats proved useless, Butler attacked the problem with the only other means at his disposal: money. He offered to buy the manuscript back from Carey, Lea & Blanchard at a higher price than the advance, but was refused. Not only did Fanny very much resent this intervention, but also the publisher's interest in the manuscript increased exponentially.

As a conciliatory gesture, Fanny allowed Butler to read her journal entries as she recopied them for the typesetter. Her concession only led to more acrimony and endless wrangles over Butler's proposed cuts.

Married less than four months, Kemble decided one evening in early autumn to pack her things and run away. Butler betrayed his

The Germantown estate outside Philadelphia where Pierce
Butler settled with his bride, Fanny Kemble.

wounded pride in his scorn for the note she left behind: "This farewell is somewhat girlish and romantic; but she had rather passed the age of girlhood at this time."

Fanny wandered the Philadelphia streets alone, unable to settle on a plan. Exhausted, cold, and disheartened after many hours on foot, she returned after dark to her brother-in-law's to find Butler in a fury. Kemble retired without speaking to her husband, or recording anything of this incident in her diary or letters.

Once the ordeal of preparing her American journal was past, once Fanny had returned to the fold after her abortive flight, she and Pierce tried to patch up their relationship. Two events in December 1834 held out hope that the Pierce Butlers might achieve domestic happiness: the repairs on Butler Place finally complete, the couple settled in to their first home; and soon afterward, Fanny confirmed that she was pregnant.

However, impending motherhood failed to have the positive effect

Pierce hoped for; his wife's mood continued to darken during the winter months of early 1835. He attributed Fanny's gloom to the physical discomforts of pregnancy and to fears about childbirth. But, as Fanny confided to Anna Jameson, she was lonely: "Human companionship indeed, at present I have not much of; but as like will to like, I do not despair of attracting towards me, by and by, some of my own kind with whom I may enjoy pleasant intercourse; but you have no idea—none—of the intellectual dearth and drought in which I am existing at present."

Her attempts to win favor with her country neighbors fared poorly. When she served beer to the Butlers' teetotaling Quaker tenant farmers, her kind intentions were interpreted as wickedness, and malicious gossip continued to plague her.

Determined to save her female intimates from such unhappiness, Fanny resorted to plain talk about the desperation of an unfulfilling partnership. On the occasion of Sarah Perkins's engagement in May 1835, Fanny vigorously cautioned her:

> Persuade your lover to embrace a profession & excite him by every means to pursue it energetically. As you are wealthy and stand in no need of support from such means it will require no little strength of character in him to follow laborious study for its own sake, & in you to urge him to pursuits which will take some of his time from you. Yet do it, do it, dear Saadi, if you value his happiness & excellence & do it before you are married.

This was a thinly veiled warning not to pursue the path she herself had chosen.

Pierce Butler's lack of profession or avocation, which may have been flattering in a doting fiancé, was most unbecoming in a husband. The two discovered they had very little in common, and Fanny found

Pierce's lackluster mental faculties as trying as he found her intellectual pursuits. However, in a letter to George Combe, Kemble was able to tint this disparity with a rosy glow: "We are fortunately different in temper. He is cheerful and contented, exceedingly calm and self possessed, and has abundance of patience with my more morbid mental constitution."

On May 28, 1835, Sarah Butler, named after Pierce's mother, was born. The birth was an ordeal. Fanny wrote to a close friend: "I cannot believe that women were intended to suffer as much as they do and be as helpless as they are, in childbearing. . . . I am sorry to find that my physical courage has been very much shaken by my confinement."

Nevertheless, Kemble quickly regained her strength and was soon up on horseback. She even boasted to an American friend about her rapid recovery: "I am myself perfectly well, and up and about as if nothing had happened. My health and strength seem to amuse everybody here. I thank God for both, and steadfastly determine to lose neither by coddling myself, which I find is very fashionable among your countrymen." Nevertheless, she would later attribute gynecological ills to returning to strenuous exercise too soon after Sarah's birth.

Although Kemble's introduction to motherhood predated F. Scott Fitzgerald's *The Great Gatsby* by nearly one hundred years, she greeted the birth of a daughter with the same mixed emotions as Daisy Buchanan. Daisy labeled her offspring a "fool," as all daughters were destined to become. Fanny took a melancholy tone: "I was at first a little disappointed that my baby was not a man-child for the lot of woman is seldom happy."

The daily routine of new motherhood left her with little time for intellectual stimulation. She described her regimen to Harriet St. Leger: "Every chink and cranny of the day between all this desultoriness is filled up with 'the baby' and study of any sort seems further off from me than ever." She took some solace, however, in the beauty of her child, "a very fine strong healthy baby—with dark blue eyes and a lux-uriant head of hair (no teeth tho', which is a pity!)."

Any pleasure she might have taken in motherhood did not improve her opinion of marriage. Shortly after Sarah's birth, Kemble philo-sophically commented, "The manner in which women are brought up render their exercising any degree of judgment and reason in the choice of a husband so very unlikely (I might say impossible) that it ap-pears to me the surest chance in the world whether this existence after marriage is happy or miserable." She was stuck with the latter, deri-sively referring to Pierce as "My lord and master."

She charged that her husband was rude and unkind, an intolerable combination. She wrote him pleading letters, suggesting a trial separa-tion and begging to go home to England. She even confessed her will-ingness to give up her child in exchange for release from the marriage. In the summer of 1835, she wrote despairingly:

> I am weary of my useless existence, my superintendence of your house is nominal; you have never allowed it to be oth-erwise; you will suffer no inconvenience from its cessa-tion. . . . If you procure a health nurse for the baby she will not fret after me, and had I died when she was born, you must have taken this measure, and my parting from her now will be as though she had never known me, and to me far less miserable than at any future time. I must beg you will take measures for my going away.

Butler dismissed this request. He believed that Fanny was suffering from the malaise, common among new mothers, which is today called postpartum depression. Pierce insisted Fanny must set aside any thought of leaving him or Sarah; if she would devote her energies to nurturing their daughter, instead of dwelling on her melancholy feel-ings, she would become less maudlin about her situation. He had faith that their lives together would improve.

Perhaps in an attempt to stem the tide of hopelessness, Kemble turned her energies outward. She was stirred by the swelling ideological currents of the day. William Ellery Channing's recently published abolitionist tract, "Slavery," inspired her to write her own "long and vehement treatise against negro slavery" during the spring of 1835. She wanted to append her antislavery essay to her journal, but was persuaded against the idea for fear of physical retaliation, a tactic increasingly favored by proslavery mobs. (Kemble may have incorporated parts of this piece into a long letter, arguing against slavery, written for *The Times* of London in 1852, but there is no extant copy of the original text.)

Always given to social commentary with a theatrical flair, Kemble saw the slavery issue as a highly charged drama, with two groups of characters on a national stage. Perhaps unaware that her own writings could contribute to the nation's mounting political and social tensions, she cast herself in the role of observer from a foreign land. In the summer of 1835, she wrote to her publisher:

> Northern people pursue the emancipation plans with all the zeal of folks who have nothing to lose by their philanthropy[,] and the southerners hold fast by their slippery property like so many tigers—the miserable blacks are restricted every day within narrower bounds. There will I fear be a season of awful retribution before right is done the unfortunate wretches. Our property lies principally in Georgia; if we are ruined I think I will come to England and take up my old trade.

Kemble's controversial opinions on slavery, expressed in Philadelphia's best parlors, added to the uproar caused by the publication of her *Journal of America*. Pierce Butler had maintained that Fanny's private writings would bring shame on their friends and family, and in many ways his prediction proved accurate. Dating from her first

months in America, passages intended as lighthearted, satirical mus-
ings came across in print as rather heavy-handed.

The book became an instant best-seller—Wiley and Long's New
York bookstore sold eight hundred copies during its first week in stock,
and curious readers clamored to inspect its allegedly incendiary contents. Kemble was an astute social critic, but her blunt style and abra-
sive criticism of nearly every facet of American society earned her
rebukes from all quarters.

The *North American Review* condemned: "In correctness of taste
and maturity of judgment she is singularly deficient." Edgar Allan Poe
commented in the *Southern Literary Messenger:* "A female, and a
young one, too, cannot speak with the self confidence which marks
this book without jarring somewhat upon American notions of the re-
tiring delicacy of the female character." In the end, however, Poe was
unable to ignore the book's merits, including its "vivacity of style."

The controversy was fueled by Fanny's derogatory commentaries on
the American press. For example, she bemoans men of literary talent
who would "accept this very mediocre mode of displaying their abilities." She disparaged journalists as writers and at one point compared
them to "insects." Eager to retaliate, many American papers allowed
reviewers to respond in kind. An Edinburgh writer likened Kemble's
attack on journalists to the way "foolish and fearless schoolboys pro-
voke a nest of hornets." Her inelegant phrasing and lively metaphors
drove one critic to respond with his own illustrated parody: *Outlines
Illustrative of the Journal of F—— A—— K——* (full of unflattering
cartoons). In addition, two other lampoons were published: *My Conscience! Journal of Fanny Thimble Cutler,* where she was caricatured as
the wife of "Fierce Cutler"; and *Fanny Kemble in America,* a fifty-page
satirical pamphlet.

The sensation was not confined to the press. Catharine Sedgwick
described to her niece the reaction in Manhattan: "The city is in an uproar. Nothing else is talked of . . . in the counting houses . . . and Wall
Street." Sedgwick believed that although Kemble had a right to ex-

To bed — to sleep —
·To sleep!—perchance to be bitten! aye — theres the scratch.
For in that sleep of ours what bugs may come,
Must give us pause —

Page 98.

An image spoofing Kemble's complaints about
the press in her Journal *(1835).*

press her opinions, publishing the journal showed "a want of tact, judgment & good sense," considering Fanny's new status as Butler's wife.

The British response to the *Journal of America* was equally negative. The reviewer in *The Times* of London politely declined to believe that Kemble had indeed written the book. The *Athenaeum* called it "one of the most deplorable exhibitions of vulgar thinking and vulgar expression that it was ever our misfortune to encounter." *The Quarterly Review* dressed Kemble down for over fifteen pages, concluding with just a few paragraphs to recommend the book. Even Queen Victoria took umbrage, confiding to her diary: "very pertly and oddly written . . . not well bred . . . many vulgar expressions . . . full of trash and nonsense which could only do harm." Fanny was not privy to the Queen's displeasure; the Kemble family's was another matter. Maria Thérèse confided to British politician and family friend Charles Greville that she was torn between admiration and disgust. Fanny's father was similarly divided, and both Kembles were alarmed at the scandal. They hoped it would soon subside, but when a comedian began to perform a spoof of the journal on the New York summer stage, no end seemed to be in sight.

Fanny and Pierce weathered this storm in silence, although Butler Place might have been echoing with remorse. More likely, baby Sarah's cries kept the couple preoccupied. During the summer of 1835, perhaps to soothe Fanny's longing for company, Butler sent his wife and child off to the Berkshires at the invitation of Catharine Sedgwick. This interlude in the mountains proved to be a watershed event: Kemble grew to love the place and the people who lived there, and the Berkshires became a lifelong passion.

At the time of Kemble's visit, the Lenox area had already been claimed by holidaymakers as "Newport in the Mountains." In 1829 William O. Curtis turned his Berkshire Coffee House in Lenox into a hotel, later improved and expanded under the direction of his son William D. Curtis. Curtis's Hotel became the best place to be seen at the height of the season, which shifted from late summer to October by the 1830s.

A Mrs. Lee of New Orleans built a pioneer summer home in 1837, and soon droves followed. By the next decade, a guidebook proclaimed: "The refined state of society in this place, the fine mountain air and scenery, and the superior accommodations at the hotel, all render Lenox a most desirable place of resort during the warm season." Kemble became a frequent visitor to Curtis's establishment, and would eventually buy her own home in the town.

Long before Lenox became a fashionable retreat, it was known as the site of some of America's earliest antislavery sentiment. The Sedgwick family had been founders of Lenox. In 1785 Theodore Sedgwick, a lawyer in the village, took on the important case of a black woman known as Mumbet, who had run away from her master, a Colonel Ashley of nearby Sheffield.

Arguing that the 1780 Massachusetts constitution did not allow slavery, Sedgwick went to court and won Mumbet her freedom. She was adopted into the family, and was buried in the Sedgwick graveyard, where Catharine Sedgwick had erected a plaque in her honor. Theodore Sedgwick went on to earn even greater respect, first as a U.S. senator and then as a federal judge.

Catharine was widely acknowledged as one of New England's leading writers. Nathaniel Hawthorne described her as "our most truthful novelist, who has made the scenery and life of Berkshire all her own." After Hawthorne moved to the Berkshires, he befriended the Sedgwicks, whom he described as "happy as summer days themselves."

Catharine's brother Theodore lived in New York, but her brother Charles and Charles's wife, Elizabeth Dwight Sedgwick, rounded out the Lenox circle. Elizabeth ran a girls' school out of her Berkshire home and was at the center of a local group of antislavery and women's rights advocates. During her summer visit, Fanny discovered in Elizabeth a true confidante, whom she regarded as highly as Harriet St. Leger.

After a season of enjoying the beautiful scenery and the adoration of the Sedgwick clan, Kemble and Sarah returned to Philadelphia in the autumn, with Fanny much refreshed. However, the harsh, dull, lonely Philadelphia winter again imposed a sense of exile.

Fanny's servants found her strange and difficult, and were unwilling to remain long in her employ. For companionship, she had only her young daughter and her husband. Butler did not forbid his wife to travel into town for company, but the weather proved foul. Kemble complained, "The cross roads in every direction were muddy quagmires, where, on foot or on horseback, rapid progress was equally impossible."

But by the following spring, as Butler had predicted, Kemble was absorbed with her daughter, now almost a year old. Sarah, she discovered with delight, had a temper, and "her little brow twists itself already into something almost as formidable as the frown of a certain young Boston lady whom I am sure you know."

Yet Fanny continued to confide to friends that life was monotonous, that it "would require a richer imagination than mine is now to draw my materials of writing (I don't mean pen, ink & paper)." Picking violets and other pleasures of country life cheered her somewhat, but most of all she longed for visitors. She described to Harriet St. Leger the long stretches of loneliness she endured: "Though people occasionally drive out and visit me and I occasionally drive in and return their calls, and we . . . at rare intervals, go in to the theater, or a dance, I have no friends, no intimates."

She continued to blame Pierce for much of her unhappiness. Her husband would not allow her even to plan for her long-promised visit to England. The muddy turnpike to Philadelphia and Butler's business interests often kept him in town, leaving Kemble, in her own words, "a disconsolate widow." She felt that she was left behind simply to protect the house from robbers, as an estate manager might. Her sense of deprivation was aggravated when Pierce's aunt fell ill in Philadelphia and family duties increased his already frequent absences.

In late April 1836, Pierce's aunt Frances died. At long last, he inherited his half of the Major's estate; he and his brother held the second largest number of slaves in the state of Georgia. Having spent almost half his life awaiting this inheritance, the Major's grandson eagerly seized control.

This was hardly the time for a journey abroad. Yet Fanny's yearning for England was palpable. She had been separated from her mother for over four years, from her father for over two—and neither parent had yet laid eyes on young Sarah. She was adamant that she be allowed to visit home.

She was nostalgic for London society, too. Married Englishwomen were allowed a rich and full social schedule, while in America, "when ladies marry they usually give up going into company and confine themselves to nursing and household duties." To illustrate her point, Kemble liked to tell the story of a young Englishwoman who was warned that living in America was nothing like living in England. When she became a bride, she tormented her husband with "such a nuisance that I used to call her the 'creaking door.'" Fanny perhaps found it necessary to follow suit; in any case, Butler finally agreed that she might spend the winter in England with her parents. He even hired a baby nurse, Margery O'Brien, to care for Sarah on the journey.

As a newly elected delegate to Pennsylvania's constitutional convention of 1837, Butler himself would have to remain behind. Although it was highly unusual for a married woman to travel unescorted, he agreed to join Fanny later.

When it was reported in the shipping news that Mrs. Pierce Butler was on board the *South America,* steaming for Liverpool on November 1, 1836, the New York *Mirror,* lest she never return, bade her a rousing adieu:

> Gone, dear Fanny, gone at last! Yes, the beautiful Juliet, the proud Lady Constance, Bianca, Julia, and the clever authoress of the "Journal," all sailed in the person of Mrs. Butler . . . What with her playing, scribbling, riding, and marrying, she has been as much talked about as a comet! . . . From the silent manner of her departure, we fear there is a settled coolness between her and our republican publick.

This send-off touched on the many scandals associated with Fanny Kemble, from her deteriorating marriage to her incorrigible outspokenness. But with his closing words, the reporter held out a morsel of charity, hinting that although Americans might find much to disparage about this flamboyant creature, she had left her mark. He ended: "We forgive you."

CHAPTER FOUR

Transatlantic Currents

Whether she was cast as a prodigal daughter returning to the Kemble ancestral seat, or as the conquering heroine returning to her family bedecked with American wealth, Fanny Kemble Butler's homecoming was unquestionably a stirring occasion. She knew not what this trip would bring, but she longed for a sense of renewal.

Procrastination and fall storms had left uncertain the date of her arrival in London during the fall of 1836. Many of Fanny's friends and relations were taken by surprise when she did indeed dock with nanny and child in December. Her parents immediately gathered her into their Park Place home, where she basked in the affection she had been denied for so long. While the unconditional love of her family was no doubt a great comfort, and she enjoyed the flattering attention showered on baby Sarah, Kemble was greatly disappointed to find that the women who had long lent a sympathetic ear to all her troubles were nowhere to be found. Harriet St. Leger was traveling in Italy, and Anna Jameson was abroad in Canada, trying to salvage her own fractious marriage.

Instead Fanny took unexpected solace in the company of her sister Adelaide, no longer the awkward teenager she had left behind. Totty at twenty-two was all grown up and about to make her professional premiere as a singer. Adelaide's reputation as a beauty, the anticipation of her performance career, and her excitement about her upcoming debut must have been a wistful reminder to Fanny of her own first night at Covent Garden over seven years before.

While Fanny had arrived in time to usher her sister onstage from the wings, her parents' stars were dimming. Preparations were already under way for her father's official retirement from the stage. Charles Kemble had just been named to the post of Examiner of Plays, a royal appointment, both prestigious and lucrative, that allowed for a graceful exit. But Maria Thérèse's health, which had long been frail, was in precipitous decline. The rigors of city life were too much for her, and she spent most of her time at the Surrey cottage she had inherited from her sister-in-law, Elizabeth Whitelock. Fanny was sensitive to not only her mother's physical infirmities, but her failing mind.

When Charles Kemble took to the stage one last time on December 23, 1836, as Benedick in Shakespeare's *Much Ado About Nothing,* his entire family rallied round. Fanny worried privately over the difficulties of giving up the "dram he has taken nightly for more than forty years." After the curtain came down, however, she was able to report to Harriet: "My father bore it all far better than I had anticipated."

Having ventured back into the London theater world, even in an offstage role, Kemble found herself swept into the social milieu of her youth. Now a young matron, she relished what she called "brilliant society, full of every element of wit, wisdom, experience, refined taste, high culture, good breeding, good sense and distinction of every sort that can make human intercourse valuable and delightful." Making up for lost time, she spent evenings in the city's finest establishments dining with entertaining companions, and weekends at the country estates of titled friends. Partaking in such luxuries spoiled young Sarah, and Kemble delighted in watching her daughter gambol across green velvet expanses of lawn. Reenchanted by the stately beauty of the Bannisters, the Fitzhughs' home near Southampton; the Hoo, Lady Dacre's place in Hertfordshire; Oatlands, the Earl of Ellesmere's home near Weybridge; and even Holland House—but she learned to decline invitations from the disagreeable Lady Holland despite the elegance of her home—Fanny emphatically dismissed Butler Place in Branchtown as a pale imitation.

With Pennsylvania now an ocean away, she chose not to dwell on her memories. Her letters to American friends boast instead of cosmopolitan activities. After six months back in Britain, she wrote to Sarah Perkins: "I have been at Ascot races all day & am going to get to my bed as fast as I can for I never achieve that before two o'clock in the morning here."

As always, she cultivated the acquaintance of writers above all, and she revived past friendships. The Greville brothers, Charles and Henry, who were both besotted with Adelaide, filled out Kemble's circle. Throughout her absence, John Kemble had tried to keep his sister abreast of literary currents in England and had sent her the first volume of poems by his college friend (and fellow Apostle) Alfred Tennyson, whose work had been embraced by London literati.

When, at a dinner party, she encountered her former flame Augustus Craven—now a minor diplomat and married to a Breton—Kemble commented that Madame Craven "sought me with apparent cordiality and I had no reason whatever for avoiding her. She is very handsome . . . with the simple good breeding of a French lady, and the serious earnestness of a devout Roman Catholic. They are going to Lisbon, where he is Attaché to the Embassy." When Craven ran through all their money, his wife turned to writing to support herself, producing, among other works, a study entitled *La Jeunesse de Fanny Kemble* (1880).

Fanny recorded in her diary the doings of the notorious Lord de Ros, who had been ostracized from society after being unmasked as a card cheat. Kemble was fascinated at the willingness of London's finest

Fanny Kemble as a young married woman.

gentlemen to turn a blind eye to de Ros's reputation as a womanizer and general reprobate—until he offended by gambling with marked cards. This irony inspired her to outline what eventually became her third drama, *An English Tragedy.* She called the play "the only good thing I ever wrote."

Spinning the moral tale of de Ros whetted Kemble's appetite for sharp social commentary. She believed that the death of William IV was a catalyst to great change in her home city: "I find London more beautiful, more rich and royal than ever; the latter epithet, by the bye, applies to external things alone, for I do not think the spirit of the people as royal, i.e. loyal, as I used to fancy it was." Ascending the throne was Victoria, who as a young girl used to watch Fanny ride at the stables, and who, like many of her countrymen, had pored over Kemble's scandalous *Journal of America* a few years earlier.

When the princess became queen, Fanny was accorded a place at court. Through her renewed alliance with Lady Dacre and her clique, Kemble was befriended by Lord and Lady Lansdowne. And when Lady Lansdowne became First Lady of the Bedchamber, she invited her new intimate, Fanny Kemble, to Parliament to witness the ceremonial first session of Victoria's reign. Kemble exulted in the grandeur of the moment: "The Queen's voice was exquisite; nor have I ever heard any spoken words more musical in their gentle distinctness than the 'My Lords and Gentlemen' which broke the breathless silence of the illustrious assembly, whose gaze was riveted upon the fair flower of royalty."

Such regal pomp and circumstance could hardly have been further removed from the muddy roads and impudent Quaker tenants of Branchtown. But as the weeks turned into months, and her wait for Pierce's arrival continued, the endless social events grew less and less appealing. She wrote, "The turmoil and dissipation of a London life, amusing as they are for a time, soon pall upon one, and I already feel in my diminished relish for them, that I am growing old." The twenty-seven-year-old Kemble surprised even herself with this confession.

The separation from her husband and America wrought subtle changes. As her allegiance to London life waned, Fanny realized that her future lay not in England, but in the United States, the home of her husband and the birthplace of her child. She came to feel that she could never abandon America or her duties there. She made a private pledge: "I should be the last person to desire that we should do so [desert America], and so I think that henceforth England and I are 'Paradise Lost' to each other." Paradoxically, it was only a visit to England that could make Kemble secure in this belief. She explained to her American confidante Sarah Perkins: "My return to my own country has been productive of many pleasures to me, but the one great benefit I expect to derive from it is a greater degree of content with my adopted one, & a more thorough resignation to its being my future residence." There was much about America to which she had become attached—primarily her husband, who was still an ocean away.

Pierce had put off their reunion several times, and Kemble struggled with the prolonged separation. He returned from Georgia in early spring of 1837 to find the Pennsylvania constitutional convention (he was a delegate, obliged to attend) once again postponed, this time until the middle of October. Now he had no reason to remain in America.

But instead of hurrying to England, Butler sent his wife an inquiring letter: Had the separation strengthened her affection for him and allowed her to reevaluate their relationship? In her long and complex response, Kemble revealed contrition: "It has led me to reflect upon some passages of our intercourse with self-condemnation, and a desire to discharge my duty to you more faithfully." Things might have boded well, if only she had ended there.

But Kemble continued: "You ask . . . how I like my independence, and whether I remember how vehemently and frequently I objected to your control. . . . [P]art of my regret . . . arises from the *manner* of my resistance, not the fact itself." She proclaimed, "There is no justice in the theory, that one rational creature is to be subservient to another," and concluded, with steely determination: "I would rather hear you acknowledge a principle of truth, than enjoy the utmost indulgence that your affection could bestow upon me."

So love and truth, in seeming opposition, remained the poles of conflict that kept the couple apart. Butler could not have been wildly encouraged by this epistle. Perhaps the long separation, combined with his lingering passion for Fanny, allowed Pierce to absorb only selected parts of her mixed signals. Whatever the case, he set sail for England to fetch his wife and daughter home. But since he had awaited Fanny's reply, he could remain in England just a month before the constitutional convention opened in Harrisburg on October 17.

Circumstances were further complicated when Charles Kemble

took ill and went to Germany to take the waters. Adelaide accompanied him, planning to offer concerts at Carlsbad, both to advance her singing career and to help defray the costs of the treatment.

Fanny hoped that she and Butler would have time to visit Carlsbad before returning to America, but bad weather delayed his arrival by a fortnight. This left just two weeks for his visit, not nearly enough time for a German sojourn and a proper good-bye to her sister and father.

Although Pierce's introduction to British society was not to unfold in quite the grand manner Fanny had planned, she was able to bring him around to meet several of her close friends, including Harriet (newly returned from Italy), the Fitzhughs, and Lord and Lady Lansdowne. Butler was in awe of the parade of attentive aristocrats who turned out to inspect him in the flesh.

In early September, Fanny, Pierce, Sarah, and the nanny boarded the *St. Andrew* for the month-long crossing. It was a difficult trip. Fanny, pregnant with her second child, complained of great discomfort and spent most of her time in her cabin.

Pierce's voyage to England signaled the couple's efforts to rekindle their affection, and the expectation of a baby seemed to mark their renewed pledge. Fanny hoped her American homecoming would be the beginnings of a brief second honeymoon. Immediately upon landing in New York, Pierce had to leave for the constitutional convention in Harrisburg, while Fanny stayed in Manhattan to recuperate from the voyage. But as soon as she could Fanny joined her husband in Harrisburg.

She was full of good cheer—agreeably taking in the bustling operations of the capital, and, especially, proud to see her husband taking such an active role. In fact, Fanny's opinion of Pierce's intellect and character was greatly improved; her love for him seemed boundless. From Harrisburg, she wrote to Sarah Perkins of the salvation of second chances: "It has been my most fortunate lot to marry a man whom I can both respect and love, but from the inconsiderate manner in which I engaged myself to him, had the result been different, I could have assured no one but myself & as it is I feel like some blind or drunken person who has been preserved by the merciful interference of Providence from falling into a precipice."

Pierce seemed to be making a positive impression not just on his wife, but on his political colleagues. Sidney George Fisher, a very distant relation of Butler, had confided in his diary, "Spoke of Pierce Butler, who has become a very active politician & Van Buren man in their neighborhood. Butler has a great deal of energy and character tho entirely without education." Prior to the constitutional convention, Butler had not been involved with politics on the local or state level. But perhaps his inheritance and his new status as a fully vested member of the planter elite led him to take a more active position, especially on the question of slavery, which was heating up the national political scene.

When Pierce and Fanny finally returned home to Branchtown, Anna Jameson stopped in for a long visit on her way back to England from Canada. It must have been a successful visit; Jameson reported Fanny was "brimful of genius, poetry, power and eloquence, yet is an excellent wife, an excellent mother, and an excellent manager of a household." And Butler must have made a special effort to ingratiate himself with this older woman who had such a hold on Fanny, for Jameson also wrote, "I like Pierce Butler very much—more than I expected. It was difficult to please me in a husband for Fanny."

A writer and burgeoning feminist, Jameson viewed Kemble as a protégée. She might have preferred to see Fanny remain within the web of London literati, where Jameson thrived and imagined that her friend might reign. Jameson's brief visit seemed to reassure her that Kemble had found a snug corner of the world which would allow her the stability and security for which she had pined during her theatrical career.

Yet after Jameson's departure, domestic relations in the Butler household began to unravel. Visits from friends reminded Fanny of the society she so missed, of the world she had enjoyed in London just a few short months before. Unsettled by the gloom of a lonely Philadelphia winter, she succumbed to the moodiness brought on by advancing pregnancy; after a quarrel of unknown cause, Kemble left her husband again. She went to her in-laws in Philadelphia and threatened to abandon the family and set sail for England. If Pierce would not pay for her ticket, she would sell her watch and gold chain to buy one. She wrote Butler, "There is abundance of time for me to reach England before my confinement: and if you will hereafter appoint means for your child's being brought over to you, I shall . . . observe them." By now, Butler discounted her demands, chalking them up to her pattern of tantrums. It is not known whether a ticket was ever purchased—but Fanny remained in Pennsylvania, and eventually returned to Butler Place to give birth.

Kemble may have been a petulant wife, but the needs of her child took priority over even the most serious grievances with her husband. Perhaps it was Sally's—Sarah's—bout with scarlet fever that prevented Kemble from making good on her threat. When one of Sally's tonsils became enlarged and interfered with her breathing, Fanny abandoned any thought of leaving. Alarmed by the little girl's worsening condition, the family physician insisted that her tonsils be removed, lest she suffocate. Fanny described the process in graphic detail: "They use a double-barreled silver tube through which two wires are passed, making a loop which is tightened around the tonsil so as to destroy its vitality and left for twenty-four hours projecting from the patient's mouth, causing some pain and extreme inconvenience. Then the tube is removed and the tonsil left to rot off."

Sally's ordeal offers insight into contemporary medical practices. Kemble herself was suffering from a painful throat and complained that she received little relief from the hundreds of leeches she had applied.

Illness plagued the Butler household for months. Kemble confided to her good friend Saadi that Pierce was an "invalid all winter." (Throughout their marriage, Pierce was frequently described by his wife as suffering from illnesses; these were never identified, but always taken quite seriously and apparently were very debilitating.) Pregnant, nursing a sick husband and child, Fanny called this season of infinite dreariness the gloomiest she could remember.

But as the blossoms of spring unfolded, Kemble, just weeks away from the birth of her second child, was feeling doubly on the cusp. She surveyed her estate with a new sense of pleasure and anticipation. After Frances Butler's death, Pierce had allowed Fanny to remodel the grounds to suit her own taste. She had supervised hundreds of plantings, most notably a double row of potted ornamental lemon trees lining the walk to the front entrance.

Frances Kemble Butler was born on May 28, 1838, her sister Sarah's third birthday. The girls' births took place at the same hour, too. Kemble always used this coincidence as an example of her mania for order. Now, like all mothers of more than one child, Kemble struggled to balance the demands of siblings, to divide and multiply her motherly love.

Illness continued to plague the household. Sarah caught the measles; then the entire family was laid low by the summer's heat wave. The hot, muggy weather dictated a waterfront retreat, but the fashionable Long Island resort Pierce Butler selected at Rockaway Beach, New York, was not to Kemble's liking. The hotel was crowded and the food, she reported, was dreadful. With only two small bathhouses available to guests, Kemble had to undress in the company of strange women. Despite the positive effects of the sea air, it was a quarrelsome holiday for the Butlers.

Amid the conflicts, Fanny was diverted by a chance encounter with Philip Hone, the former mayor of New York who had been kind to her when she was an actress. Fanny's conscience must have stung her at the moment of recognition, for she had repaid Hone's generosity with a less than flattering portrait in her published journal. Although Hone had been wounded when the book was first published, apparently all was now forgiven. Newly swayed by her charms, Hone danced and talked with Kemble for hours. Relieved that her youthful transgressions had done no permanent harm, Fanny vigorously declared her appreciation: "Mr. Hone, I cannot express to you how happy you have made me by the notice you have taken of me on this occasion. Believe me I am extremely grateful." Relations with her husband remained stressful, however. Butler refused to be placated with a dance and a smile.

In the Berkshires lay the antidote to the disappointment of Rockaway Beach. For an autumn holiday, Butler sent Fanny and her daughters to the Red Lion Inn in Stockbridge, Massachusetts. They could easily visit and picnic with the Sedgwicks in nearby Lenox. Fanny also befriended the Appleton sisters, Fanny and Mary. Mary Appleton would later marry Henry Wadsworth Longfellow, one of Kemble's staunchest admirers.

Kemble was in high spirits until news came from England that her mother had died suddenly in September at her Surrey cottage. Waves of grief and regret, coupled with an overwhelming sense of loss, rolled over Fanny. The Atlantic seemed an unbridgeable abyss, where she might drown in her own loneliness. As she made her way back to Pennsylvania, Fanny was plunged into one of the deepest depressions of her life.

She blamed her marriage for her crushing sorrow. While Butler remained in Philadelphia and she at Butler Place, Fanny wrote him a long letter pleading for release from the marriage. She begged him to cast aside his "regard for appearances" and recognize that they were doomed to unhappiness. She took her share of the blame: "In part this is my own fault; for I married you without for a moment using my own judgment or observation to ascertain whether we were likely to be companions and fellows to each other." But now that "the sentiment which drew us together is waning and perishing away," their union was nothing more than an onerous burden. Although she recognized she was tied to her husband by economic necessity, this dependence was "doubly irksome then to me, who have had and still have the means of perfect independence." Although the available means to this end, her acting career, was distasteful, it had the saving grace of being "unfettered by the very odious restraint of obligation without affection." In consideration of all, she proposed "that we may henceforward live apart."

There are hints in this letter of extenuating circumstances. Kemble reminded Butler of her "painful and exhausting indisposition" since the birth of their younger daughter, suggesting that conjugal relations may have been suspended. She concluded, "I think your comfort will probably be increased by your absence from me." There may have been underlying sexual tensions and jealousies, which boiled over after her daughter's birth.

Kemble had been faithful to her husband during her long absence in England. But he, Fanny suspected, may not have been. In later years, she found proof; for now, his suspicious behavior was hurtful nonetheless. But whether from a sense of propriety or from stubbornness, Pierce Butler refused to entertain the idea of a formal separation and declared that he and Fanny would continue to live as man and wife.

While the couple wrangled over questions of power and authority within their own household, national politics moved threateningly into the foreground. The sanctity of union became a matter of urgent political debate within the larger society. Irreconcilable differences were straining the national fabric.

Fundamental disagreements over states' rights and the westward extension of slavery were becoming more volatile in legislatures around the nation. Headlines screamed dire warnings; mention of the issues brought down impolite silence in well-appointed parlors and provoked barroom brawls.

English by birth, American only by marriage, Fanny might have distanced herself from this national imbroglio. But neutrality was not in Kemble's nature; she could never play the sphinx. British politics during her youth had been consumed with debates over slavery, which she had avidly followed in print. Arguments for liberty and emancipation were frequently heard in the Kemble parlor. During John's Cambridge days, his activism in the movement to free Spain brought him into close association with those fighting to end slavery in the British colonies. Young Fanny absorbed both sides of every contest, which she then floated in the pages of her journal, even including bits and pieces of Parliamentary debate in her diaries and letters.

A voracious reader, Fanny would have been well acquainted with the Somerset case of 1772, a landmark decision whereby Africans in bondage brought into Britain were declared free. The nation's highest court ruled that no one had the power to hold slaves in England and thus outlawed slavery in the British Isles, paving the way for future reforms in the colonies. While ideological opposition to slavery was beginning to take hold on both sides of the Atlantic, England and America were severely tested by the entrenched economic realities of the system, which so greatly benefited empire builders.

The question of the slave trade would continue to plague world governments. In the 1780s the founders of the United States wrestled to limit the extent to which their new republic would participate in the international slave trade. They settled on prohibiting the trade after 1807.

The efforts of the fledgling American government were overshadowed by the ongoing demonstrations against slavery throughout the British colonies. Begun by radical Quakers in the mid–eighteenth century, abolitionism soon outgrew its evangelical origins. Broad and effective agitation, fomented by diverse political and religious motives, led to a Parliamentary ban on slavery within the British Empire after 1833. This triumph was effected in great part by the much revered William Wilberforce, who opposed slavery from his seat in Parliament until ill health forced his retirement from the House of Commons in 1825. He died just weeks before Parliament voted the ban on slavery in British colonies.

The status of persons of African descent had been disputed in Kemble's adopted nation from its very founding. Significant numbers of African Americans, both slave and free, had fought the British during the American Revolution. Yet legal discrimination, against all blacks, persisted following independence: from a ban on black emigration to the United States to a prohibition against militia service for free blacks, even decorated veterans of the Continental Army.

Although delegates to the U.S. Constitutional Convention outlawed the external slave trade (after January 1, 1808), and federal legislators banned slavery in the territories of the Northwest Ordinance (1787), slaveowners made significant gains. The Constitution provided that congressional apportionments would be based on numbers "including those bound to service for a term of years [indentured servants], and excluding Indians not taxed, three fifths of all other persons." This provision not only protected slaveowners' property, but legitimated human bondage in the founding document of the great American experiment in democracy.

In its infancy, the United States attempted to sidestep the divisive issue of slavery—allowing it to flourish in states where it was embraced, and to wither where it was opposed, especially New England. This fence-straddling worked until Missouri (part of the Louisiana Territory, purchased in 1803) made a bid to enter the union in 1819. With Missouri's application, the delicate balance between free states and slave states within the U.S. Senate was threatened. Congress worked out the 1820 Missouri Compromise: Maine broke off to form a separate free state; Missouri entered the union as a slave state. All future territories were to be free or slave according to their geographic location, above or below a line designated by Congress along Missouri's southern border. Slavery's defenders and detractors became more vocal and more combative in the wake of this congressional conflagration.

An increasing resentment of slaveowners fueled opposition to the South's "peculiar institution." In response, Southern statesmen stopped characterizing slavery as a necessary evil. Rather, the slavocracy boldly pronounced it a positive good. Slavery rescued "inferior Africans" from their "Dark Continent" and delivered them to "civilization and Christianity," where slaveowners shouldered the burdens of this "God-given mission."

As emancipation movements formed in the North and the ranks of free blacks swelled along the urban seaboard, a significant proportion of the white antislavery community advocated only gradual emancipation and the relocation of free blacks outside the United States. To this end, the American Colonization Society formed in 1816.

Throughout the 1820s, the society strengthened its cause by presenting itself as an antislavery organization. Terrified that the society's program might succeed, free blacks began to pour their energies into the immediate emancipation of slaves. They declared themselves in favor of "abolitionism," rather than the "gradualist" approach of an earlier generation of antislavery advocates. David Walker, a free black in Boston, published a famous *Appeal to the Colored Citizens of the World* in 1829, condemning colonization as "white supremacy." Walker joined with other black activists in demanding emancipation and genuine freedom for blacks within American society.

Eventually a radical core of white evangelicals shifted their position, transforming themselves into abolitionists as well. Adopting the slogan "Am I not a brother and a man?," their movement gained greater social prominence, especially through white women's growing involvement in grassroots organizations.

Radical abolitionism shifted into high gear with the appearance of William Lloyd Garrison's newspaper *The Liberator* in 1831, and a growing dissatisfaction with "the slave power." That same year, the slave preacher Nat Turner led a revolt that left more than fifty white residents of Southampton, Virginia—including women and children—dead.

As an Englishwoman, Fanny Kemble claimed she was "on principle" opposed to slavery, and this opinion was fixed in her mind when she set sail for America in 1832. Kemble professed she was appalled at the way in which skin color determined all interactions in this alleged democracy. On her first voyage to America, she witnessed racial prejudice:

> The steward of our ship, a black—a very intelligent, obliging, respectable servant—came here the other morning to ask my father for an order [of theater tickets], at the same time adding that it must be for the gallery, as people of color were not allowed to go into any other part of the theater. . . . The prejudice against these unfortunate people is, of course, incomprehensible to us. On board ship, after giving that same man some trouble, Dall poured him out a glass of wine, when we were having our dinner, whereupon the captain looked at her with utter amazement, and I thought some little contempt, and said, "Ah, one can tell by that that you are not an American;" which sort of thing makes one feel rather glad one is not.

It is true that Kemble shared many of the racial attitudes she condemned. Her first week in New York, for example, she remarked that "several of the black women I saw pass had very fine figures, but the contrast of a bright blue, or pink crepe bonnet, with the black face, white teeth, and the glaring blue whites of the eyes, is beyond description grotesque." Nevertheless, from an early age she offered every indication of empathy with those held in bondage. Although she believed in the inferiority of slaves, she held it to be an outgrowth of slavery rather than vice versa.

When, in 1834, Kemble took up residence in Philadelphia as Mrs. Pierce Butler, she found herself in a city with a complex racial dynamic. A mid-Atlantic port with a sophisticated urban atmosphere, situated in a border state, Philadelphia became a battleground for slave catchers, for antislavery radicals, for blacks and whites locked in bitter opposition.

Philadelphia had a long African American heritage, of which the Mother Bethel African Methodist Episcopal Church on Sixth Street below Pine was a shining example. In 1790, the U.S. census reported only three hundred slaves in the town, and by 1820 the number had shrunk to less than a dozen, while the free black community had burgeoned through reproduction and in-migration. Many of Philadelphia's free blacks had achieved wealth and standing, primarily as owners of their own businesses, mainly services such as barbering, catering, and millinery.

Blacks played a prominent role in Philadelphia's maritime contingent. Having earned fame as a cabin boy who remained on a British prison ship rather than betray his loyalty to the Revolution, James Forten set the tone for Philadelphia's African American elite: patriotic, enterprising, and fiercely proud.

A sailmaker worth over $100,000 in 1832, Forten had a long and righteous career as an activist, beginning in 1800 when he sought to repeal the Fugitive Slave Law of 1793. The House of Representatives' swift and negative response to Forten's petition did not deter his pursuit of black equality. On December 4, 1833, he hosted William Lloyd Garrison and other white abolitionists as they joined with African American activists to form the American Anti-Slavery Society. The proud tradition was carried on by Forten's granddaughter Charlotte, who went south during the Civil War to teach freedpeople on one of the Union-occupied South Carolina Sea Islands.

One visiting Englishman pointed out that abolitionist sentiment had far from won the day: "Philadelphia appears to be the metropolis of this odious prejudice [against blacks] and that there is probably no city in the known world where dislike amounting to hatred of the coloured population prevails more than in the city of brotherly love." Another antebellum commentator observed that in Philadelphia "everything southern was exalted and worshipped," presumably including slavery.

Through her connections to the Sedgwicks, through her contact with William Ellery Channing, and finally, through her close relationship with Philadelphia's leading Unitarian cleric and antislavery advocate, the Reverend William Furness, Fanny Kemble was drawn into a circle of contacts preoccupied with these debates. But as much as she might sympathize with the abolitionist cause, the peril of speaking out was genuine: "Our fellow citizens [may] tear our house down and make a bonfire of our furniture . . . a favorite mode of remonstrance in these parts with those who advocate the rights of unhappy blacks."

During the 1830s, antislavery men and women repeatedly petitioned Congress for abolition. Northern and Southern legislators were so bitterly divided over this paper flooding Capitol Hill that Congress passed a gag rule in May 1836. After this date, all antislavery petitions would be tabled upon submission to the House of Representatives.

Denied their most effective outlet for expression, antislavery activists undertook alternative measures. Many, like Lydia Maria Child, took up their pens. Child published widely in antislavery journals; her most notable work was an 1833 treatise, *An Appeal in Favor of That Class of Americans Called Africans.* In 1837 the lecturer Angelina Grimké took her grievances to a committee of the Massachusetts legislature. Her daring inspired female abolitionists to hold open meetings of their own. In May 1837 the first Anti-Slavery Convention of American Women was held in New York City.

The printed word, antislavery activists soon discovered, was their most formidable weapon, and those who used it were not uncommonly the targets of physical attack. No less a figure than William Lloyd Garrison was tarred and feathered for his abolitionist editorials. On November 7, 1837, antislavery editor Elijah Lovejoy was fatally shot in the act of defending his press in Alton, Illinois, and was instantly heralded as a martyr, a symbol of the bloodthirsty forces of slavery.

Fanny Kemble as painted by Henry Inman.

In spite of escalating violence, abolitionist women determined to hold a second national meeting in 1838, convening at the newly erected Pennsylvania Hall. Built with funds from Philadelphia reformers, this imposing structure—located on Sixth Street between Mulberry and Sassafras—featured a pillared facade reminiscent of a Greek temple. Nicholas Biddle, an influential city father, had visited Greece in 1806 and upon his return had commissioned several neoclassical buildings, among them the Second Bank of the United States, completed in 1824. The gleaming white Pennsylvania Hall housed John Greenleaf Whittier's antislavery newspaper, the *Pennsylvania Freeman,* "free produce" stores (stocked with *no* goods made with slave labor), a small auditorium on the ground floor, and a large blue-and-white meeting room on an upper floor. There the second Anti-Slavery Convention of American Women opened on May 14, 1838, with Whittier reading a poem he had written for the occasion.

The next day, May 15, women delegates, black and white, from across New England and the Middle Atlantic states, passed a resolution calling for the end of slavery in the District of Columbia. Hostile onlookers lurking outside the hall became incensed over the mixing of the races in a public forum.

On May 16 a "Call to Citizens" was posted, a bold threat against any further "integrated" gatherings. The mayor of Philadelphia pleaded with the convention's organizers: if they would not suspend their meeting, they must at least prohibit black women from attending. Refusing, the abolitionists convened for a second day, while as many as seventeen thousand protestors gathered outside the hall. Crowds blocked the streets, and the mayor shut down the convention. Women antislavery leaders, directed by Lucretia Mott, defiantly marched from the hall in integrated pairs.

The night of May 16, arsonists broke in to Pennsylvania Hall. Eyewitness accounts suggest the local fire company let the building burn to the ground. Emboldened, the mob moved on, vandalizing first the Mother Bethel AME Church and then the nearby Shelter for Colored Orphans. The violence raged until the early hours of the morning, yet the Philadelphia police were nowhere to be found. The abolitionist women reconvened the next day in a nearby schoolhouse, where they pledged to continue their campaign.

At home in Branchtown, just miles from where these events were unfolding, Kemble was preparing for the impending birth of her second child. She strayed little from her domestic routine. On May 7, she described the pleasant spring setting to her friend Harriet: "I am sitting on the veranda, or piazza as they call it here, watching Sally in a buff coat zigzagging about the lawn."

Ever since Pierce had inherited his Georgia property in 1836, Fanny, bent on discovering the realities of slavery, had begged to go south. But Pierce demurred and delayed, perhaps aware that as long as Kemble remained in the North, shielded from grim details, her amorphous abolitionist leanings would not take shape.

Kemble's views often mirrored the abolitionist radicalism embraced by many of her New England intimates, but her name never appeared on the rolls of the Philadelphia Anti-Slavery Society or the American Anti-Slavery Society (both founded in 1833); nor was she affiliated with any other political abolitionist group. Perhaps England's slow elimination of slavery led her to assume that the institution in America was on a similar course of decline.

This notion was not so far-fetched. Many hundreds of Virginia slaveowners granted slaves their freedom in the wake of Nat Turner's rebellion of 1831; state legislators in Richmond debated abolishing slavery as well. As a dramatist, Kemble saw Southern slaveholders as an audience—a Christian audience that would doubtless be swayed by abolitionist exhortations concerning the hellfire and damnation due slavery's master class.

As Mrs. Pierce Butler, the wife of the second largest slaveholder in Georgia, Fanny found herself in a precarious position. Her husband had provided his wife with sugar-coated tales of the Butler plantations, where Major Butler had for decades presided as beneficent master. But her willingness to believe that her husband's family were "good" slaveowners, indulgent and paternalistic, made her a target of the very abolitionist ideology she—however tacitly—supported. Butler recognized that his wife's abolitionism was built on sentiment and intuition rather than on observation. He understood that her penchant for hygiene, competence, and Christian morality would make her recoil from the slaves who lived in sinful squalor on plantations. But Butler miscalculated where Kemble would lay the blame for that degradation.

Late in the fall of 1838, Butler finally consented to bring his family south, away from the escalating antislavery agitation and, he hoped, from Fanny's protracted grief over her mother's death. On the eve of her journey, Kemble wryly catalogued the perils she might confront: "Whether I shall die of a yellow fever or the jaundice or [illegible] whether I shall be shot at from behind a tree for my abolitionism, or swallowed horse and all by an Altamaha alligator or whether indeed we may not all have the pleasure of being blown half way up to heaven [in a steamboat] on our way to Charleston are matters yet folded within the unopened slumbers of time." And once she had survived the journey, her principles and faith would be severely tested by all she saw and heard in residence on a Georgian plantation.

CHAPTER FIVE

The War Over Slavery

Butler hoped a season at his Sea Island plantations would inspire in his wife a view of slavery that mirrored his own. Complacent as landowner, slaveholder, and head of the family, he failed to realize what an adversary he faced in Fanny, who, even at her most vulnerable, was fighting—for her marriage, against slavery, to come into her own as a writer.

At the time of his death in 1822, Major Pierce Butler, the second largest slaveholder in Georgia, passed that mantle to his heirs, Pierce and John Butler. Just as their grandfather practiced seasonal migration, spending the winter months in Georgia, watching over his kingdom, now, so did the Butler brothers. Upon taking possession in 1836, they traveled to Georgia to inspect their inheritance, a magnificent conglomeration of estates along the Altamaha River, near the port of Darien, and nearly a thousand slaves. The family landholdings included a seventeen-hundred-acre tract at Hampton on the northern end of St. Simon's Island; the majority of what became known as Butler Island; and all of neighboring Little St. Simon's Island near Hamp-

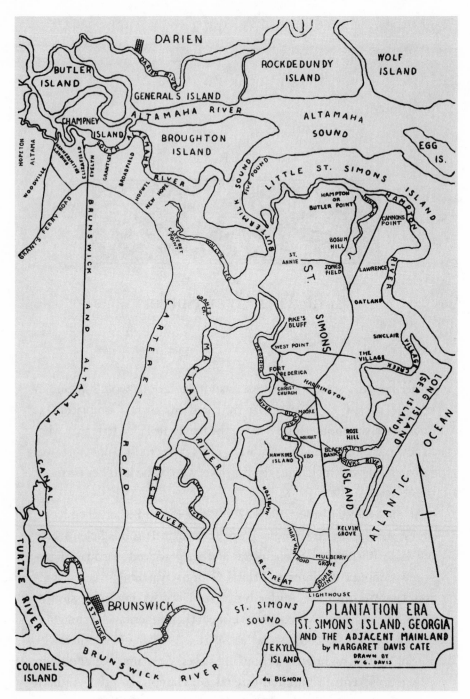

*Butler holdings in the region included Butler Island and Hampton
Point, at the northernmost part of St. Simon's Island.*

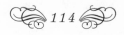

ton Point, including a six-hundred-acre tract originally known as Experiment. Slaves sent to this distant "pound" for up to five years' hard labor renamed it Five Pound Tree.

Aunt Frances had kept accounts and managed operations as well as she could, and the King family—Roswell King, Sr., and his son—had for decades tended to the land and to the laborers who worked it. But the extended absence of a resident Butler patriarch had taken its toll. Gone was the grandeur of the Butler heyday.

Major Pierce Butler (1744–1822) had given up his post in the British army to marry a Low Country heiress, Mary Middleton of South Carolina. Eager to strike out on his own, Butler commandeered several hundred of his wife's slaves (he lost 138 to the British when they ran away during the American Revolution) to cultivate rice and cotton on the Georgia Sea Islands. "Butler cotton" commanded such a high price on the British exchange that it became the standard to which others aspired.

After his wife's death in 1790, Butler made a permanent home in Philadelphia and became a director of the Bank of the United States. In 1804, when Aaron Burr killed Alexander Hamilton in a duel in Weehawken, New Jersey, Burr traveled south under the name of "R. King" (perhaps after Butler's overseer Roswell King), and eventually took refuge at Butler's estate on St. Simon's, where his exploits were much admired by local planters.

Burr's visit was eclipsed by the hurricane that year, which swept away six hundred barrels of Butler rice and drowned nineteen slaves, sixteen at Butler Island. Butler's driver, a slave named Morris, bravely prevented over a hundred slaves from attempting to cross the Hampton River, instead guiding them to shelter on Little St. Simon's Island. For his courage, Butler presented Morris with an engraved silver tankard, known as the Butler Cup.

A storm of a different sort broke in January 1815, when over 130 Butler slaves liberated themselves during a British occupation of Cumberland Island. After the War of 1812, many of these emancipated

"Butler Cup," presented to a heroic slave named Morris,
whose bravery saved lives during the hurricane of 1804.

African Americans, some still calling themselves Butler, were resettled by the British in Bermuda and Nova Scotia.

By 1810 Butler ceased his seasonal migrations, making his last visit to Georgia in 1815, but he remained loyal to his fellow planters. In 1820 Butler purchased a mansion called the St. Clair house, which he rented for a nominal fee to the "St. Clair Club," whose well-to-do members held monthly dinners so exclusive that only three outside guests were permitted.

At each gathering, rival plantation chefs tried to outdo one another; the clear winner was a free black named Sans Foix, who cooked for the Couper household at Hampton Point. After the meal, a punchbowl filled with rum, brandy, sugar, and lemon peel was brought out and toasts were made all around as each member offered a song or a story, accompanied by slave fiddlers.

These stories of mirth and bounty made the South loom large in Kemble's imagination. Well aware of the property's state of decline, Pierce warned her that accommodations on the island would be primitive, yet she was not deterred. In a vividly detailed travelogue she kept for the benefit of Elizabeth Sedgwick, the South emerged, with its stunning beauties and cruelties, as a character in its own right.

The journey—by boat, train, and coach—from Philadelphia to the Sea Islands proved arduous. Although the Butlers purchased first-class accommodations at overnight stops along the way, even the most basic amenities proved scarce. Fanny struggled to care for three-year-old Sarah and infant Fan; she described the constant lack of privacy, of clean towels, and even of milk for the children. She herself "preferred washing to eating," and missed breakfast in favor of a toilette, only to discover that there was no towel, nor glass, nor "chambermaid to appeal to."

At Portsmouth, Virginia, however, the tone of Kemble's chronicle altered markedly, as she recorded her first encounter with slaves. "The sight of them in no way tended to alter my previous opinions of them. They were poorly clothed; looked horribly dirty, and had a lazy recklessness in their air and manner as they sauntered along, which naturally belongs to creatures without one of the responsibilities which are the honorable burden of rational humanity." Abolitionist leanings notwithstanding, her ignorance showed as she stretched to "prove" philosophical fundamentals through casual observations. The realities of plantation life led her to choose her words more carefully.

She was soothed by the sight of Charleston, where they debarked on Christmas day. "It is so very long since I have seen anything old, that the lower streets of Charleston, in all their dinginess and decay, were a refreshment and a rest to my spirit." She embraced the city's

The overseer's house where Fanny Kemble stayed
during her 1838–39 visit to Butler Island.

The coastal waters along St. Simon's Island.

"air of eccentricity," and her promenade along Charleston's bayside esplanade perhaps reminded her of happier days in Brighton or Bath.

Kemble landed on Butler Island, Georgia, on December 30, 1838, brought to shore by "the measured rush of the Atlantic unfurling its huge skirts upon the white sounds of the beach." Surrounded by natural beauty, she was inspired to explore the island on horseback, marveling at the "thick and close embroidery of creeping moss . . . the most vivid green and red." The place, she concluded, was like "a fairy tale." Yet the fairy tale had a monstrous underside. Kemble confessed, "I should like the wild savage loneliness of the far away existence extremely if it were not for the one small item of 'the slavery.'"

Kemble had arrived believing that "people on this plantation are well off, and consider themselves well off, in comparison with the slaves on some of the neighboring estates." After living among them for four months, she found herself praying for a watery apocalypse to "wash my soul and the souls of those I love clean from the blood of our kind!"

This transformation was not immediate. Fanny's descriptions of her early days on the plantation rely heavily on racial stereotype. Curious about their new mistress, the slaves (up to fourteen at a time) came to her cabin to watch her write. "One after another," she recorded, the men and women "squat down on their hams in a circle, the bright blaze from the huge pine logs, which is the only light of this half of the room, shining on their sooty limbs and faces, and making them like a ring of ebony idols surrounding my domestic hearth."

Unsure of the motives of her visitors, Kemble fashioned the episode into a story, whose language reveals prejudice tinged with humble honesty.

> Sometimes at the end of my day's journal, I look up and say suddenly, "Well, what do you want?" when each black figure springs up at once, as if moved by machinery; they all answer, "Me come say ha do (how d'ye do), missus;" and then they

troop out as noiselessly as they entered, like a procession of sable dreams, and I go off in search, if possible, of whiter ones.

Despite Kemble's sanguine rendition of these encounters, the slaves' proximity seemed distressingly constant. "Whether I be asleep or awake, reading, eating or walking—in the kitchen, my bedroom, or the parlor—they flock in with urgent entreaties and pitiful stories, and my conscience forbids my ever postponing their business for any other matter; for, with shame and grief of heart I say it, by their unpaid labor I live—their nakedness clothes me, and their heavy toil maintains me in luxurious idleness."

Fanny found herself increasingly drawn to the plight of the slaves. She struggled to overcome her aversion to the physical unpleasantness of their dirt-encrusted bodies (especially her housemaid, Mary) and attempted to treat them with kindness and decency.

The children became her constant concern. Kemble fretted, "How horridly brutish it all did seem" that "there is not a girl of sixteen on the plantations but has children, nor a woman of thirty but has grandchildren." Searching for a logical explanation, she reasoned: "A woman thinks, and not much amiss, that the more frequently she adds to the number of her master's livestock by bringing new slaves into the world, the more claims she will have upon his consideration and good will."

Her own husband was quick to demonstrate just how little he cared for the women's suffering. One winter evening, Kemble reported: "Mr. [Butler] was called out . . . to listen to a complaint of overwork from a gang of pregnant women. I did not stay to listen to the details of their petition, for I am unable to command myself on such occasions and Mr. [Butler] seems positively degraded in my eyes as he stood enforcing upon these women the necessity of their fulfilling their appointed tasks."

With her husband's craving for mastery aroused, Kemble feared, slavery was sure to have similar ill effects on young Sarah. "I was observing her today among her swarthy worshipers, for they follow her as such and saw, with dismay, the universal eagerness with which they sprang to obey her little gestures of command . . . think of learning to rule despotically your fellow creatures before the first lesson of self-government has been well spelled over! It makes me tremble; but I shall find a remedy, or remove myself and the children from this misery and ruin."

Resolved to realize this impassioned pledge, Kemble established a slave hospital and a slave nursery and instructed the overseer to heed the complaints of the ill and infirm. She paid wages to those slaves who were her personal servants. With the children, she made a game of hygiene, rewarding cleanliness with trinkets. In her last weeks on the island, she even went so far as to teach the alphabet (in violation of Georgia law) to a bright slave called Aleck. Her reforms most certainly did some good, as later visitors to the plantation commented on the whitewashed cabins and the neat appearance of slave facilities.

But her relentless interference brought public humiliation. The local doctor defended Butler's longtime standing as a model master: "I can state truly that Butler was humane. . . . Indeed he was indulgent almost to a fault when one compares his management to that generally found in plantations." He scoffed at Kemble's "utter ignorance of the Negro character, particularly Negro women *enceinte,* who delight in complaints and have a constitutional weakness about facts."

The overseer advised Butler to bar his wife from hearing further petitions. She scorned the overseer's advice: "Perhaps he is afraid of the mere contagion of freedom . . . my way of speaking to the people, of treating them, of living with them . . . the infinite compassion and human consideration I feel for them."

In truth, Kemble cared little for any aspect of planter society; she especially disliked its female contingent. "I pity them for the stupid

*James Hamilton Couper was a planter and
a Butler neighbor at Hampton Point.*

sameness of their most vapid existence, which would deaden any
amount of intelligence, obliterate any amount of instruction, and render torpid and stagnant any amount of natural energy and vivacity. I
would rather die—rather a thousand times—than live the lives of
these Georgia planters' wives and daughters."

But far more sinister was the subtlety of slaveholders' oppressive
hold. Making "pets, playthings and jesters" of favorite slaves, Kemble
remarked, was "perfectly consistent with the profoundest contempt
and injustice, degrades the object of it quite as much, though it oppresses him less, than the cruelty practiced upon his fellows."

Kemble now knew to a certainty what one South Carolinian had
confided: "Abolition is impossible because every healthy negro can
fetch a thousand dollars in the Charleston market at this moment."

That the outcry against slavery had been "raised with threefold force within the last few years" was little comfort when she was living with a man who willfully perpetuated it. Privately, she hoped that "this sojourn among Mr. [Butler]'s slaves may not lessen my respect for him, but I fear it."

Kemble's discomfort over her station may have intensified her antislavery rhetoric. She took to culling atrocities from Southern papers, a technique popularized by Angelina Grimké and her husband Theodore Weld in their 1839 exposé, *American Slavery as It Is*. Each tale—a pregnant woman tied to a tree by her thumbs, with her clothes rolled about her waist before she was whipped with a cowhide; slaves prevented from attending the church on St. Simon's by their Christian masters; "owners [who] have a fancy for maiming their slaves—some brand them, some pull out their teeth, some shoot them a little here and there"—is more unspeakable than the last.

Fanny claimed not to embellish or comment in her journal for Elizabeth Sedgwick: "I do not wish to add to, or perhaps I ought to say take away from, the effect of such narration by amplifying the simple horror and misery of their bare details." But while she may not have deliberately crafted "bare details" into abolitionist propaganda, these writings do have a sensational effect. Even as she tried to counter racist rhetoric with provocative reversals—Would blacks "smell any worse if they were free" instead of slave?—Kemble's daring made her vulnerable to scandal.

In the face of oppressive daily battles with her husband, Fanny snapped under pressure. Repeating a pattern from her past, she fled the scene of her distress. We will never know what drove her. She made a lone dash for a rowboat, determined to escape, and rowed into the silent night, landing in the darkness at Darien. She must have paused—worn down by the exertion of her escape and the intensity of her emotions—just long enough to realize, in the warmth of the rising sun, that she had no real means to make her way to Philadelphia. The next day she returned to her children, but this time the rift between her and

Pierce never seemed to heal. Its cause, a descendant has suggested, was Kemble's discovery of her husband's illicit sexual liaison with a slave woman.

Kemble came to believe that she was little different from Butler's other property, subject to her husband's will. Perhaps in response to the powerlessness she felt in her marriage, Kemble's writings turned increasingly to white men's sexual exploitation of slave women. "Almost every Southern planter," she asserted with authority, "has a family more or less numerous of illegitimate colored children." On the taboo subject of "miscegenation," she told of Judy, forced to have sex with "Mr. K——," who flogged her and sent her to Five Pound, a miserable exile, where she gave birth to a mulatto son, Jem Valiant.

Although she replaced names with dashes in the published version of her journal, the identifying factors she included were recognized instantly by Georgia's planter elite. Butler and his overseers were not immune from her excoriations. She reported that Roswell King (both father and son) coerced and impregnated slave women.

It was Butler's disregard of a particular slave, ironically named Psyche, that Kemble felt most deeply. Psyche, who was married to another slave, Joe, sought Kemble's protection against the couple's separation. (Many Butler slaves were arbitrarily given to Roswell King, then sent to his holdings in Alabama.) In a flash of understanding, Kemble saw her husband's utter power not only over his slaves, but over herself and her children.

Unnerved by a sense of impotence, Kemble cursed her feeble attempts at charity. "A long chain of all my possessions," she lamented, "wound in glittering procession through my brain, with many hypothetical calculations of the value of each separate ornament." She was doubtful that "among the whole [she could make a sum] equal to the price of the poor creature [Psyche] and her children." After a long and emotional series of events, Joe and Psyche were able to remain together in Georgia.

Quantifying the tragic inequality of material wealth and human life

*Images of slave women being flogged were rare; this one
was featured in an antebellum abolitionist tract.*

allowed Kemble to understand, for the first time, what abdicating her financial independence had truly cost her. "For the last four years of my life that preceded my marriage," she wrote, "I literally coined money, and never until this moment, I think, did I reflect on the great means of good to myself and others, that I so gladly agreed to give up forever for a maintenance by the unpaid labor of slaves."

No longer able to carry the burden of her own private war against slavery—on the plantation and in her marriage—Kemble succumbed to depression, confessing: "I think I should die if I had to live here." During this bleak time, her only solace was to record the stories of the

Stereotypical antebellum-era image of plantation harmony.

slave women who visited her, so that others might one day know of
their suffering, and of her own.

- Fanny has had six children; all dead but one. She came to beg
to have her work in the field lightened.
- Nanny has had three children; two of them are dead. She
came to implore that the rule of sending them into the field three
weeks after their confinement might be altered.
- Leah, Caesar's wife, has had six children; three are dead.
- Sophy, Lewis's wife, came to beg for some old linen. She is
suffering fearfully; has had ten children; five of them are dead.

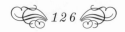

The principal favor she asked was a piece of meat, which I gave her.

• Sally, Scipio's wife, has had two miscarriages and three children born, one of whom is dead. She came complaining of incessant pain and weakness in her back. This woman was a mulatto daughter of a slave called Sophy, by a white man of the name of Walker, who visited the plantation.

• Charlotte, Renty's wife, had had two miscarriages and was with child again. She was almost crippled with rheumatism, and showed me a pair of swollen knees that made my heart ache. I have promised her a pair of flannel trousers, which I must forthwith set about making.

• Sarah, Stephen's wife—this woman's case and history were alike and deplorable. She had had four miscarriages, had brought seven children into the world, five of whom were dead and was with child again. She complained of dreadful pains in the back, and an internal tumor which swells with the exertion of working in the fields; probably, I think, she is ruptured. She told me she had once been mad and had run into the woods, where she contrived to elude discovery for some time, but was at last tracked and brought back, when she was tied up by the arms and heavy logs fastened to her feet, and was severely flogged. . . .

• Sukey, Bush's wife, only came to pay her respects. She had had four miscarriages; had brought eleven children into the world, five of whom are dead.

• Molly, Quambo's wife, also only came to see me. Hers was the best account I have yet received; she had had nine children, and six of them were still alive.

This is only the entry for to-day in my diary, of the people's complaints and visits. Can you conceive a more wretched picture than that which it exhibits of the conditions under which these women live?

Kemble's account of her days on Butler Island portrays her husband—and any man who believed as he did—as an indifferent tyrant. Upon their return to Philadelphia in May 1839, Fanny gave Pierce an ultimatum: if the family livelihood continued to be drawn from slave labor, she no longer wanted to stay with him. Butler dismissed this as the height of hypocrisy: "The act of marrying a slave owner made her also a slave owner; and her support as well as mine was derived from the product of slave labour."

Kemble denied her husband the marriage bed. She may have feared the prospect of an additional child, but she also recognized sexuality as her sole means of control. At the height of their misery, she quoted to Butler his own words: "'What need of intellectual converse, have you not an affectionate husband and two sweet babies?'" Her acerbic reply, "You might as well say to a man who told you he had no arms—Oh! no, but you have legs," was ignored.

Alarmed at his wife's rebelliousness, Pierce wrote to her friends Charles and Elizabeth Sedgwick in Lenox, claiming to be afraid for Fanny's mental health. He repeated her threat to take Sarah to London with her and leave him with one-year-old Fan. Butler begged the Sedgwicks to intercede on his behalf, carefully concealing that he was spending more nights in Philadelphia than he did at home.

Although Fanny likely suspected Pierce of infidelity, her strict code of privacy prevented her from sharing these fears with the Sedgwicks, who lent Butler their sympathy. Elizabeth Sedgwick wrote Fanny a strongly worded letter: "Your mind is positively and greatly diseased . . . . You have no right . . . to deprive your husband of his children . . . you inherit, undoubtedly, from your mother, those morbid tendencies which poison and spoil all." At the same time, Sedgwick counseled Butler to be "soothing" and "compassionate" toward Fanny, as if she were gravely ill.

The Sedgwicks also invited Fanny and the children to Lenox for a prolonged visit. Butler, complaining of his own poor health, spent the summer at Hot Springs, Virginia, a therapeutic resort where invalids sought water cures.

Butler's letters during this period exude a philosophic melancholy: "If I cannot have happiness in my own home, it is nowhere for me. I may not be happy with you; but oh, most true it is, I cannot be happy without you." But even the sweetest epistle could not overcome the disharmony that reigned in October 1839, when the couple were reunited at Butler Place.

Against Pierce's express wishes, Fanny continued to rail against slavery and allowed her journal to circulate among abolitionists. He retaliated by giving her just one day's notice that he planned to winter in Georgia—and intended that she stay behind. Although ill health delayed his parting, he felt no regret over leaving Kemble alone.

During their prolonged separation, Butler fell seriously ill yet again, and his Georgia attendants feared he might die. News of his condition filled Kemble with despair and regret. She wrote to her husband on his sickbed:

> God bless you, my darling, dearest Pierce; when you think of me—*if* you think of me—think as one whose love for you has been a source not of joy or delight, but of pain and agony. . . . forgive me, my dearest Pierce, if I have so bitterly cursed your existence. I cannot write more; I am blinded with crying.

Butler recovered enough to travel home that spring. So grateful was she for his safe return that Kemble promised never again to mention slavery. During the summer of 1840, the couple lived together in relative peace.

They planned to spend a second winter together in Georgia, then travel to Europe the following spring. But when Fanny received news that her father was gravely ill, the entire family set sail on December 1 for London, taking with them Ann Martin, their new nursemaid. (Fanny had fired her former nanny, Margery O'Brien, for teaching Catholic catechism to Sarah and Fan. Martin was a Protestant.) They would not return to America for nearly three years.

By the time the Butlers arrived in England, Charles Kemble had already begun to recover. The Butlers rented a house near Piccadilly, where they were joined by Charles Kemble, Harriet St. Leger, and—after her triumphant Italian debut at La Scala—Fanny's younger sister Adelaide, now a professional singer.

During the summer of 1841, Adelaide toured the Rhineland with the pianist and composer Franz Liszt. The Butlers, equally enamored of Liszt and the German countryside, enjoyed themselves immensely in his traveling entourage, finding the pianist "radiant with the fire of his great natural gifts." Upon her return to London, Adelaide debuted at Covent Garden, performing before packed houses in *Norma* and *Le Nozze di Figaro*. Fanny was suitably proud of her sister's success. She wrote to Harriet: "Adelaide sang beautifully and looked beautiful and was extremely admired and praised and petted."

In October 1841, Pierce Butler decided to prolong their stay in England. He rented a grand house on Harley Street so that he might reciprocate the social invitations extended to the Butlers throughout the previous season. At the peak of their popularity, Kemble was presented to Queen Victoria, and Pierce was "out in search of amusement from morning till night." But his gambling and the couple's increasing incompatibility made them notorious.

Charles Greville gossiped: "Now after wasting the best years of her life in something very like solitude near Philadelphia, with two children, whom she is passionately fond of, what is her situation? She has discovered that she has married a weak, dawdling, ignorant, violent tempered man who is utterly unsuited to her and she to him and she is aware that she has outlived his liking as he has outlived her esteem and respect."

Although Butler had quite a fortune, Philadelphia knew what Lon-

Fanny's sister, Adelaide Kemble, had a brief but celebrated
career as an opera singer, 1837–42.

don only guessed—that Butler's expenses exceeded his resources. Over Butler's prideful objections, Adelaide lent Fanny money whenever she exceeded her allowance. Kemble frequently turned to her pen as an additional source of income. She peddled essays and reviews to her brother John, editor of the *Quarterly Review,* using her earnings to pay off her milliner, dressmaker, and other accounts.

Pierce and Fanny both knew that her work with the greatest potential value was her Georgia "Journal of a Residence," which had been circulating privately among New England abolitionists. By the early

1840s, Northern activists were exhilarated that a "wide and deep feeling" against the South "was silently stealing upon the hearts of our people." In 1839 the founding of the Liberty Party, with a "free soil" agenda, stirred up even more interest in abolitionist campaigns. Antislavery activists were seeking new and more powerful propaganda to advance their cause.

Lydia Maria Child, the well-known abolitionist and New York editor, expressed interest in publishing Kemble's letters to Elizabeth Sedgwick. She also wanted to serialize the Georgian journal in her antislavery newspaper. Butler demanded that his wife ignore the offer. Kemble insisted she must respond, if only to explain that her diary was *not* for sale. She gave Butler her letter to Child—to read, seal, and mail—then found it weeks later still in his desk drawer. Torn between fury that Butler would disregard her wishes and embarrassment that Child had been kept waiting, she sent an apologetic letter to her explaining the circumstances of the delay. The couple's heated dispute over both Child's offer and Kemble's response demonstrated their irreconcilable differences over a married woman's right to a separate identity. Butler demanded Kemble's absolute obedience to him, that she accede to his wishes without reproach. She repeatedly failed him in this regard. But Butler failed her in significant ways, as well.

In April 1842, Kemble overheard rumors of Butler's involvement in yet another adulterous affair. In a rage, she packed up her belongings and headed for Liverpool, determined to sail back to Philadelphia. But Pierce caught the next train and persuaded her to forgive him.

The Kemble family assigned Fanny a great deal of the blame for these marital histrionics. Adelaide speculated that her sister would have been better off with less artistic talent (and temperament), and a greater "sense of domestic duty." In her opinion, Fanny should have "studied the character of her husband for the purpose of improving it, and corrected the faults of her own in order to make him happy."

Perhaps Adelaide felt justified in her criticism because she had just made her own happy match. She had decided to give up her career in the opera to marry Edward Sartoris, a rather plain gentleman with a country house in Hampshire. Fanny herself expressed polite reserve over her sister's choice, but one acquaintance bluntly dismissed him as "a pea jacket." Henry James, who would later become a great friend of the family, described Sartoris as very pleasant, although "unprepossessing."

The wedding plans were interrupted by the continuing financial woes of Covent Garden. Against his children's strict advice, Charles Kemble had once again become involved in managing the theater. When he fell into arrears on performers' wages, Adelaide was prevailed upon to prolong her run until her father could clear his debts. Fanny offered her own theatrical services, but Pierce forbade her to work.

Annoyed because Butler had repeatedly postponed their departure and because he was solely in charge of their timetable, Fanny wrote to a friend in February, "Mr. Butler *thinks* he should go in the middle of April, but for my part I shall not think any thing about it until I am on board the packet." Ann Martin, the girls' much-loved nanny, gave her notice and sailed home to America. Unperturbed, Butler hired a new governess, Amelia Hall, whose presence would intensify the discord between Fanny and her husband in the years to come.

Butler's infidelities continued over the summer of 1843, when his seduction of a household maid once again provoked Fanny to run off for several days. He tried to placate his wife by sending her and Sarah to visit relatives in Edinburgh, but in a letter dated shortly after her return, she exhorted him: "Do not, for God's sake, give yourself up to unworthy pursuits and pleasures; remember your children." Refusing to find himself at fault, Butler replied, "On my soul and conscience I have done every thing in my power to make you happy and contented."

Even Fanny's continuing passion for her husband—"my heart still answers to your voice, my blood in my veins to your footsteps"—was not enough to curb the escalation of their mutually destructive behavior. Desperate for relief, Kemble pleaded: "I propose an entire separation . . . if you still refuse me an entire reconciliation."

At this crucial juncture, one of Butler's desperate illnesses distracted the warring couple, and their tender feelings resurfaced. Fanny begged Pierce to let her nurse him back to health, and Butler believed her motivations to be genuine: "I am quite satisfied with the promises you have made . . . our reunion will be happy and lasting."

Once again living, according to Butler, "as man and wife," the couple completed their plans to return home to Philadelphia. In mounting a farewell party for two hundred, Butler spared no expense, even though he had to borrow from the newlywed Sartorises to settle his accounts. But that debt seemed to matter little. Butler had extracted from his father-in-law a deed that, upon Charles Kemble's death, granted Fanny the trust income she had arranged for her father in 1834.

Still, the Butlers arrived in America cash poor. Forced to let Butler Place, they moved into a boardinghouse on Walnut Street in Philadelphia. Kemble had always found Branchtown isolated, and had longed for urban society. But the current arrangement was "detestable." "Anguish," she wrote to Sarah Perkins—now Sarah Cleveland—"has come over me like a flood." When her watch and chain were pilfered from her room, she complained to Harriet, "Of the discomfort and disorder of our mode of life, I cannot easily give you a notion, for you know nothing of the sort, and until now, neither did I." She wept with gratitude when Harriet replaced her stolen treasure.

But Butler proved a far more nefarious thief, robbing Kemble of any lingering illusions about the sanctity of their marriage. In October 1843, she stumbled upon letters providing proof of her husband's illicit sexual conduct as far back as five years. When she confronted him about his philandering and infidelity, he was more indignant at Fanny's prying than embarrassed at her discovery of his liaisons. His indifference to her confirmation of the rumors that had plagued their marriage for years and his unwillingness to conceal his dalliances drove Fanny to retain Theodore Sedgwick as legal counsel. In November 1843, she asked Pierce for a formal separation agreement.

In light of the sordid details of Butler's infidelities, Elizabeth Sedgwick was especially remorseful, having frequently advised her friend to reconcile with her husband. Elizabeth and Charles, along with Theodore and Catharine Sedgwick, traveled to Philadelphia in a last attempt to urge Butler to agree to Fanny's terms, to reach an amicable settlement.

Butler would not concede any fault but rather demanded that the Sedgwicks cease what he saw as their harassment. Theodore Sedgwick began to build a legal case, making discreet inquiries about Butler's sexual and romantic adventures during the couple's over two-year stay in London; he focused especially on the character of the governess, Miss Hall, with whom, Kemble was sure, Butler had become sexually involved. Butler discovered the investigation and lashed back with vituperative attacks on both Fanny and her cohorts.

But in 1844, one of his escapades became commonly known, and he was powerless to prevent dishonor and ill will from blackening his reputation. On April 15, James Schott of Bladensburg, Maryland, had challenged Butler to a duel, from which both parties escaped without injury. Schott, believing that he had been denied satisfaction, published a tract alleging a sexual tryst between Butler and Mrs. Schott: "On the night of Saturday [March] ninth [1844] at midnight, a circumstance occurred to which I have no desire to give publicity nor to say one word more of it than it was of a character to justify—in fact render imperatively necessary—all the steps which I took in consequence of it."

Butler denied Schott's charges. Perhaps seeing her husband mired in a scandal of his own making emboldened Kemble to promise that she would "never in any way to any one again advert to the circumstances of your past life, never to refer to them by word or letter to any human being, in short, to bury them." Butler replied imperiously,

"There is no 'circumstance' or act of the 'past life' which I desire to bury."

To stress the point, he brazenly took the girls and Miss Hall (with whom he was reputedly having an affair) to Newport for the summer of 1844. That fall, he drew up a contract specifying that—in return for room and board, a monthly allowance, and one-hour daily visiting privileges with her daughters—his wife would refrain from "reprobation and reproach," as well as from "interference" with the upbringing of Sarah and Fan. Finally—in retaliation for the Sedgwicks' attack on him—the contract called on Fanny to cease "forever" all acquaintance with the family.

The marriage laws left Kemble no recourse; she could submit or lose her daughters. Yet she remained defiant until February 1845, when six-year-old Fan fell and broke her arm. Unable to bear the thought of her daughter alone and in pain, Kemble relented. She wrote her farewells to the Sedgwicks, and signed the document Butler had prepared.

From the moment she rejoined the household, Kemble claimed, Pierce plotted to be rid of her. She believed the contract had been a ploy to drive her away, and that he had never expected her to submit to his Draconian conditions. After only a month, the pact was broken, on the ground that Kemble had read a letter from Elizabeth Sedgwick, even though Pierce himself had handed it to her.

From that moment, he absolved himself of any responsibility for Fanny; he announced that she would no longer be allowed to raise the children and would be allowed to see them only with his express permission. This time, Kemble did not fight. She sailed for London in October 1845.

CHAPTER SIX

Fighting for Her Rights

Pierce "has sent me penniless as well as husbandless and childless home," Fanny wrote to Sarah Cleveland in November 1845. While society matrons readily incorporated the infamous Mrs. Butler's problems into their steady stream of gossip, Charles Kemble simply, and without ceremony, welcomed his daughter home.

Charles's prestigious sinecure as Examiner of Plays had recently passed to his son John. But since the principal of Fanny's theatrical earnings continued to generate interest, he had sufficient income. His annotated and abridged Shakespearean scripts were widely regarded as masterworks, and he earned twenty pounds an evening reading from the texts (although his growing deafness hindered his abilities). Still, as Fanny was well aware, her father's resources could not support them both. She sold some poems for a small sum, but it was a source of worry that all earnings and any assets she accumulated legally belonged, under the rule of femme couverte, to her husband.

Under American law, an unmarried woman was femme sole, but a married woman was designated as femme couverte and, as such, had no separate legal personality: her property (unless specifically protected by a prenuptial agreement) was subject to the control of her husband, and any earnings she might accumulate could be seized by her husband. Further, the minor children were also under the total control of their father, with the mother having no rights under the law. At the same time, since the Revolution, divorce law in America was shifting over time—very gradually, but much faster than in European nations—to recognize the rights of women, especially mothers.

"If I want to institute a process for the recovery of my rights I must be in America myself," Fanny determined, but friends urged her to remain abroad. Harriet St. Leger invited Fanny to join her and her companion, Dorothy Wilson, in Hastings. Lady Dacre offered Fanny refuge at her estate, the Hoo. Charles put forth a decisive plan of his own. He would accompany his daughter to America to obtain her money by legal means; that failing, the two would embark on a theatrical tour. But Fanny resisted, haunted by memories of the desperate financial circumstances that had precipitated their 1832 American tour.

Fanny finally accepted an invitation from Adelaide and Edward (who were living on the Continent at the time) to spend the winter at their Italian home. On December 20, Kemble set out for Rome on borrowed funds. That her only companion was her Irish maid, Bridget Hayes, made for a lonely Christmas. Even her reunion with Adelaide was only briefly joyous. While Edward Sartoris was gently supportive of her decision not to remain with Butler, Adelaide was indifferent at best, remarking, "'Sooner than lose my children there is *nothing* I would not do.'" This sentiment, Kemble was certain, reflected "the feeling of the great majority of women."

Fanny remained with her sister's family for nearly a year. Still in need of money, she took up a mercenary pen and wrote a travel book. "I have a great contempt for the barren balderdash I write, but a thing is worth what it will fetch, and if a bookseller will buy my trash, I will sell it to him, for beggars must, in no case, be choosers." The British publisher Edward Moxon obliged by offering her a handsome sum for her Italian journal.

Year of Consolation contained no direct references to her personal situation, but both the title and numerous poetic asides revealed her profound despondency:

> Sorrow and sin, and suffering and strife
> Have been cast in the waters of my life
> And they have sunk deep down to the well-head
> And all that flows thence is embittered.

Concerning these poems an American critic sniped, "We can hardly give the reader better advice than to skip them all. . . . But what would have made her writing better, would doubtless have also made her life happier—something less of the predominance of self."

But the *North American Review* called Kemble's writings on Roman politics "much the best account we have yet had" and suggested that the social chameleon might easily make a third home for herself in Italy. This was unlikely. Kemble felt deeply isolated—from England and America, from her husband, and most especially from her two young daughters. In December 1845 she wrote to Harriet St. Leger: "It would be impossible for me to tell you how sad I am." She suspected that Butler was using her absence to endear himself to Sarah and Fan, and to ease her out of their lives.

As May 28—Sarah's eleventh birthday and Fan's eighth—approached, Fanny longed for news of the girls. She turned to Sarah Perkins Cleveland for help: "I do not suppose Mr. Butler would take your visiting them [but] . . . at any rate I should have [the] consolation of having your report of them."

In search of ever-elusive happiness, Kemble made a pilgrimage to the Trevi Fountain, where, according to custom, she took a sip from its waters. Then she returned to England to spend yet another holiday without a home of her own. In January 1847 good news must have arrived, for Kemble wrote thankfully to Sarah Cleveland:

> This my dearest friend is the greatest, the only service you can render me—the misery of such separation as mine absent of but one consolation—the receiving from all who can furnish me with every particle of information of my girls which can be gleaned or gathered for me by those who more fortunate than their Mother have opportunities of seeing them.

By this time it had become well known in aristocratic circles that Butler had refused Kemble money for a period of nearly a year and a half. It is unclear whether he intended to punish her or if he was simply short of funds (bad investments and gambling made him the bane of creditors throughout the 1840s and into the 1850s). Indeed, Charles Sumner, acting on Kemble's behalf, was still trying to pry from Butler documents vital to the settlement. He advised Fanny that she might be forced to sue for divorce, a step she was loath to undertake.

When Fanny was asked if she wanted to return to the stage, her response was "Never!" She remembered her acting career as "positively odious." But the work would "enable me to secure something for my girls" and provide a "means of independence," so she reconsidered, even pledging to improve upon her technique: "I hope that in spite of the loss of youth of person and feeling, I may be able to fill some parts better than I did formerly." Her plan was to tour England for two years, billing herself as Fanny Kemble Butler, until she had worn out her "public favor." Then she would return to America to live modestly on her savings.

Although Kemble found the audiences generous, and the critics kind, the rigors of touring proved more than she could bear. After only a few months, she found herself completely debilitated by a painful affliction "suffered for years indeed ever since my Fanny's birth . . . the

Fanny Kemble (Butler) as Isabella.

*During her return to the stage in the 1840s,
Fanny reprised the role she had popularized in
her youth, Isabella.*

piles." Horrified by aristocratic ladies' tendency to take "chloroform as a pastime," Kemble underwent an operation without benefit of anesthetic, preferring to endure the pain rather than "lose all self government."

She returned to the London stage in her most triumphant role, that of Julia in *The Hunchback*. One critic found her voice enhanced and her performance improved by "mature judgement and acute perception." Although she still drew audiences, Fanny was no longer a box-office

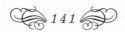

William Macready was a leading actor of his
generation, but proved a great trial to Kemble during
their joint performances.

sensation. Nevertheless, Butler became aware of her return to the stage, thanks to notices in the London papers. The distance to London did nothing to lessen his fury. He forbade the children to write to their mother, and kept her letters from them. Without her knowledge, he also initiated proceedings under Pennsylvania law to "ask for divorce as a matter of absolute right," as he could do if he proved desertion for a period of two years.

Without letters from her beloved Sarah and Fan, Kemble was propelled even further into the depths of loneliness. She accepted the female lead in a charity performance of Victor Hugo's *Hernani*—opposite, as it turned out, her first love, Augustus Craven. Her journal reveals nothing about what transpired at this initial reunion. But a year later, following one of his visits to her dressing room, she commented enigmatically on the "improbability" of life.

Soon after *Hernani,* Kemble reluctantly agreed to perform at Covent Garden in aid of the restoration of Shakespeare's home. She was ambivalent about the prospect of returning—over a quarter of a century later—to the site of her youthful triumph. This was the first time she had faced a Covent Garden audience since her farewell performance in 1832. Following her brief onstage appearance, she was overcome with emotion and, refusing curtain calls, "left the house as quickly as possible."

In January 1848, Kemble won a month-long contract to perform four nights a week at London's Princess Theatre with the notoriously temperamental actor William Macready. She seized this lucrative opportunity without hesitation. Kemble had known Macready for years, and although he had declined to produce her play *An English Tragedy,* he very much admired her writing. They proved, however, remarkably ill-suited to share the stage.

Kemble resented Macready's bullying manner, while he thought her a poor actress who put on airs unjustified by her skills. Macready fumed about Kemble's inadequacies in his diary: "I have never seen [a Desdemona] so bad, so unnatural, so affected, so conceited." While Kemble later conceded that there may have been some truth to Macready's assessment, at the time the savage bluntness of his criticism pushed her toward a second retirement.

Just then, Charles Kemble—whose infirmities would soon keep him from performing altogether—passed his annotated scripts to his daughter, in hopes that she would continue the Shakespearean readings he had begun. In the early years of her marriage, Fanny had given readings for charity or drawing room entertainment, but it had been many years since she had performed solo with just her voice to hold an audience.

Upon resuming her stage career in 1847, she had asked theater managers for £100 per week but was quickly forced to lower her price to £50 to maintain steady bookings. Out of that sum came the cost of a dresser (Bridget Hayes), costumes, rehearsal space, and travel—and very little profit. However, if she could launch a career as a solo performer and charge £20 per performance (the same price her father had commanded), she might reduce her expenses and perhaps generate steady income. Three to four bookings per week would provide a healthy income, and allow her to save.

Kemble hired Henry Mitchell, an associate of her father's, to schedule readings outside London. In Manchester, she wore a satin dress of bright red, her favorite color, and sat by a table bearing only a glass of water and her script. The audience was enchanted: she interpreted with bewitching ease each individual character, as if personifying an entire cast of players.

At first, Kemble scheduled her afternoon readings around a full roster of evening performances. But after just a few weeks, Mitchell had booked £500 worth of engagements, and by March 1848, she gave up theatrical engagements entirely. Recalling a performance from her first American run, Kemble underlined the wretched excess required to mount a full-scale drama:

> How I do loathe the stage! these wretched, tawdry, glittering rages, flung over the breathing forms of ideal loveliness. . . . how I do loathe my most impotent and unpoetical craft! . . . lying over [Romeo's] corpse, and fumbling for his dagger . . . I, Juliet, thus apostrophized him—Romeo being dead—"Why, where *the* devil *is* your dagger?" . . . What a disgusting travesty. . . . it's an absolute *shame* that one of Shakespeare's plays should be thus turned into a mockery.

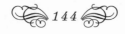

Shakespearean readings in drawing rooms and lyceums were
a theatrical legacy from Charles Kemble to his daughter.

In contrast, she wrote to Harriet, "The happiness of reading Shakespeare's heavenly imaginations is so far beyond all the excitement of acting them." In her new guise, she drew an entirely new audience: those who might never have considered attending the theater because of religious or moral scruples, but were willing to be entertained by an evening of Shakespeare read aloud.

Kemble cared deeply about educating her audiences to all the great works of the Bard. She heeded her advisers' admonition not to read the plays in their entirety, instead performing her father's abridgments, which ran two hours. But she insisted on presenting a full cycle of two dozen dramas.

When she performed Shakespeare's most popular plays, among them *Hamlet, Romeo and Juliet,* and *A Midsummer Night's Dream,* she regularly drew a full house. While Mitchell could easily have charged ten shillings per ticket, she allowed him to charge only five.

She also limited her performances to four per week, even though Mitchell could have sold seats enough for six. Keen to capitalize on his client's popularity, he proposed to bill her as "celebrated" in advertisements of future readings. Kemble quashed this idea, forbidding any "florid prose" in connection with her performances.

Perhaps most exasperating to Mitchell, however, was Kemble's insistence on offering—in the tradition of a bygone era in British theater—a benefit performance in each city she visited. The profits from one out of five readings went to local charities; this made her beloved by audiences but maligned by Mitchell, her financial adviser.

Adelaide and Edward were due to return from Italy that spring, and her bookings were going so well that Kemble put off indefinitely plans for transatlantic travel. But her hopes for a pleasant season were dashed when, on March 28, 1848, a Philadelphia court sent Kemble a summons announcing that Butler was seeking a divorce and sole custody of the children. Following to the letter the shrewd advice of his lawyers, Butler had silently waited out the full two-year period that entitled him to claim desertion. He wanted a clear-cut case against his wife, as the custody laws in Pennsylvania were more progressive than most, perhaps due to the influence of the Quakers.

In 1816, Pennsylvania became one of the first states to liberalize laws on marital dissolution. In a landmark custody case in 1813, the judge considered what are now referred to as the best interests of the child—a decidedly revolutionary reading of the law, especially because in this particular dispute, the husband charged his wife with adultery. Nevertheless, Pennsylvania Chief Justice William Tilghman ruled: "It appears to us, that considering their tender years [a seven-year-old and ten-year-old daughter], they stand in need of the kind of assistance which can be afforded by none so well as a mother." Justice evolved slowly, however, and courts continued to allow American fathers presumptive—though not absolute—rights in cases of divorce. Thus, proof of Fanny's desertion of the marriage and her girls was of paramount importance to Pierce's case. But beneath any emotional satisfaction he might glean from a custody victory lay a clear financial objective—to avoid sustaining any losses (taking a profit if at all possible).

Under the doctrine of marital unity, Butler was entitled to claim any or all of his wife's earnings. As they were gearing up for a battle royal, Kemble felt it necessary to protect herself. In August 1848 she preempted any attempts at legal robbery by investing £3,000 in British bonds under the name of a never-married friend, Emily Fitzhugh. Her nest egg safely tucked away in England, she crossed the Atlantic to fight for her girls.

Upon landing in America in mid-September 1848, Kemble immediately sought legal remedy. Theodore Sedgwick filed a formal answer to Butler's allegations with the Pennsylvania court. In Massachusetts, the Sedgwicks pledged their support. In Philadelphia, the Biddles, the Joshua Fishers, and the Reverend William Henry Furness rallied to her as well. Afraid to antagonize Butler further, however, Fanny dared not resume her Shakespearean performances; in fact, she rarely ventured out in public.

Although divorce was available, it was still relatively rare. Further, the Butlers' split attracted a great deal of interest on both sides of the Atlantic. Preliminary proceedings were scheduled in Philadelphia in November 1848. To keep Fanny's mind off her legal ordeal, Sally Cleveland offered to buy her a horse, but Kemble refused: "I shall be obliged to deny myself the luxury" until "I am allowed to resume my lucrative activity." Her staunch devotion to deprivation produced intermittent optimism—"I really have grounds for thinking that before long my children may be restored to me"—but more pronounced in her letters from this period are gloom and fright.

On November 14, just prior to her summons date, she wrote: "I am driven half crazy with this anticipated horror of having to make my appearance in a Court of law there to encounter the man who has destroyed my life and dragged me to this intolerable issue." A little over a week later, she declared: "Upon this afternoon to Philadelphia—I feel as if I were going to execution—" Above all, she was dismayed to see her private anguish turn to public drama with her daughters' futures in the balance.

Like most couples going through divorce, the Butlers allowed their daughters to become pawns in their marital battles. In the months before the trial, Kemble had decided not to see Sarah and Fan because "a momentary or even temporary enjoyment of my children's sight would be an awful agony." For his part, Butler wanted to prolong the separation in any way possible. He had intended to enroll the girls in a Georgia boarding school in the fall of 1848, but he settled on an academy near Philadelphia. Kemble's continued prayer that "God will in his own good time *restore* my precious lost ones to me" was finally granted that November when Butler allowed them one brief visit— the first in over three years—at Fanny's Philadelphia hotel.

At the November hearing, Kemble's lawyers moved for a court date, which was set for April 16, 1849. Of greatest concern was the possibility that Butler's lawyers would have persuaded the judge to set aside the sixty-page "Narrative" Fanny had written in response to her husband's version of events. Convinced that she could persuade any jury of her worthiness as a mother, she insisted upon the opportunity to introduce evidence in her favor in open court.

Before the judge could rule on this sensitive question, however, the matter had a very public airing, for newspapers throughout the United States—and eventually Britain—printed purloined copies of the "Narrative." Although many were moved by her descriptions of Butler's brutality, her testimony mattered little to Philadelphia's elite, who were disposed to take Butler's side. Kemble wrote dejectedly to the Boston lawyer Samuel Ward that Butler projected "a hallucination so strong that I think if I remain here much longer I shall come to perceive that he is a paragon of every earthly virtue and myself a monster of iniquity."

Just as Butler's fellow planters had found him a model slaveowner, they deemed him a faultless husband: "Now the charge of cruelty against Mr. Butler by his own acts or by the acts of others approved by him falls harmlessly to the ground in the community where he was best known and most highly esteemed and respected."

But even the most vigorous claims of his sterling character might be challenged by witnesses to the contrary, witnesses who under oath might attest to Butler's checkered past. For that reason Butler was determined to avoid a trial. He could ill afford testimony regarding his extensive infidelities, especially his recent involvement with a Miss Coleman.

In an undated letter to Sally Cleveland, Kemble reported that his "devotion to Miss Coleman is more open and [illeg.] than ever and the whole posture of his affairs and crime is I think as curious as any that can or will be disguised." Kemble and her lawyers gambled that if they kept what they knew under wraps, they might be able to use it as leverage for an out-of-court settlement.

Kemble was buoyed by the legal expertise of Joshua Fisher (his wife, Eliza, was a Middleton by birth, and thus a blood relative of Butler) and by additional visits with Sarah and Fan. Meanwhile, Butler was summoned to his Georgia estates. John Butler's 1848 death from dysentery during the Mexican War had left Pierce in sole charge of the plantations, and his management supported his sister-in-law, Gabriella (Ella), and her children, as well as his own.

While his brother's family could depend on Pierce, Fanny knew just one way to earn the money she needed to pay off her mounting debts. In the weeks after Butler's departure for the South, she wrote to Sam Ward, "I am not without hope too that by giving up my plan of reading hear [sic] my children may be allowed to finish the winter in place among their friends instead of being dragged down to Georgia." But when she changed her mind and applied to hire a lecture hall at the University of Pennsylvania, she was "respectfully declined," most certainly because of Butler's influence.

Kemble proved more successful in New York City. Philip Hone described her routine:

> She reads Shakespeare's plays three evenings in the week, and at noon on Mondays in the Stuyvesant Institute in Broadway, a room which will hold six or seven hundred persons, and which is filled when she reads by the elite of the world of fashion; delicate women, grave gentlemen, belles, beaux and critics flock to the doors of the entrance, and rush into such places as they can find, two or three hours before the lady's appearance.

Hone correctly predicted that she would become a phenomenon. But his calculation of her earnings at $2,000–$3,000 per week failed to deduct from gross receipts agent's fees, room rentals, and travel costs. Further, Hone's estimates were based on figures published in the local press of Kemble's take at charity events, for which tickets were always pricier than for normal performances. For example, Kemble's reading at the Manhattan branch of the St. George Society (which supported indigent British expatriates) drew the atypically high sum of $1,100.

Nevertheless, she earned enough to pay her considerable legal fees, and, at long last, to buy a two-story house a half-mile outside her beloved Lenox, Massachusetts. "The Perch" was set in a glen of oaks and boasted a three-story observation tower.

The hearing was postponed until September 1849; as the months wore on, Kemble's side threatened to exercise their most powerful legal option—the right of dower, by which a wife might claim one-third of her husband's estate. On the defensive, Butler eased his posturing and let Sarah and Fan spend two months in Lenox with their mother. Shortly after their July 1849 arrival, Kemble reported jubilantly, "I am happy to say that both the girls appear already to have prospered physically from this visit to Berkshire."

*Kemble's beloved Berkshire home, the Perch, in
Lenox, Massachusetts.*

The notoriety of the divorce proved especially damaging to Butler.
The diarist Sidney Fisher was frankly sympathetic to Kemble: "It is
quite notorious that she was driven from his house by his own barbarous treatment, I think he can hardly succeed. . . . [Her] position is
certainly a painful one. She is obliged to return to the stage . . . as Butler makes her no allowance." An equally impartial observer, J. K.
Paulding, remarked over dinner to former president Martin Van Buren
that Fanny had married into "a family which for three generations has
been the curse of every woman connected with the name."

By the end of the summer, news of Butler's chronic financial troubles was spreading by the day. Joshua Fisher strategically parlayed the
embarrassment into a settlement advantageous to his client. In return
for giving up her right of dower and withdrawing her challenge to the
petition for divorce, she would receive "an income of fifteen hundred
dollars a year settled upon me to go to the children at my death." For

*Sarah and Frances Butler as young girls—they were born
exactly three years apart, sharing a birthday.*

his part, Butler would "get his divorce" and custody of the children for
ten months per year except "two months of every year with me . . . and
uninterrupted intercourse with them at all other times personally or by
letter."

The divorce was granted on September 22, 1849. Fanny declared
her liberation from Butler by boldly adopting the professional title
"Mrs. Fanny Kemble." She went back out on the road, trying to cure
her troubles with stiff doses of work. And audiences flocked—perhaps
as much to gawk at the celebrated divorcée as to hear Mr. Shakespeare's dialogue.

We know all too little about Kemble's feelings about her separation
from her children and the very public failure of her marriage. She sug-

gested she was like Ceres, deprived of her offspring seasonally, but she was granted only two months rather than the Greek myth's proverbial six. The extant marital correspondence between Fanny and Pierce suggests a relationship of passionate excess. But in eleven volumes of published memoirs (under six separate titles), Kemble reflected on her relationship with Pierce Butler only in thickly veiled abstractions. Even after he was long dead, she never directly described their conflicts in her publications. And she burned letters she felt might compromise her privacy.

In 1850, however, Butler felt no such compunction. Still fuming over his wife's "falsehoods and exaggerations" concerning him (he believed he had been especially maligned in Boston), he began a defense of his marital conduct. He privately published and discreetly distributed his 188-page tirade, *Mr. Butler's Statement*.

Although he presented the *Statement* as a "self-vindication" in his own words, Butler included long excerpts from Fanny's letters to him. Some of these show the depth and clarity of Kemble's innermost feelings, as when she remarks with firm conviction: "We are not all made up of affections—we have intellects—and we have passions—and each and all should have their objects and their spheres of action, or the creature is maimed." Pierce and Fanny's alternating, side-by-side accounts are the clearest testimony we have to the true nature of their relationship.

In Butler's opinion, his wife's "peculiar" views were to blame for the breakup of their marriage: "She held that marriage should be companionship on equal terms—partnership, in which, if both partners agree, it is well; but if they do not, neither is bound to yield."

For her part, Fanny proclaimed, "It is not in the law of my conscience to promise implicit obedience to a human being, fallible like myself, and who can by no means relieve me of the responsibility of my actions before God." This interpretation of the marriage vow might square with a modern sensibility, but Butler found it "deranged."

Widespread speculation focused on the couple's conflict over abolitionism. One close friend of Butler's concluded that slavery "was the rock that wrecked the domestic peace. But it is cruelly unjust to charge *him* with the disaster. . . . Everybody knew that the lady was an uncompromising abolitionist and no one knew better than herself that he was a slaveholder . . . on the *one subject* she was a hopeless monomaniac."

But while Butler could have rested his argument on these shaky foundations, he had more to add. His wife's abolitionism was just one of her many moral flaws. Her evidence of his sexual dalliances, Butler claimed, was misleading. The letters in question, he insisted, were "old, written several years before, without signatures, and apparently in the handwriting of a female." Further, he claimed, he "had never opened or read them." He denied, too, that he had withheld funds from Fanny; any financial hardship she suffered was her fault, because "she did not scrupulously keep within the limits prescribed." He claimed he never prevented reasonable contact between his wife and daughters, but that "her letters became so objectionable as to compel me to place an interdict upon further communications." Pierce's reaction to the dissolution of the marriage was characteristically defensive, with no hint of regret.

For Kemble, the early days of independence were not easy. She labeled this period her "post-emancipation crisis" and went into a deep malaise in which nothing pleased her. While touring in Cincinnati, Milwaukee, and St. Louis, she wrote long, disconsolate letters to friends. To Theodore Sedgwick she confided: "I was intended by nature for quite another sort of existence than this strolling independence. . . . a home where I would have been excessively spoilt and petted would have suited me far better than this vagabonding freedom and the general affections of a whole population."

In an attempt at stability, Kemble decided to settle in Lenox in 1850. Joshua Fisher would continue to represent her interests in Philadelphia, while Theodore Sedgwick would manage her finances (as well as retain all legal documents pertaining to the divorce settlement and custody) in New York.

But shortly thereafter, Kemble received word her father was seriously ill. She sailed for London immediately. While Charles Kemble once more regained his health, his finances were in shambles thanks to his mismanagement. Father and daughter were forced by the need for economy to set up housekeeping together. Kemble struggled, as usual, to offer her father the support and assistance he always seemed to need.

Adelaide was back in London, but the sisters were ill-prepared for the next round of Kemble family crises. Their younger brother, Harry—whose doomed youthful romance with an heiress above his station would later be immortalized by Henry James in 1881 as *Washington Square*—had taken to drink and other vices while stationed as an officer in Dublin. In 1851 he returned to London, bringing with him a three-year-old bastard son, "literally in tatters, swarming with vermin." The child's mother, an Irishwoman, had abandoned him and gone to America.

Fanny and Adelaide took the boy in, and decided to give Harry, as he was called, a good Protestant upbringing. Only then did their brother reveal the whole truth—that his common-law wife had also left him with an infant daughter who would have to be taken in as well. Shortly thereafter, he succumbed to the mental illness that had plagued Maria-Thérèse, and was committed for life to a sanitarium outside London. He survived his daughter, who died in childhood, but left his two sisters to rear his son.

Added to these familial burdens were reports from America that Butler was not honoring his promises. He had already fallen behind on his support payments, and now Fanny feared that he would refuse her the prescribed two-month annual visit from the children. Kemble decided not to risk the trip to America, but instead to spend the summer of 1853 with the Sartorises in Sorrento, Italy; she stayed on for the fall in Rome.

Always at home among her artistic counterparts, Kemble socialized with fellow expatriates Robert and Elizabeth Barrett Browning and befriended the young American sculptor Harriet Hosmer. She became fast friends as well with the painter Frederick Leighton, who later became the first artist to be elevated to the English peerage. Leighton's lovely portrait of Adelaide's daughter, May, bore a striking resemblance to Fanny. Although his portraits were popular, Leighton's work most often featured draped Pre-Raphaelite figures that were considered daring in their day; Kemble had a difficult time finding Leighton patrons among her American friends.

She spent hours touring Rome, directing the coachman with abandon: "Go where you will, only go." But horseback rides, festive literary gatherings, and singing duets with Adelaide only thinly veiled Kemble's persistent melancholy. Anne Thackeray (daughter of the Kembles' good friend William Thackeray) commented in 1853, "It was a hard and difficult time of her life when she needed all her courage to endure her daily portion of suffering."

By the early summer of 1854, Butler had not yet resumed his support payments and Kemble was forced to return to London, where she found her father once again in failing health. In less than six months, Charles Kemble was dead. To pay for settling her father's estate, as well as for her brother's upkeep at the sanitarium and young Harry's education, Kemble began, once again, to stage Shakespearean readings.

Animosity between her and Butler continued; they wrangled through their lawyers. As early as June 1852, Kemble wrote to Joshua Fisher in Philadelphia that she had resigned herself "to wait for the event of my eldest child's majority which may restore to me some portion of what I have lost." Although she might wait for time with her daughters, Fisher advised her to launch a countersuit to force Butler to honor his financial obligations. But she refused, believing such efforts were fruitless.

As a divorced woman, Kemble was vulnerable to the scrutiny of her peers. That she had voluntarily separated from her children was an especially sensitive matter, which elicited coolness if not disdain from some friends, including Sarah Perkins Cleveland. In 1856, following a six-year hiatus in their correspondence, Kemble elliptically referred to the breach between the friends: "I have had but one reason for not writing to you all during all these years of my absence from this country—your not writing to me." But even if Cleveland had shunned her, Fanny was "very grateful" for her "quiet kindness" toward Sarah and Fan.

True to her word, Kemble found renewed joy in motherhood once Sarah came of age and was finally free from any legal tie to her father. Absorbed with her maternal role, Kemble wrote to Sarah Cleveland, "My life now chiefly hangs upon Sarah and all my projects revolve around her."

For over a decade, since she had first left her husband in 1845, Kemble had fruitlessly harbored affections for her daughters. She wanted to lavish on them all that she had had to withhold during the years the girls were kept from her. And her patience was finally rewarded, through Butler's misfortune.

As early as 1856, Philadelphians had become aware of Pierce Butler's profligacy. Huge losses forced him to take boarders at his Philadelphia home to reduce expenses. Diarist Sidney George Fisher gossiped on June 3, 1856: "Heard from Henry that [Pierce] Butler has well nigh ruined his splendid estate by stock gambling." His affairs were in such disorder that he was required to turn over management of his finances to three trustees: Henry Fisher, Thomas James (his co-trustee on his late brother John's estate), and George Cadwalader (who was married to Pierce's sister Frances).

By 1857 Butler's financial plight had become acute. In August, Fisher reported to his diary that "this beautiful old place [Butler Place] is to be cut up in lots." When the railroad offered to buy York Farm (a parcel of land with a farmhouse which was a part of the Butler estate in Branchtown) for $700 an acre, Butler pleaded with his ex-wife to release it from the trust for his daughters. But Kemble would not allow the property to be sacrificed, even when Butler promised to pay her the $12,000 he owed in back alimony. This proved a shrewd financial decision in the long run.

Fanny faced financial crises of her own when both her brothers died penniless in 1857. Henry Kemble died in an asylum, leaving Fanny and Adelaide to continue to care for Henry's son, their nephew Harry. Kemble contributed £700 toward a fund established to support John Mitchell Kemble's German widow, Natalia, and their offspring, Gertrude, Mildred, and Henry—who were nearly indigent by his death.

When instability in the financial markets brought on the panic of 1857, the New York trustees of her savings decided it would be prudent to transfer Kemble's money from risky high-yield stocks in America (earning 7 percent) to more conservative investments in Britain, which returned only 3 percent. Fanny was supremely vexed at having her investment income cut in half, but she continued to reap revenues through her Shakespearean readings.

When family or work commitments did not conflict, her income allowed her to visit the Alps, where she spent each summer, from June 1 to September 1. She often met up with fellow mountain enthusiasts, such as Arthur and Mary Anne Malkin of London and the Harvard naturalist Louis Agassiz.

While fortune smiled on his ex-wife, Butler's woes grew worse. His mismanagement of his brother's estate had pitted him against his sister-in-law Ella's lawyers, and his own debts were dire and mounting. Kemble reported shortly before New Year's Day 1859 "the ruin of my girls' worldly prospects," which she blamed on Pierce Butler's stock speculation: he had cast away half a million dollars "with a wanton folly."

CHAPTER SEVEN

Battle Cries for Freedom

By 1859, Pierce Butler, heir to one of the great fortunes of Georgia, had sunk so deeply into debt that he was forced to consider the unthinkable: selling half of his slaves. Sidney George Fisher explained the impact of the sale on enslaved families:

> It is a dreadful affair, however, selling these hereditary Negroes. There are 900 of them belonging to the estate, a little community who have lived for generations on the plantation, among whom, therefore, all sorts of relations of blood & friendship are established. Butlers half, 450, to be sold at public auction & scattered over the South. Families will not be separated, that is to say, husbands & wives, parents & young children. But brothers & sisters of mature age, parents and children of mature age, all other relations & the ties of home & long association will be violently severed. It will be a hard thing for Butler to witness and it is a monstrous thing to do.

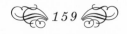

Fisher added a sobering reminder: "It is done every day in the South."

After years of speculation, gambling, and high living, Butler was finally being forced to answer to Ella on behalf of herself and her heirs. Trustees had already sold off Butler's once grand, now neglected Philadelphia mansion for $30,000. Other Butler properties were forfeited for debt as well. But they did not fetch enough to satisfy Butler's creditors, much less to ensure that he could continue to live in luxury. Ella Butler herself took up residence in her brother-in-law's prized Butler Place, since he could no longer afford the upkeep.

In February 1859, while visiting her Charleston relations, Ella was summoned by her lawyers to Savannah, where she signed a document approving the division of the Butler slaves. Half would go to the estate of John Butler, and thus would remain on the plantations. The fate of the other 450—Pierce's half—was more precarious. About twenty elderly slaves would continue to live on Butler property. The remainder were boarded onto railway cars and steamboats and brought to Tenbroeck Race Course near Savannah, where each man, woman, and child would be sold to the highest bidder.

Joseph Bryan, a well-known Savannah slave trader, was engaged to promote the sale. He widely circulated bills advertising that a "Gang of 460 Slaves" would be "sold in families" on March 2–3, 1859. Although the Butler name was not mentioned, the identity of the distressed owner was well known.

Those days in early March were perhaps among Butler's worst. As owner, he was not obligated to attend the sale. But he keenly felt his duty to acknowledge the event, and took it upon himself to personally greet each of the nearly five hundred people being sold, giving each of them four newly minted quarters as a farewell token. During the two days of the sale, rain fell unceasingly on the racetrack, as if mirroring the tears shed by the men, women, and children up for auction. The sale would thereafter be known among the slaves as "the weeping time."

The harsh realities of slavery dictated the separation
of African American families, often at auction.

The event featured prominently in local newspapers, and within days the story had spread to the Northeast. Horace Greeley's star correspondent, Mortimer Thomson (under the byline "Q. K. Philander Doesticks"), wrote a sensational six-column article that appeared in the *New York Tribune* on March 9 and was reprinted on March 11 by popular demand. The Philadelphia *Sunday Dispatch* (March 13) embellished the story with details of the Butler family fortune. The London *Times* carried the piece on April 12, 1859, calling special attention to Butler's marriage to Fanny Kemble. In 1863, Thomson's article was republished as an antislavery pamphlet, "What Became of the Slaves on a Georgia Plantation"; it was billed as a sequel to Fanny Kemble's *Journal of a Residence on a Georgian Plantation,* which appeared in June of that year.

Thomson described the heartrending scene: "All the clinging ties that bound them to living hearts were torn asunder, for but one-half of each of these two happy little communities was sent to the shambles, to be scattered to the four winds, and the other half was left behind."

Butler netted $300,205. The average price per slave was just over $700, more than $100 over the presale estimates. The highest sum paid for one family—a mother and her five grown children—was $6,180. The highest price for an individual was $1,750; the lowest, $250. Soon after the last slave was sold, the rain stopped. Champagne corks popped in celebration. And Pierce Butler, rich again, made a trip to southern Europe before returning home to Philadelphia.

With Pierce well out of the way, Fanny was reunited with her daughters. In May 1859, Fan turned twenty-one and was free to spend as much time with her mother as she chose. Kemble grieved over the upheaval the Savannah sale would surely visit on the unfortunate Butler slaves, even as she counted on the proceeds to bring an end to her daughters' poverty.

Her prayers for her daughters' happiness were partially answered when, in October 1859, twenty-four-year-old Sarah wed Owen Wister of Germantown, ten years her senior. In previous years, several beaux had courted Sarah. She had been attached to a Mr. Kane of Philadelphia, and had even been engaged to a Mr. Sanford of New York, before her betrothal to Wister.

Wister, a well-respected doctor with a thriving practice in the Philadelphia suburbs, had served in the U.S. Navy as a surgeon during the 1840s and 1850s. His family were Quakers who had built their estate, Grumblethorpe, a few miles outside Philadelphia, in 1744. They also owned nearby Belfield, built by the artist Charles Willson Peale. Wister was related to the Fisher family, who owned the adjacent Wakefield estate, and to whom Sarah was kin on the Butler side as well.

The young couple was fortunate to set up housekeeping next door to Grumblethorpe, not far from Butler Place where Sarah was born. Sarah Butler Wister had finally found a home, happily anchored amidst family, friends, and familiar surroundings.

In those heady days, Germantown was undergoing rapid improvement. Although it was a good six miles from City Hall, urban amenities were extending outward. Sidney Fisher reported in 1859: "They have now gas & water from waterworks in every house. Shops & mechanics follow the rich population of the villas, and soon every luxury of a city can be had in the neighborhood." Further, the price of real estate was escalating, so that "all the families"—including the Wisters and the Butlers—"who own much land here have been enriched."

By all accounts, Owen Wister was a model son-in-law. He shared Sarah's every sentiment—except where Fanny Kemble was concerned. His affection and indulgence toward her far exceeded his wife's. (Sarah once wrote: "My mother was the most stimulating companion I have ever known. She was also the most goading.") Owen's ability to get along with his mother-in-law caused tension at times between the couple, especially in the early years of the marriage. However, both sides of the family considered it a brilliant match. Even Pierce Butler, who may have been suspicious of his son-in-law's Quaker background and especially of his abolitionist leanings, expressed no dissatisfaction with Sarah's choice.

With Sarah happily ensconced in her new home in Branchtown, Fanny focused her attentions on Fan. Both children had suffered terribly during their parents' tumultuous marriage and divorce, but Fan, being the younger, was affected far more deeply. In a grand gesture of affection, Fanny brought her to England, showing her off to London society. But news of Sarah's pregnancy in the spring of 1860 drew them both home.

Fanny was in Philadelphia on July 14, 1860, when her first grandchild, Owen Wister, Jr., was born, but she did not attend the birth. Sidney Fisher, noting that Dr. Wister had only a servant girl to assist him when his son was born at five in the morning, recalled the old saying that "blacksmiths' horses and shoemakers' wives are worse shod than any other people."

Sarah chose the baby's legal name, but Owen had wanted to name his son Daniel, in memory of his grandfather, so he insisted the child be known as Dan. Soon Fanny settled in with her daughter and grandson. Fisher visited the extended family on August 27, and, after "a very pleasant evening," recorded his impressions: "Always liked Mrs. Kemble. She is a woman of genius & of noble impulses & kind feelings. Too much will & vitality & force of character, however, to be very happy in domestic life, more especially with such a man as Butler, her inferior in all intellectual endowments, but her equal in firmness & strength of character." He observed that Fanny's notorious temper seemed pleasantly improved since the divorce:

> Her manners & conversation this evening more quiet than they used to be and she was very cordial, easy & pleasant. We talked of books, authors, politics, English country life & Sarah put her oar in, too, & always with effect. She has much of her mother's talent & character & looks very well, tho somewhat thin & pale after her confinement.

During the fall of 1860, the family was excited by a visit to America by the Prince of Wales. Fanny, who was tending to a sick friend, did not gain a personal audience with the Prince, but Fan was able to meet him and even to dance with him at a New York ball. When her mother suggested she might preserve her dancing shoes as a memento of her brush with a future king, Fan Butler "shrugged her shoulders and laughed, though she said he was a 'nice little fellow, and danced very well.'" In Fan, Kemble concluded, she had raised a "monkey of a democratic damsel."

While she maintained her Lenox property, for the sake of economy Fanny remained with Sarah and Owen and baby Dan. Living in Branchtown elicited nostalgia for her early years as a Philadelphia matron and mother, but American politics competed fiercely for her attentions. The presidential election of November 1860, Kemble reported, brought "distraction and uproar" to the household. "The southern states are loud in vehement threats of secession if the Republican candidate is elected; but their bluster is really lamentably ludicrous, for they are without money, without credit, without power, without character—in short, *sans* everything but so many millions of slaves."

Just how indelibly Sarah Wister had been influenced by Kemble's political views was confirmed when she wrote to her mother: "I suppose the impressions you gave me as a child had never been effaced." Sarah recalled in annotations to her diary that as a young child "of six or seven in England I remember crying in secret over the taunts I heard on the subject of slavery. At the same period I began saving my pence to pay the Pennsylvania bonds, a naive scheme that all the children in America should unite in paying off the states & sectional debts."

The Butler sisters were not united in abolitionism. Fan resented Sarah's open contempt for slavery and complained that her sister went so far as to refuse to "receive a Southerner in her house." Sectional divisions inflamed family tensions in every state of the endangered union, but the circumstances of the Kemble-Butler-Wister clan were exceptional, the debate over slavery having played such a prominent role in the Butler breakup nearly two decades before. By 1860, this conflict had already begun to break down social civility throughout the nation. Kemble and her daughters certainly recognized that the political consequences for themselves, as well as the country, would be severe.

Following Lincoln's election, the country was rocked with explosive outbursts. In the North, Charles Francis Adams (son and grandson of presidents) proclaimed: "The country has once and for all thrown off the domination of slaveholders." The *Charleston Mercury* responded: "The tea has been thrown overboard." North and South squared off with equally strong responses to the changes about to take place now that a Republican was about to move into the White House. Kemble wrote to a friend in England: "The United States schism . . . has become a wide yawning cleft, like your favorite Swiss abysms. . . . it seems to me slavery has made the Southerners insane egotists, and the pursuit of gain has made the Northerners incapable egotists." What

*The American Civil War erupted at Fort Sumter in
Charleston Harbor in April 1861.*

would resolve this? Perhaps the force of arms: "A grievous civil war, shattering their financial and commercial idols, and compelling them to find the connection between public safety and private virtue may be the salvation of the country; a blessed, bitter blast of adversity."

Pierce Butler had retreated to Europe in deep humiliation after the sale of his slaves, but the political crisis brought him back to take control of his affairs. Following South Carolina's Ordinance of Secession, passed in December 1860, a Philadelphian reported,

Butler is eager for secession & has just returned from Georgia, where he says there is no difference of opinion. He said that he came here only to *buy arms* and intends to return immediately and join the army. He will take his daughter Fanny with him and has bought a rifle for *her*, too, for he says even the women in the South are going to fight. What madness, yet one cannot help admiring the knightly spirit these southern men are displaying. They rush recklessly on fearful odds & fearful dangers and talk like men insane. Yet is there not reasons for the wild excitement they exhibit? Is it not really terror, the instinctive dread of approaching peril which they think they can baffle by fronting and defying? The power of the North is overwhelming if it should be used against them.

Indeed, Pierce and Fan Butler did make a trip South, on March 27. Butler even served as the escort of Eliza Middleton Fisher—a loyal friend of Fanny Kemble's, from whom he had been estranged for many years—and her daughter, Sophie. Eliza's brother-in-law explained: "Odd changes sometimes occur in people's relations to each other, and that Mrs. Fisher should travel with Butler is one of the oddest. . . . Both Fisher [a Butler trustee] & his wife were not long ago loud in the denunciations of Butler & Mrs. Fisher even went so far as to refuse to speak to him."

The reconciliation was a comedy of manners. "About a year ago," the observer recalled, "Fisher wished to invite Mrs. Owen Wister to a party, for her mother's sake chiefly. She did not like to do this without also asking Fanny Butler, and she could not ask her without including her father. So she left a card for Butler & invited him. Butler went to the party and as he well knows how to do, if he pleases, made himself acceptable to Mrs. Fisher." So Butler took Eliza and Sophie to the home of their Charleston kin, and they were present when gunfire erupted at Fort Sumter.

The firing on the federal fort in Charleston harbor by Confederates marked the beginning of armed conflict. Lincoln's call to arms and the defection of the upper South to the Confederacy signaled no turning back from war. On April 13, 1861, Sarah Wister described the scene in Philadelphia following the federal surrender in South Carolina. Thousands assembled in the streets of Philadelphia and swore "revenge on all disunionists." Pierce Butler being a conspicuous member of that minority, during the melee Sarah uttered a private, heartfelt prayer: "Oh how thankful I am for Father's absence."

Response to the dissolution of the Union ranged across the spectrum of emotions. Sophie Fisher, for one, was "standing at the window of her uncle's house on the Battery at Charleston when Ft. Sumter surrendered, & burst into tears as she saw the Stars & Stripes lowered: her aunt ridiculed her for affectation & sentimentality."

Throughout the spring and summer of 1861, Sarah Wister kept a diary of these astonishing times. (She also described Owen Junior's progress in a separate journal, "The Early Years of a Child of Promise.") During the week following Lincoln's call to arms, her writings seesawed between her private concerns and the larger public sphere: "Practised [piano], read & drew all day. The baby is to be fed now, previous to weaning him, & I spent ever so long messing and mixing & boiling his food for him; I fancy it will not be easy to make the nurse take so much trouble when she had it so much easier a mode of satisfying him. I shall hail the hour when I wash my hands of my last wet nurse."

The next day in town she found "even the book sellers place the red, white and blue bindings together; the streets are filled with a crowd of idle, eager, hurrying, lounging, talking, listening people, men & women, old & young, rich & poor, wherever there is a telegraph office, there is a regular jam at the corner to read the last message which has just been pasted up on a board." Then her husband came to town, and went out to drill with the local Union company on April 20, even though he had been unable to procure a musket.

The following day, in a fit of nostalgia, Sarah went to Butler Place in search of violets: "still finer than any others, with a richer purple & sweeter perfume. I picked quite a bunch & strayed back with them." The fragrance and the surroundings combined to make her feel possessive of the place: "Next to Owen, Father & Fan I love it above all things." She went on to confess her fears: "Before long it may be confiscated, for who knows whether even now Father is not in the Southern Army?"

Sarah pointedly did not include Kemble among those she loved most. As a prolonged houseguest, Fanny was a bit much—excitable about politics and overgenerous with advice about child rearing. Four days later, on April 26, Sarah reported,

> Owen in a moment of insanity begged Mother to prolong her visit. She had made all her arrangements to go tomorrow morning, her trunks are packed, her carriage ordered, while I have engaged a parcel of chimney sweeps, chorewomen & upholsterers to come on Monday & clean the house & get it ready for summer. Of course there was a scene. She said she would stay if I wished, as long as I wished, & of course I was placed by my silence in the agreeable posture of declining a further visit. I froze hard as usual & went to bed more angry with Owen for his thoughtlessness & folly than I have been since our marriage.

But the next day Sarah mustered enough affection to bid a fond farewell at the station, where she saw her mother off to New York: "I wish I could say 'peace go with her,' but that it never will."

With her mother gone, Sarah resumed worrying about her father and sister. On April 27, she finally received a letter from Fan, who remained in Darien, Georgia:

> Thank goodness she says nothing of any talk of his [Pierce Butler's] joining the Confederate army, & speaks confi-

dently of being here next week. . . . She thinks that the taking of Ft. Sumter will put an end to the hostilities as the North will see that the South is in earnest, & is so very unwilling to fight itself!!! She will open her eyes a little when she arrives here & finds every man of her acquaintance enlisted.

From April 1861 onward, nearly every entry in Sarah Wister's diary reported some political event, some story of war, some telling detail of the harrowing existence of those who remained at home. "Half a dozen Southern school girls, very young were leaving Bethlehem [Pennsylvania] where they were at boarding school on the first breaking out of this trouble some two weeks ago: on getting into the cars they saw some little national flags stuck about the windows, they rushed upon them, tore them down, stamped & spat upon them."

Times were hard. In a short span, Sarah Wister had gone from pampered girl to prudent matron to harried mother in wartime. Shortages plagued her. With exasperation and pride, she reported "spending two hours over a parcel of fashion plates & a heap of cast off raiment devising how I might make a new jerkin out of an old coat."

Between the ages of twenty and thirty-five, Sarah had an annual allowance of $500 a year, not a sum to allow her the extravagances of other young matrons in her circle or the unbridled expenditures of her youth. Wartime economic pressures devalued currency even further. Sarah found that "the tightness of the times in addition to my constitutional impecuniosity admonished me to make as much as I can out of what I have this summer." Wardrobe options were curtailed for women of all stations, but Sarah was less selfish than many of her well-to-do peers. The summer of 1861 she spent an enormous amount of her free time at the sewing rooms organized to supply Union troops.

On May 7, Fan arrived unannounced: "She came by Kentucky, Tennessee & had not changed her clothes for six days, till this morning, & has not been in bed for six nights. Nevertheless she looks fat & fresh."

Sarah's joy at seeing her sister was tempered with alarm when Fan could give no report of their father, who had returned to Georgia after bringing her as far as Cincinnati.

Pierce Butler's continuing absence preyed upon the sisters, who were "tormented by rumor." Sarah told of an acquaintance who had been arrested in Baltimore for furnishing ammunition to secessionists; she feared he might pay with his life. Pierce Butler's daughters must have feared that he risked a similar fate.

By May 28, their shared birthday, Sarah was dreaming of her youth with Fan at Butler Place, for fear those happier times might be forever lost. "Feeling that it might be the last of these double birthdays we might spend together I looked through all my jewelry to find something for [Fan]. . . . I have a choking ball in my throat."

Despite her abiding affection for her only sibling, Sarah was displeased by Fan's open fascination with all matters military and especially with her championing of Confederate soldiers. When Fan prattled on about invasions and events that proved to be mere rumor, Sarah reported with annoyance: "Like mother like daughter, a wonderful pair, not a word of it true."

With her husband drilling in the local Union militia, the prospect that her father might join the Confederate army became frighteningly real to Sarah. But Butler soothed his daughter's fears in a June letter, pledging his continuing loyalty to Pennsylvania: he "would not take up arms against his own country," Sarah reported to her diary, "even if Fanny & myself not in existence as a restraining motive."

The sisters were distinctly relieved when their father reappeared in Philadelphia on August 3, 1861, after nearly five months in the South. Owen Wister, Jr., later recalled that Butler made both his daughters adore him. They were enraptured to have him back and they basked in his presence.

But on August 18, Pierce Butler was arrested by special order of the secretary of war, Simon Cameron. He was taken to New York for incarceration. Sidney Fisher reported:

It is said that he had been in correspondence with the secessionists in the South, which I do not believe, unless about
private business. He has expressed, however, since his return
the strongest opinions in favor of the southern cause and
wishes for its success in earnest language, as he did here the
other day, and in such times as these that alone is sufficient
to justify his arrest.

Like many Butler family acquaintances, Fisher "felt sorry" for Butler and his daughters. But he stood firm in his belief that "it was right
to commit him." He went on to reflect, "Perhaps also it is a good thing
for him, as it will keep him quiet and out of harm's way. I suppose he
will be comfortable at the Fort and he will meet there a number of gentlemen from Baltimore, prisoners like himself & congenial companions."

On August 20, Sarah traveled alone to join her mother and Fan in
Lenox. The long journey gave her ample opportunity to reflect upon
the troubles that had lately befallen her family. Her most immediate
concern, perhaps, was for Fan. "Poor little thing, this will come more
heavily on her than on anyone else after her winter & spring of anxiety
and harassment." In her journal, Sarah also confessed suspicions that
her father indeed might be guilty of aiding the Confederacy.

Her mother had already come to the same conclusion. "The charges
against him is that he acted as an agent for the Southerners in a visit he
paid this spring, having received large sums of money for the purchase
and transmission of arms. Knowing Mr. B——'s Southern sympathies,
I think the charge very likely to be true; whether it can be proved is
quite another question."

Butler might be released only if someone powerful intervened for
him in Washington. The Wisters turned to the Fox family—a relation
was assistant secretary of the Navy—who lived at the nearby estate of
Champlost. On August 22, Sarah appealed to President Lincoln for

permission to visit her father. On August 23, she heard from Butler himself, who wrote that he had been detained at Fort Lafayette on Staten Island and denied all visitors. She was devastated by his complaints about conditions: "Whatever right the government may have to arrest & imprison men on suspicion, it cannot have the least to herd them together . . . & deprive them of all necessaries and decencies of life."

Before leaving for Massachusetts, Sarah had charged her husband with two important responsibilities—the care of their son and the campaign to free Butler. Sarah arrived in Lenox on August 26, followed closely by the good news that the federal authorities' search of her father's papers had turned up no incriminating material. On August 31, Owen wrote Sarah that through the intercession of the Fox family, she and Fan would be permitted to visit Pierce in prison, which they did.

But Owen also included a stern warning that Fan's unchaperoned visits to military camps outside Philadelphia had become the subject of unpleasant speculation. He implored Sarah to warn her sister about her potentially dangerous behavior, adding, "If Fan refuses to take immediate steps to break up that intimacy, I will put a stop to it by any means that may be necessary." He added apologetically: "I am sorry to add to your troubles dearest Sarah and I am very unwilling to interfere in this affair, but it has gone quite sufficiently too far."

With her ex-husband imprisoned, Fanny Kemble put aside any lingering ill will toward him to be a mainstay for her daughters, especially Fan, who had taken to her bed several times with crying spells, and seemed unhinged by the crisis. Kemble remained steadfast in her belief that Butler was capable of treasonous activity, but feared that even if no evidence could be found, he might be detained for the remainder of the war. She was prepared to take full charge of her younger daughter in the interim. She wrote to a friend: "Perhaps if she does not (mis) bestow herself in marriage in the mean time she will return to Europe

with me next year. I am making huge plans of travel, and live surrounded by maps." Kemble may have been feeling especially magnan-
imous, for both Sarah and Fan seemed to cling to their mother during
this visit. Indeed, Sarah told Owen she would not cut her trip short
because, for once, she and her mother were getting along so well.

However, Owen resented Kemble's usurping his protective role toward his wife. This was their first prolonged separation since they were
married, and he was quite lovesick for her: "I am beginning to count
the days, that must still be passed with no better hope than coming
home to an empty house & lonely bed at night."

As the time for their reunion in Lenox drew near, Sarah returned
her husband's longing: "Good bye my own dearest, three more nights
& you will be here. I absolutely faint for you." She had sent him long
letters to convey her strong feelings: "I long for you, unspeakably, especially in my long rambles in the copse of which I generally rest for
nearly an hour in some sunny spots right in the midst of the woods or
on some great rocks by one of the many lovely brooks." Doubtless,
Wister was reassured when his wife wrote: "You are the only human
being with whom I could have these moments, the only one whose
presence would not make me self-conscious. In the long silences even
before we were married you know I told you in the copse woods that
I had lost the sense of another person in your company." Sarah's deep
attachment to her husband, she believed, stemmed from her unhappy
childhood: "All the old vague yearning of my empty heart which I had
from a child for some human love to fill my being." She closed
amorously: "I so miss you & crave you. . . . such a longing for you for
your clasping arms & burning kisses comes over me."

Owen's reply was equally passionate: "I have been haunted by vi-
sions of us being there together which have sometimes set me nearly
wild with intense longing for the reality & I have always looked forward to their fulfillment some day. . . . Oh Sarah you cannot know the
state I have been in since I know that long cherished ecstasy about to
be tasted." Once they were reunited, at the end of September, they

pledged never again to spend more than two weeks apart—a promise that would prove impossible to keep.

The letters Sarah and Owen exchanged during this period also detail strategies for Butler's release from prison. Owen's plan hinged on Sarah's producing the letter in which Butler had pledged his loyalty to Pennsylvania; he believed that forwarding it to Washington would prove Butler was no traitor.

One of Butler's friends advocated a more daring tactic: "The President should be told that Mr. Butler was a very peculiar man, that he inherited a large fortune when a boy & that his pleasure then was to play the flute in the orchestra of a theater, which was thought well of by his friends, that he was very successful among the ladies, and could have married any lady in the country; instead of which he had married—as he did—which didn't turn out very well." Wister retorted that Butler's friends could secure his freedom "without finding it necessary to represent him as a lunatic."

After a prolonged series of letters between Lenox and Philadelphia, and between Philadelphia and Washington—with family and friends calling in all markers—Pierce Butler was released by order of the State Department on September 21, 1861, and welcomed home with open arms by his daughters.

But their joy in Butler's freedom would soon be eclipsed by the gravity of protracted civil war, of carnage and burials. Even before Butler was imprisoned in mid-August, the war had begun in earnest. On July 21, 1861, in the battle of Bull Run, 18,000 men engaged, and thousands lost their lives in the Union defeat.

An autumnal pall had replaced the initial exhilaration of the previous spring's call to arms. Butler's loyalties rankled staunch Unionists, among them Sidney George Fisher, who complained that Butler "refused to take the Oath of allegiance." So Butler remained under a cloud of suspicion, which forced both him and Fan to muzzle their unpopular views.

For her part, Kemble was heartened by rising Unionist fervor. In residence in Lenox during the fall of 1861, she freely voiced her hopes: "After some bad and good fighting, and unlimited amount of brag and bluster on both sides, the South, in spite of much better state of preparation, much better soldiers, better officers, and, above all, a much more unanimous and *venomous* spirit of hostility, will be obliged to knock under to the infinitely greater resources and less violent but much more enduring determination of the North. With the clearing away of the storm, slavery will be swept from among the acknowledged institutions of America."

When Kemble returned to Philadelphia, she did not modify her strident views. One observer reported: "She is very enthusiastic about the war & predicts from it the destruction of slavery." While many Northerners fervently prayed to defeat the Confederates and restore the Union, only a radical vanguard saw the war as a means of abolition. Many thought there was no going back once military mobilization began; Wendell Phillips proclaimed, "We have passed the Rubicon."

With all the eligible young men off to war Fan Butler grew restless. When her mother proposed a tour of Switzerland, Fan readily agreed. The pair planned to winter in Hampshire, England, where Adelaide Sartoris had found them a cottage near her own. But when Sarah requested Fan's company at Butler Place during the winter of 1862–63, Fan sailed home.

Kemble was sorry not to have Fan with her, but the feeling was ameliorated by the knowledge that her daughters were together. She described to a friend Fan and Sarah's "great satisfaction of their present fellowship under the same roof." Fan helped out with Dan, now a toddler, while Sarah traveled frequently to Germantown to check on her husband and the progress of the new house they were building there.

Sarah's life as a young mother in Branchtown differed little from the circumstances her mother had known twenty years before. "Of social pleasures outside my own house I had nearly none," she recalled. "I taught my child & had him a great deal with me, I sewed constantly; I kept up my music, French & German; I corresponded regularly with ten or twelve friends besides my weekly letter . . . to my Mother."

Oddly, Kemble noted that Sarah typically "says little of public affairs"; in fact, most of her letters are full of war news. In January 1863, Kemble received a letter Sarah had written while the "last disastrous engagement at Fredericksburg was going on and before its horrible result was ascertained." In this bloody battle on December 13, the Union army suffered perhaps its most crushing defeat to date. Lincoln commented when he heard the news, "If there is a worse place than hell, I am in it." The grim word of retreat and casualties was slow to spread throughout the North, but, once known, quick to excite among citizens a venomous anger—against the Union generals, against the federal government, against Lincoln himself.

Back in England, Kemble had long been skeptical of Lincoln's wisdom in the area of foreign policy. It was commonly held that France and England, whose textile industries suffered at the hands of the Union blockade of the South, instituted in July 1861, might well renege on their proclamations of neutrality. The year before, Kemble had announced at a Philadelphia society gathering that while she regretted "the hostile opinions exhibited by England . . . we have much more to dread from France." If not for the "remonstrances & advice of the English government," she maintained, the Emperor, Napoleon III, would long "before this have recognized the South & opened the blockade."

As early as September 1861, Kemble suspected that her beloved England might cave in and recognize the Confederacy, which could scuttle the chance of Union victory. She voiced her concern to her friend Arthur Malkin: "I hope to God that neither England nor any other power from the other side of the water will meddle in the matter—but above all, *not* England."

As 1862 wore on, the Confederates tallied a string of victories, thereby raising their position in the eyes of Europe. Pro-Unionists braced themselves for apocalypse. But in mid-September, the push toward European intervention was thwarted, narrowly, by General George McClellan's triumph at Antietam (September 17) and its political and ideological aftermath—the announcement of Lincoln's plans for emancipation. The preliminary Emancipation Proclamation, in September 1862, came as quite a shock to white Southerners. They were even more dismayed on January 1, 1863, when by presidential edict Lincoln freed all the slaves of rebel masters, as the preliminary proclamation had promised to do.

At this dramatic juncture, Fanny Kemble plucked up her courage and consented to publish *Journal of a Residence on a Georgian Plantation,* the vivid and haunting diatribe against human bondage composed during her stay on the Butler plantations in the winter of 1838–39.

Over two decades had passed since 1841, when Lydia Maria Child had identified Kemble's eyewitness account of slavery as a boon to the abolitionist cause. At that time, Pierce Butler succeeded, as he often did during their marriage, in suppressing the publication of his wife's writings. But by 1863, their divorce sufficiently permanent, Kemble was free to put her journal to the purpose she had always intended: swaying public opinion against slavery.

At the urgings of friends and concerned politicians, Kemble also attached a letter that she had composed in 1852 for the London *Times,* in response to the intense controversy over Harriet Beecher Stowe's *Uncle Tom's Cabin.* (Kemble had not published the letter because at the time Pierce still controlled the children, and she did not dare to antagonize him.)

Upon the journal's publication in May 1863, the British praised its truth and power: "A more startling and fearful narrative on a well-worn subject was never laid before readers," said the *Athenaeum.* Passages were read aloud on the floor of the House of Commons and to cotton workers in Manchester. The Ladies' Emancipation Society of London culled excerpts for publication in a pamphlet entitled "The Essence of Slavery," then printed hundreds of thousands by demand.

Kemble was undoubtedly proud and happy, but it is impossible to assess the journal's contemporary significance exactly. It would be safe to say that the book has more greatly influenced twentieth-century historians than Civil War–era politicians. Nevertheless, that her opinions were circulated so widely leaves little doubt that her words touched countless hearts and minds. And the *Journal* confirmed Fanny Kemble as an international figure not only celebrated but influential.

An American edition was published in June 1863; the Northern press responded as enthusiastically as London's had. (In the Confederacy, needless to say, the *Journal* was reviled.) Frederick Law Olmsted found Kemble's indictment to coincide with his own, and, under the pen name Yeoman, wrote a ringing endorsement of her observations as "deep, thorough and detailed." A lengthy review in the *Atlantic Monthly* intoned:

> The book is a permanent and most valuable chapter in our history; for it is the first ample, lucid, faithful, detailed account, from the actual head-quarters of a slave-plantation in this country, of the workings of the system—its persistent hopeless, helpless, crushing of humanity in the slave, and the more fearful moral and mental dryrot it generates in the master.

Horace Greeley's *Tribune* published its extended praise of Kemble's Georgian journal on the same July day as news of the victory at Gettysburg splashed across the front page.

Perhaps owing to his long acquaintance with both Kemble and Butler in Philadelphia, the diarist Sidney George Fisher brought the symbolism of the events portrayed to bear on the participants themselves. "Filth, squalor, cruelty & wretchedness are painted in very strong colors, as well as the discomfort and inconvenience of Butler's own house. . . . I am surprised at the picture they draw of the miserable condition of the Negroes, which is very discreditable to Butler." He then trained his eye on Kemble's motives for publishing: "These letters are now printed for the first time, partly, I suppose, for the sake of annoying Butler, partly to aid the cause of abolition & partly for the money they will bring."

In typical fashion, Fanny's daughters found themselves divided over their mother's latest literary efforts. As a sometime poet and essayist and longtime antislavery sympathizer, Sarah had been involved with a Quaker writing circle whose members regularly and dutifully contributed to *The Liberty Bell*, an annual volume published to benefit abolitionist societies. She even wrote poems sympathetic to the plight of slaves, which appeared in print after the war. And she joined her husband's family in forswearing any tolerance to Rebel sentiments, a pledge that cemented her sympathy for her mother's publication as powerful propaganda.

But Fan was scandalized. She railed at Kemble's disregard for Pierce and saw the book as a familial betrayal. Fan later said that she would never have the *Journal* in her house, and, even fifteen years after publication, claimed, "I have never lost in the least degree by the feeling of bitterness I have always felt about the publication of your first Southern book and nothing would ever induce me to." What Fan and her father said to each other, we don't know; none of the family's extant correspondence touches on it.

According to one Philadelphian, Butler's own sister-in-law, Ella Butler, unexpectedly embraced Kemble's views: "Altho her father & some of her brothers are . . . great sufferers by the war and all violent secessionists, she is loyal to the Union & the government. She approves of emancipation."

In any case, Ella's response to her brother-in-law's public humiliation was probably overshadowed by a private grief. Her only daughter, Lizzie, had died in 1862, leaving behind three daughters and a son, young Francis McAllister, who had taken the surname Butler. His sex and his name change entitled him to inherit his grandfather John Butler's fortune. But Francis's own death in 1863 cruelly, or so it must have seemed to Gabriella, returned to Butler complete control over the major's legacy. Pierce's girls would inherit it all—or what was left of a once-great patrimony.

The Butler estate had been threatened by the Union army from the early days of the war. As early as October 1861, Federal ships were posted off St. Simon's to maintain the blockade. To protect the waterway into Brunswick harbor, planters fortified the island's southern tip with the large guns known as Columbiads. Nearly 1,500 Georgia troops were stationed there. But when Union troops swarmed onto Hilton Head, just miles up the coast, the slaveowners of St. Simon's recognized their peril and moved themselves and their chattel onto the mainland for protection. Butler slaves were evacuated with their overseers to Waycross, near Savannah, where they expected to remain until the end of the war.

In February 1862, Robert E. Lee ordered Confederate troops to abandon the island and move the valuable Columbiads to Savannah. The Union troops moved in and the outpost they established at the Retreat Plantation became a magnet for blacks seeking freedom. As one Federal soldier reported, "The marshes, or savannahs, in this part of the country, which border the rivers are almost impassable for human beings, yet many a slave had waded through them toward the North star of Freedom."

By April over fifty African Americans had arrived at the Union camp. This count climbed to three hundred by May and almost five hundred by August; it eventually reached nearly a thousand. Patrolling Union gunboats, Georgia planters complained, "encourage the escape of negroes, and by stealing and reselling them aid in swelling personal wealth and in defraying the expense of war."

It was true that Union officers were willing to use these escaped slaves—so-called contrabands—to further their cause. The escapees were not resold into slavery, but rather drafted into Union service. The officer in charge at St. Simon's was instructed thus: "Select, if you can do so, thirty stout contrabands for work on boats and bring them with you to Port Royal. They should be single men of course." Those newly liberated slaves were paid from $8 to $10 per month upon enlistment. Those left behind, including many women and children, foraged on the island or looked to Federal soldiers for aid. In June 1862, the Union commander reported, "my supplies have been mostly from Pierce Butler's place."

Late that summer, a regiment of black Union soldiers, the 1st South Carolina Volunteers, landed on St. Simon's and embarked on a spree of raiding and burning. The white commander testified, "I started from St. Simon's with 62 colored fighting men and returned with 156 fighting men (all colored). As soon as we took a slave from his claimant we placed a musket in his hands and he began to fight for the freedom of others."

Naturally this was disturbing news to the planters on the mainland. Reports of destruction and mayhem in the Sea Islands circulated rapidly, from Darien, Georgia, to Philadelphia. In the eastern theater of war, losses mounted on both sides; stakes escalated as plantations were burned, family graveyards desecrated, and churches (most notably Christ Church, near Fort Frederica) vandalized.

During June and July, Abraham Lincoln drafted his preliminary Emancipation Proclamation, which threatened Rebels with the freeing of their slaves. Lincoln made no secret that, among his wartime goals, restoring the Union ranked above eradicating slavery; he agonized over just how far to go toward enacting emancipation. In September 1862, he offered to protect the institution of slavery for those who remained loyal to the Union—a plea that was, not surprisingly, ignored by Confederate planters. Most along the Eastern Seaboard were already witness to a mass exodus of slaves, who more and more frequently took up arms against their former masters.

On January 1, 1863, this extraordinary Union war measure, the Emancipation Proclamation, became Federal policy. Lincoln officially welcomed ex-slaves into the Union as soldiers—and eventually perhaps as citizens. This outraged Southern planters, helpless to prevent the flight of countless able-bodied African Americans looking to trade their ragged osnaburg clothing for Yankee uniforms. The black troops became a fearful sign of things to come. By May, African American soldiers began to distinguish themselves, at the battles of Milliken's Bend, Mississippi, and Port Hudson, Louisiana. But the most famous of these "colored" troops—the 54th Massachusetts—were soon to earn their glory.

In June 1863 this regiment, composed mainly of free black volunteers from the New England states (including two of Frederick Douglass's sons), joined with troops from the South Carolina Volunteers on an expedition along the Georgia coast. Their commander, Colonel Robert Gould Shaw, was the son of Boston abolitionists, great friends of Fanny Kemble's. They had met her in 1853, when she was on holiday with Adelaide in Sorrento, Italy.

In Georgia, Shaw took the opportunity to visit Butler's Hampton plantation. He wrote to his family:

> Today I rode over to Mr. Butler's plantation. It is an immense place & parts of it are very beautiful. . . . there are about ten of his slaves left here, all of them sixty or seventy years old. . . . they maintained that "Massa Butler was a good Massa" and they would give anything to see him again. When I had told them I had seen "Miss Fanny," they looked much pleased & one named "John" wanted me to tell her I had seen him.

Perhaps these men and women recalled with fondness the passion and integrity with which Kemble had exerted herself on their behalf. She had paid her household help with her own money, struggled to keep families together, and tried to lighten the workload for nursing mothers and pregnant women—fighting bitterly with her husband for each concession. Though she had spent only a few months on the estate, over twenty-five years earlier, her memory was revered by the recipients of these kindnesses, long after her departure, long after she ceased to use the name Butler.

This visit to Hampton predated the infamous raid on Darien of June 1863, in which Shaw's regiment participated. The unprovoked burning and pillaging of this deserted village was widely condemned as savage. Shaw himself complained, "It seems to me very barbarous to turn women and children adrift in that way—and if I am only assisting Col. Montgomery [his commanding officer] in some private enterprise it is very distasteful to me." To his family, Shaw attempted to explain his commanders' motives: "The Southerners must be made to feel that this is a real war, and that they were to be swept away by the hand of God like the Jews of old."

Soon after, Shaw led the vain charge against Fort Wagner, a Confederate stronghold just south of Charleston. His six hundred men volunteered to lead the assault, then bravely navigated the narrow band of land between the marsh and the sea. Frederick Douglass's son Lewis recalled how Confederate shelling tore a twenty-foot swath in the wall of advancing soldiers—blood, bodies, bayonets exploding into noise and stench. Shaw drew his sword, raised it in the air, and urged his men onward. When the soldier carrying the regimental colors fell, Sergeant William H. Carney took them up, carrying the flag to the top of a parapet. He sustained multiple wounds, but kept the flag held high. (For his heroism that day, he later became the first African American to receive the Medal of Honor.)

Although Carney planted the flag triumphantly on the Rebel ramparts, the fort was not taken that day, nor would it be for many weeks. At battle's end, 31 men from Shaw's regiment had died (including Shaw and three other white officers); 135 were wounded, and 92 were missing.

The Northern press reported black heroism rhapsodically and was voluble in offering tales of Confederate depravity. It was rumored that Shaw's body was stripped of its uniform and paraded in the Rebel fort

*Men and women, black and white, adults and
children, became war refugees.*

before being thrown unceremoniously into a mass grave alongside
those of his men. The Rebels responded to Union requests for Shaw's
body with the taunt "We have buried him with his niggers." Shaw's father simply asked that no effort be made to recover his son's body, as
it was right that he be buried with his men.

Fanny Kemble was devastated by the loss of this heroic young man,
of whom she had been so fond. She and other abolitionists saw Shaw's
death as a martyrdom; and they cultivated a movement to exalt his
memory and mythologize his role, which culminated in the erection
on the Boston Common of an elaborate monument designed by Augustus Saint-Gaudens.

Pierce Butler, too, endured painful loss during the war. In July 1863,
Lieutenant Pierce Butler Holmes—Pierce's namesake, his godson, and
the son of Dr. James Holmes, his Sea Island physician and close friend
—had been captured at Gettysburg. From a Baltimore prison hospital,
young Lieutenant Holmes wrote to Butler. Butler came at once to
visit, bringing Fan along. "Generous and kind attention was given by

Pierce Butler's godson, Pierce Butler Holmes, served with a company of young Confederates such as these.

Mr. Butler to every Confederate in the prison." Dr. Holmes reported that "they took affectionate leave after providing my son with a purse of gold to supply his wants and fancies and to pay his way home when able to travel." Following a furlough in Georgia, Holmes returned to active service. He died of wounds sustained in the Battle of the Wilderness in May 1864.

As Pierce Butler neared fifty-five, his health, always fragile at best, began to decline, his spirit breaking under the weight of death and destruction. A Philadelphia friend reported: "He said his life had been prosperous, that he was now old, and nothing more to do or enjoy in the world & was quite ready to go. He said he should leave an estate of $400,000 to his family, which I was very glad to hear, as with what they have already it will make them well off." Certainly Butler must have been relieved to recapture his stature as generous and indulgent father, a role he had enjoyed playing until creditors intervened.

It pained Fan Butler to watch her once-lively father adopt a funereal air, but outwardly at least, she appeared a young woman in full bloom. A member of her Philadelphia set described her as "charming . . . gay, graceful, thorobred, clever, cultivated & more than pretty. She has a good figure & an expressive face, beautiful hair, & good features." Yet she remained an excessively devoted daughter, presumably content without a husband as long as she could play hostess for her father.

In January 1864 Pierce Butler bought Ella's house, which his sister-in-law had been trying to sell for eight years. Perhaps the purchase was intended to soften the financial blow of Ella's grandson's death, which had caused inheritance rights to the major's estate to revert to Pierce. In any case, the stately Philadelphia mansion would make a proper home for his younger daughter, after her many years adrift. Kemble reported that Fan, ensconced in her new home, was "in great satisfaction," having escaped "the discomforts & inconveniences & annoyances of boarding house life."

Perhaps Fanny feared she was being displaced. She showered her daughter with gifts and invitations. Fan agreed to return to England in the spring of 1864, where they stayed in a Hampshire cottage. Kemble reported to Harriet St. Leger that she was also splurging on a trip to the Continent: "What I provide for Fan is full twice what I should provide for myself if I was alone & you know I am greedy and extravagant." On a summer visit to Geneva, Fan received a batch of letters reporting on the death of a childhood acquaintance. Kemble wrote to a friend: "When I see my poor child weeping her eyes out over the news of this one death & think that the lad was *only* her friend & then remember the mothers, sisters, wives & lovers whose every bereavement is going up to Heaven day after day I feel sick with horror."

A less personal but painful anxiety was the political news of 1864. Sarah wrote her mother that a Democratic victory—by way of an alliance between the Northern and Southern wings of the party—was widely predicted. Kemble feared a Democratic government might derail the Republican commitment to ending slavery, so that "all the heroic courage of the past years [would] hav[e] literally been for nothing." But once Federal troops captured Atlanta on September 2, Lincoln's reelection seemed secure. Thousands from the Union army were offered furloughs to go home to vote. After Lincoln's reelection, the death throes of slavery were hastened by General William Tecumseh Sherman's famous March to the Sea.

Pierce Butler's apprehensions over Union victories in Georgia—and the impending Confederate doom they forecast—undid him emotionally. He was particularly disheartened in January 1865 by Sherman's Special Field Order No. 15, whereby the South Atlantic coast from Charleston to Florida was "reserved and set apart for the settlement of negroes now made free by acts of war." The last shreds of his economic security now permanently compromised, he became unhinged, challenging a business partner to a duel and in consequence being charged with disturbing the peace. Butler's activities had long wagged the tongues of Philadelphia. This time he fled the scandalmongers, withdrawing to the rural privacy of York Farm.

In April 1865, when bulletins announcing the fall of Richmond finally reached London, both Kemble and Fan wept over the news: "I with joy and she with sorrow." In rapid succession, Lee surrendered, Lincoln was assassinated, the largest manhunt in American history was launched; John Wilkes Booth died a fugitive and his co-conspirators were put on trial and hanged or imprisoned. Fan had already determined to sail home to her father, knowing there would be hard times ahead, certain he would need her now more than ever.

This prediction was correct. On May 5, a mob gathered around Butler's Branchtown home. The windows were bare of any black mourning ribbons in memory of Lincoln, a flouting of the national grief his neighbors could not abide. Only the intervention of a local leader known for his staunch abolitionism prevented violence.

The war's end left Kemble hopeful for America's future: "In countless thousands of lamentable graves the bitter wrong lies buried—atoned for by a four year fratricidal war: the beautiful Southern land is lifting its head from the disgrace of slavery and the agony of its defense." But former Confederates felt none of Kemble's uplift, only the bleak erosion of their tarnished pride. The plantation economy was destroyed, for planters were ill equipped to cope with the wholesale emancipation of slave property. Pierce Butler might have thanked his lucky stars that he had converted to currency half his human property in the slave sale of 1859. But his guilt over the dispersal of his human chattel remained with him until the end of his life.

Although he could not undo these events, Butler hoped to prove himself a man of honor, to reclaim his good name. He wanted to go South, where he would minister to "his people" and manage his plantations.

Sarah Wister was skeptical of her father's insistence on restoring his Georgia estates, but Fan volunteered to accompany him on this great crusade. As for Kemble, she feared her daughter's pledge to stay by her father's side would only lead to grief.

CHAPTER EIGHT

Lost Causes

The Union may have brought about Confederate defeat and the destruction of slavery, but peace was not among the victor's spoils. Both
North and South dug in for a long struggle.

The South's defeat left Butler a broken man. While he was still in
possession of his Philadelphia property, the estates in Georgia had been
pillaged and his future was uncertain. The land, however, retained its
value, especially the fertile rice fields of the Sea Islands. St. Simon's was
centrally located on the rice coast, near the mouth of the Altamaha
River, which flowed south from the upcountry Piedmont region
nearly 150 miles, delivering fresh water into the tidal region and thus
providing the planters with a natural hydraulic system for flooding and
draining the fields. This rich system needed tending, or it would, over
time, revert back to swampland. Now the labor planters had for generations counted upon to toil over the planting and weeding was dis-
persed.

In early 1866, a plan presented itself. Butler was offered $20,000 a
year to lease half of his Sea Island plantations. Such a sum could never

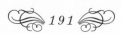

have been realized before the war, even with a full complement of slaves (505 in 1860) in place.

Butler also discovered that many of his former slaves, including some who had been sold away in 1859, had returned to Butler Island and Hampton Point. He saw an opportunity to redeem himself.

Fanny Kemble had characterized Butler as a despot; Butler's friends portrayed him as a peerless master. The truth lay somewhere in between. Testimony from Southern and Northern observers—Robert Gould Shaw, it will be recalled, among them—confirms the loyalty of many of Butler's slaves. Before the sale in 1859, Butler's overseers and managers had augmented his slave holdings, by "natural increase" as much as by purchase. Some planters sold off women and children, then used the cash to buy prime hands, young male slaves. This strategy maximized profits, but there is no evidence that Butler resorted to such tactics.

Dating back to the American Revolutionary era, African American families enslaved on Butler plantations generally were kept together. With few exceptions, elderly slaves were given lighter duties and remained on the plantations where they had worked and where their children remained, until the sale of 1859. In the economic chaos provoked by the end of slavery, Butler might have seized the opportunity the lease presented to reap a comfortable income in his declining years.

However, in addition to that offer, Butler received two letters, one from a Freedmen's Bureau agent and another from a neighbor. The neighbor told him that his ex-slaves had "all" returned and wanted to work, but "refused to engage themselves to anyone else, even to their liberators." The Bureau agent warned that unless Butler appeared, "the negroes would be removed and made to work elsewhere." So Butler refused to grant the lease and decided to head south himself.

Philadelphians, including his own family, were shocked. Owen Wister claimed that Butler would soon "make ducks and drakes of it." Sidney Fisher concurred that Butler had "an unfortunate propensity for attempting to manage business, comprised [sic] with a total incapacity for such work." Fisher found it especially unfortunate that the war had increased the value of Butler's Southern property. But Butler did have one loyalist: his daughter Fan. And the bond between the two, which had always been strong, was strengthened by her faith in his dream of rebuilding their plantations. In March 1866, Fan and Pierce left Philadelphia "to look after our property in Georgia and see what could be done about it."

In many ways, Fan's trip south in 1866 was a melancholy echo of her mother's journey nearly thirty years before. Just as her mother had done before her, Fan would publish a journal of the time she spent on the plantation. Kemble had complained bitterly about travel conditions, and by Fan's account these were little improved: "The hotel was a miserable tumble-down old frame house, and the room we were shown into more fit for a stable than a human habitation." She spent the night pounding the floor with her umbrella to frighten away the rats.

Fan grieved bitterly over the ruin wrought by war. Stopping in Richmond to visit a friend's grave, she saddened at the sight of the memorial to a single fallen soldier, but the spectacle of row upon row of small wooden boards serving as headstones overwhelmed her. "I was glad to leave the town before daylight the next morning and I hope I may never be there again." She was horrified by General Sherman's handiwork in South Carolina: "Street after street was merely one long line of blackened ruins, which showed from the size and beautifully laid out gardens, how handsome some of the houses had been. It was too horrible!"

When they arrived in Savannah, Butler bade Fan stay behind while he surveyed conditions on St. Simon's. Fan found the once-gay port city desolate: "It was piteous to see so many mere girls' faces shaded by deep crape veils and widows' caps. . . . the women live in the past, and the men only in the daily present, trying, in a listless sort of way, to repair their ruined fortunes."

Butler's house on St. Simon's had been stripped bare, so he slept on the floor with a piece of wood for his pillow. Most of the surrounding plantations were idle and deserted. The Freedmen's Bureau reported that over 17,000 deaths from disease and starvation had depopulated the region. Yet Butler found his property crowded with former slaves, and "they received him very affectionately, and made an agreement with him to work for one half the crop."

Butler prepared for planting and charged his daughter with the task of stocking the household. Fan made the journey to the island in a boat laden with furniture, arriving at one o'clock in the morning because of various delays and the need for a good tide. The conditions at St. Simon's were primitive. Fan reported to her sister: "I have relapsed into barbarism total. . . . I feel like Robinson Crusoe with three hundred men Fridays."

But, much as her mother had done, she marveled at the abundance of nature: "On the acre of ground enclosed about the house are a superb magnolia tree, covered with its queenly flowers, roses running wild in every direction; orange, fig and peach trees now in blossom, give promise of fruit later on, while every tree and bush is alive with red-bird, mockingbirds, blackbirds, and jays, so as I sit on the piazza the air comes to me laden with sweet smells and sweet sounds of all descriptions."

Fan received the same warm reception the former slaves offered Butler himself: "The negroes seem perfectly happy at getting back to the old place and having us there, and I have been deeply touched by many instances of devotion on their part." Butler, like other former slaveowners, faced the problem of former slaves returning who were too young or too old to work. But Fan confessed that, with their property in the North, the Butlers, unlike most coastal planters, could afford to feed their workers' families.

Some of Butler's former slaves had spent what little cash they had to make their way back to the plantation. An elderly couple presented Butler with a bag full of silver half-dollars, given them the second year of the war by a Union soldier as compensation for chickens confiscated. Fan was amazed that they had kept the coins during all their wartime hardship, never wavering from their intent to turn the silver over to Butler. He paid the couple its worth in currency, but planned to cast it into a keepsake to commemorate their faithfulness.

Butler quickly discovered, however, that loyalty wasn't commercially viable. Fan Butler complained about "the influence of Northerners, some of whom had filled the poor people's minds with all sorts of vain hopes and ideas, among others that their former masters would not be allowed to return, and the land was theirs, a thing many of them believed." Butler despaired that too many workers left the field by early afternoon. "Half a day's work will keep them from starving," Fan fretted, "but won't raise a crop."

Many blacks simply wanted to work their own stakes. In a bid to reestablish his authority, Butler instructed the fifty blacks in residence who were farming his land that they might keep the corn and cotton they had already planted only if they each put in an additional twenty acres for him. The following year he promised they would sharecrop: he would provide seed and tools and the land, in exchange for a portion of the crop. The workers apparently accepted these terms and Fan reported, "To show what perfect confidence my father had on his side in his old slaves, the day after starting the work here [near Hampton Point] he returned to Butler's Island leaving me and my maid entirely alone, with no white person within eight miles of us."

Fan Butler claimed she felt safe, although she did report a disturbance down by the river late one night. Despite her fear of firearms, she took two small pistols Butler had given her and set out to investigate. (It turned out to be a boatload of mules sent from Butler Island.) But generally Fan discounted the rumor mill, which, she grumbled, churned out alarms about "negro insurrections."

Primitive and harsh conditions prevailed. Fan reported that the island had been "absolutely swept," and she lived on hominy, rice, and fish, supplemented occasionally by a piece of venison. The kitchen roof leaked, so she "often had to cook holding up an umbrella in one hand

Fanny Kemble's elder daughter, Sarah Butler Wister.

and stirring with the other." Snakes were common. After encountering a large rattler, Fan could no longer take the long walks she had previously enjoyed. Yet her spirits were surprisingly buoyant; she wrote to her sister in July, "Three times have I settled upon a day for leaving, and three times have I put it off; the truth is, I am very busy, very useful and very happy."

Just as her mother had discovered in 1838, transcending the challenges of plantation life would prove exhilarating. Fan learned to cook and doctor, skills for which she had had little need before now. "I was rather nervous about [dispensing medicines] at first, but have grown bolder since I find what good results always follow my doses." Fresh bass and bluefish—occasionally caught by Fan herself—graced the daily table. She adopted two pet bears, six weeks old, feeding them milk and watching them turn somersaults. The house at Hampton Point, she envisioned, "might, by a little judicious clearing and pruning, be made quite lovely, and if I am here next winter, as I suppose I shall be, I shall try my hand at a little landscape gardening."

But her concern for her father was considerable. Butler spent his days under the hot sun, supervising the workers in the rice fields. To reach his sleeping quarters, he rowed a mile across the river, then rode six miles through the pine woods. From Saturday until Monday he stayed with his daughter at Hampton Point on St. Simon's, a schedule that suited her.

Fan wished to remain in Georgia through the summer, but, fearing the onset of the malarial season, Pierce insisted that she return to Philadelphia. Fan anxiously wrote her sister that "with no doctor, no nurse, no medicine, and no proper food nearer than Savannah, it would be a serious thing to be ill here." Despite her misgivings, she returned to Philadelphia in late July without her father. She was accompanied north by a black servant boy, also named Pierce.

Drought conditions prevailed all that summer and Butler struggled to bring in a decent crop. He spent the fall and winter preparing the house on Butler Island for Fan's return. In February 1867, Sidney Fisher heard from the man who managed Butler's affairs in Philadelphia that "he is obliged to stay there and . . . is again in trouble about his money matters, which is a thing of course with him & would be if he were worth a million. He undertook to manage the plantation himself last year & it did not pay expenses." Alarmed at Fan's plans to return south, Fanny Kemble appealed to Sarah to stop her, only to receive "rather fanciful words of rebuke."

Perhaps to provide Fan moral support, Sarah and the seven-year-old Dan made the trip to Georgia that spring; according to Sarah's reports, the two Wisters lifted the mood considerably. "It is a great pleasure to Fanny to have us here . . . he [Butler] said yesterday morning that it made him so happy it seemed like a dream." The elderly former slaves looked to young Dan as the heir apparent and entertained him with tales about his great-great-grandfather Major Pierce Butler.

Sarah had received long and detailed reports about conditions on the plantation and Fan's failing health, none of which prepared her for what she found. The kitchen "stands apart from the house & the sun shines in through walls and roof by day & the moon shines in by night. A few blackened kettles are the only utensils & a rickety shelf the substitute for dresser table." The rudimentary household required nearly constant supervision, and Sarah noted that her little sister rose mightily to the occasion: "She has the most minute directions to give about everything & to see that they are carried out." Fan, "who put in with her own hands or superintended the putting in of all the vegetables that have been planted this spring," earned her authority through her own labor, although it was taking a physical and emotional toll.

Ever mindful of the purpose of her journey, Sarah was glad to be of comfort to her father and sister, but she found even the briefest separation from her husband difficult to bear. "I was sad in Savannah and I am sad here, but not in low spirits," she wrote. "I enjoy the changes & calms & quiet & summer weather & rich peculiar scenery, excessively but feel as if I had been away from home for many weeks."

Owen, too, felt the separation keenly. "I am guilty," he told his wife, "of the weakness of putting your miniatures under my pillow every night." The passage of another month made him positively lovesick: "For several nights I have made an ass of myself reading your old letters of 56–7 from the very first after our talk in the dining room at Butler Place, instead of going to bed as other husbands would." Sarah's absence made Owen anxious under any circumstances, but he particularly feared her exposure to such a dangerous climate: "I become maddened with the ideas there are more possibilities of losing you my dearest, dearest love."

But Sarah stayed well, and recorded that by the time of her May departure, Fan was recovering her physical health. Her sister "looks much better than when she left home, but is pale & rather thin & I

A photograph of Liverpool Hazzard taken in the 1930s. As a
young man, Hazzard had been Pierce Butler's boatman.

think dejected by the uncertainty of her future." Sarah's characteriza-
tion of her sister's outlook could not have been more accurate. During
the early summer, Fan was troubled by "news of political disturbances,
and a general growing restlessness among the negroes, which [Butler]
feared would end in great trouble and destroy their usefulness as
labourers."

When authorities in Washington ordered the former Confederate
States divided into five military districts, Fan Butler indignantly commented: "If they would frankly say they intend to keep us down, it

would be fairer than making a pretence of readmitting us to equal rights." The Republicans, who were "exciting the negroes to every kind of insolent lawlessness to goad the people into acts of rebellion and resistance," became the primary target of her hostility.

Her father, she believed, was threatened with ruin if political hostility toward the planter class continued. In January 1867, Fan, in a state of extreme agitation, catalogued to Sarah the dire consequences of black suffrage. She warned that the law known as "the Oath" (former Confederates were required to pledge allegiance to the United States before being restored to citizenship) was being "forced upon us, whose very heart it pierces and prosperity it kills," and would mean disaster. In the late spring, Fan Butler came down with a fever. At her father's insistence, once she had recovered she departed for Philadelphia.

That was early July 1867. Just over a month later, Pierce Butler was dead. He had suddenly taken ill with what Sidney Fisher later identified as "country fever" (malaria). His boatman, Liverpool Hazzard, rowed Butler to Darien and delivered him to his townhouse in an area north of Darien known as the Ridge. But by the time his personal physician, Dr. James Holmes, arrived, it was too late. Pierce Butler was buried on Butler land in Darien with little ceremony. His family was absent from his graveside.

Fisher summed him up as "a man of strongly marked character with some good qualities & many faults. He led a very unsatisfactory life & threw away great advantages. He was handsome, clever, most gentlemanlike in his manners, but uneducated, obstinate, prejudiced & passionate."

During much of his life, Butler had retained legal counsel for one purpose or another, but he had never made a will. His administrators struggled with a complex tangle of debts and obligations, including $27,000 owed his brother John's estate. The remainder of Pierce's wealth was divided equally between his daughters, with cash and investments (exclusive of real estate) valued at over $56,000. Landed properties included the houses (and their contents) at York Farm, at Butler Place, in Philadelphia, and of course the Sea Island plantations.

Fanny may have believed that Pierce Butler's death would remove an obstacle from her path to full reconciliation with Sarah and Fan; she boarded a ship within a week of hearing the news. Her arrival to take her place by the side of her grieving daughters was made much of by Philadelphia gossips. "Mrs. Kemble has returned to this country," Sidney Fisher reported, "I suppose to live here with her daughters, or rather near them, for I doubt her being able to live in the same house with either." In fact, she did move into the Wisters' Germantown home (with her English maid), paying $50 a week for her board.

She resumed her reading career with style and verve. Henry Lee, a devoted fan since his Harvard days, heard her read *Richard III* in 1867: "From the entrance soliloquy to the shrieking of the ghosts over the sleeping Richard, her reading was so inspired that we were all electrified; and the next morning I wrote: 'What was the matter with you last night? You never read so in your life . . . something extraordinary must have happened.'"

Lee was quite right. Kemble had just inherited a priceless theatrical legacy. Her cousin Cecilia Siddons Combe had died and left her not only five Kemble family portraits but also a pair of gloves that Garrick had given to Mrs. Siddons and that were believed to have belonged to Shakespeare. "I had seen the flame," Lee wrote. "Now I had discovered the fuel."

But while Kemble made a dizzying ascent to her former glory, both her girls were fading. In the months following Pierce Butler's death, it was Sarah more than her sister who seemed incapacitated by grief. Her mother's visit proved an unwelcome intrusion, and she complained that "I w'd gladly pass the winter in Siberia if I cd have solitude there." Sidney Fisher confirmed that, as ever, Kemble dominated any setting:

And now this woman, divorced years ago by reason of her own fiery and impetuous temper & her husband's dogged & iron will, comes here as soon as he is in his grave, prosperous, victorious, triumphant, to play the part of mother to his & her children, & to live, if she pleases, in his ancestral home— a success fairly achieved by courage, energy, genius, making determined battle against adverse powers & finally subduing them.

While Sarah dreamed of flight, Fan actually quit her mother's presence so that she could preserve her father's legacy. If Butler's plantations lived on, Fan believed, so would his memory. She headed for Georgia to take up the reins of plantation management.

Matching her father's plantation ledger with the over three hundred sets of credit and debit records held by Butler workers proved to be no simple task. "Before anything else could be done the negroes had to be settled with for the past two years, and their share of the crops divided according to the amount due each man." Going over sums into the early morning hours, she was able to straighten out the accounts. But in the daytime, disputes erupted, mainly because of individual workers' disbelief that two full years of labor could have yielded such minimal financial returns. They grumbled bitterly, "Massa not treat us so," finding it easier to blame her than him or the system he had instituted.

Fan became so weary of the endless disputes that she just handed out wages, refusing to engage in debates. In total, Fan Butler distributed over $6,000 to the sharecroppers, some of whom received $200 or $300.

With cash in hand, some left to buy land of their own. Ill-equipped to cope with the rapidly changing business and social climate, Fan lashed out at the "common class of men" who "cheated the freedpeople." She worried as much that fluid trends in real estate—pioneered, she noted, by "small shopkeepers and Jews"—represented a threat to her ability to secure a workforce.

Equally problematic to Butler was the "lawlessness" of the Freedmen's Bureau courts, which dispensed a justice so whimsical that even her brother-in-law, "a Northern man and a strong Republican in his feelings," was offended. Wister wrote a letter about the "real" state of race relations in the South (kindness from former Confederates and roughness from Republican enforcers), which Fan Butler declared unprintable in any Northern Republican journal. Nevertheless, Wister sent his letter to a Philadelphia newspaper, which, Fan reported, refused to print it.

For her part, she maintained antebellum racial stereotypes, calling the freedpeople "lazy and childlike." She felt it unwise to do business during the Christmas season and instead tried to reestablish the lapsed plantation tradition of decorating a large Christmas tree and distributing presents to the children and sweets to the adults at a holiday levee.

In January 1868, her first order of business was extremely challenging: getting blacks to sign labor contracts. She complained, "My agents were quite powerless to make them come to any terms." Deciding to appeal to the workers personally, she spent six hours meeting with a steady parade of former employees, listening to their concerns, endlessly patient with their requests to have parts of the contract reread. By the end of the day, she had been able to convince nearly a fifth of her former workforce to sign on for the coming year. Butler recalled: "I thought sixty-two the first day, good work, though I had a violent attack of hysterics afterwards from fatigue and excitement." She continued campaigning until she had contracted the full force required.

Butler always believed that a firm, fair manner and her hereditary ties to the workers were all that prevented order from degenerating into chaos. She witnessed disruptions on neighboring plantations, where the new Northern owners wasted as long as three months into

Former slave cabins on St. Simon's Island.

the new year—nearly one-quarter of contract time—trying to secure workers. Like her neo-Confederate planter friends, Fan had no patience for Yankee reform.

Butler set about putting her plantation in order. Her priorities were not so different from her mother's thirty years before. She ordered repairs on the cavernous former hospital building. The crumbling structure had four large rooms, one of which had been commandeered by the freedpeople for a chapel. Butler allowed them to keep it and also designated a schoolroom, for which she employed a teacher. She, like her mother before her, was committed to providing rudimentary education to African Americans: "I had school in the morning for the children, and in the evening for the young people who worked in the fields. This is decidedly the most popular, and we have over fifty scholars, some of them quite old men—much too old to learn, but so zealous that I could not bear to turn them away."

Butler also wanted one of the rooms in the hospital to shelter the old women who couldn't work—presumably so they might tend young children whose mothers were working in the field. But the memory of enslavement was fresh. The grannies refused to be housed together, preferring to live with their extended families, regardless of the mistress's wishes.

The freedwomen resisted even more strongly Butler's attempt to establish a maternity ward in the former hospital. The strongest opposition came from "the old plantation midwife, who is indignant at her work being taken away from her." Butler bribed pregnant women with blankets, better food, and the promise of clothes for newborns delivered in the infirmary. But the hospital beds stayed empty; Butler confessed, "I never did succeed . . . and after several attempts, had to give it up."

She was equally defeated in her attempt to provide the workers at Butler Island with "good things at cost price." Shops in Darien sold inferior merchandise at three times cost. After the war, Pierce Butler had instituted the practice of shipping goods from Philadelphia, absorbing the expense of freight and spoilage. The Butler plantation store was kept stocked and open for business two hours every afternoon, but after a year, Fan had lost $3,000. More discouraging, the store wasn't even serving its intended purpose—her workers "much preferred" to shop in Darien.

When she first came to the islands in 1866, Butler had felt free to ride alone across their expanse as "the serpent had not entered into my paradise." Butler may have used this metaphor of Eden unconsciously, but allusions to evil and deceit appear throughout her postwar memoir. Butler believed that if not for the malevolent intervention of the Northern agitators known as carpetbaggers, she and other planters would have struggled along, tempering their sacrifice with black progress.

Butler reported in March 1868 the appearance around Darien of posters proclaiming that all freedmen must attend political meetings "on pain of being fined five hundred dollars or exiled to a foreign land." Unable to convince her workers to ignore these scare tactics, she took the unusual step of seeking assistance from Union authorities, whom she typically found contemptible. She was in part encouraged by her personal acquaintance with, and confidence in, General George Meade, the Union commander in charge of McIntosh County.

She wrote a formal letter asking for his help in dispelling the myths surrounding these political meetings, and assured him that she would allow her workers to vote once they had finished their day's work. (Voting took place over the course of four days and the nearest polling place was at Darien, only a short distance away.) She also sent along a personal note with more particular complaints. Meade replied immediately with a long, solicitous letter, including an official order that anyone falsely threatening workers, brandishing arms, or committing any other trespass would be prosecuted. Butler was extremely pleased, indeed triumphant. She read Meade's order to her workers, then had it posted in Darien. With the law behind her, she threatened with dismissal any one of them failing to show up for work—although voting after work would be permitted.

But the very next day Meade dispatched an addendum clarifying the matter of freedmen's voting: "You seem to think you have the right to decide when your people shall vote. . . . This is not so, and I would advise you not to insist on it." Butler pocketed the letter and disregarded Meade's directive. This incident strengthened her conviction that black suffrage was a "wicked farce" perpetuated by "agents belonging to the Republican Party, mostly Northern adventurers."

Around six A.M. on the first of the election days, Butler got word from her field manager (a white man) that over three hundred workers, her entire crew, had gone to vote. He protested that dismissing them, as she had threatened, would leave no one to plant for her. Disheartened, Fan took a boat to St. Simon's, where "the people were working like machinery and gave no trouble at all . . . and at the head of the fifty was Bram [the son of white overseer Roswell King and a slave mother], with eight of his family at work under him." Less than a handful of workers had deserted the fields. Located, as they were,

*Northern newspaper illustration of African American
participation in Southern elections.*

twelve miles from the nearest polling booth, these workers had been insulated from what Fan considered disruptive outside forces.

Later in the day, her manager sent word from Butler Island that all her workers had returned to the fields. Some even promised extra labor the next day to make up for lost time. Planting went on as usual in Butler's rice fields during the last three days of the election. But Fan's experience was exceptional. Most of her neighbors complained that their workers turned the occasion of voting into a four-day siesta. To Butler these events signaled the onset of a "new order," one in which African American males voted and made decisions for themselves. Although freedpeople felt this jubilee was long overdue, white planters resisted the gradual dawn of this new age.

A formidable opponent to planter hegemony arrived in the Sea Islands in the form of Tunis G. Campbell, an individual who figured prominently in Fan Butler's Georgian memoir. Campbell was a remarkable figure, whose political struggles in Georgia personified the forces at work during the tumult of Reconstruction.

Born a free black in New Jersey in 1813, Campbell had been educated in a white Episcopal school in New York until the age of eighteen. He converted to Methodism, became a polished speaker on both religious and political topics, and involved himself in radical abolitionism. While working as a hotel steward in New York City during the 1830s and 1840s, Campbell became vehemently opposed to the colonization movement, which advocated the migration of free blacks back to Africa. In the 1850s, he had been an active participant in the free black convention movement, where men of color in the Northern states had participated in annual gatherings to create their own political agendas.

When the war broke out in 1861, Campbell was fifty; married and the father of four, he was living in Manhattan and working as a baker. Despite his age and his family responsibilities, Campbell volunteered for military service. But in the early days of the war, the Union army barred men of color. Following the Emancipation Proclamation in 1863, plans were under way to resettle freedpeople within the occupied South and to educate them. Campbell petitioned President Lincoln to let him accompany the government workers involved in these campaigns, but was ignored.

Eventually Campbell was able to secure a military appointment and was ordered to South Carolina to work with General Rufus Saxton, in charge of contraband operations in the region. In August 1863, Campbell reported for duty at Port Royal near Hilton Head, South Carolina.

In January 1865, General Sherman ordered the coastal regions to be reorganized with his famous Order No. 15. Saxton designated Campbell "superintendent" of the Georgia Sea Islands. Campbell took boatloads of black refugees to Ossabaw, St. Catherine's, and St. Simon's for settlement. After the Confederate surrender and Lincoln's assassination, Campbell reported, "Everything is in confusion."

Emboldened by that chaos, Campbell advocated "separatism for

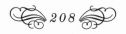

strength." He launched an independent black colony on St. Catherine's Island, and forbade whites to enter. He established an all-black government, headquartered on the family estate of Button Gwinnett, a signer of the Declaration of Independence, and named himself as head. Under the protection of a militia, he preached economic self-sufficiency. By 1866 over four hundred freedmen and their families had been given parcels of forty acres, scattered around the entire island at St. Catherine's, and Campbell was weaning his people off government rations. Both children and adults attended schools, moving toward social autonomy. But this postwar progress would soon be interrupted by outside forces.

In January 1866, President Andrew Johnson fired Rufus Saxton and replaced him with Davis Tillson. Tillson insisted that white men have access to St. Catherine's Island, and imposed his authority by force. Next, white planters and leaseholders moved in, reclaiming land from African American farmers and offering them labor contracts instead. Campbell urged the freedpeople to resist, but Tillson won out, dismissing him on charges of misconduct.

Unfazed, Campbell spent some money of his own on a down payment on the BelleVille plantation in McIntosh County, on the mainland. In 1867 he organized the BelleVille Farmers Association, an independent black community of over a hundred freedpeople.

Tunis Campbell was an imposing figure—over six feet tall, with a distinguished gray goatee—and a spellbinding orator. In 1867, he emerged as a formidable leader in electoral politics; he was appointed to the Board of Registration (the single black on the three-man board) for Georgia's Second District, where he helped to add 675 blacks and 128 whites to the McIntosh County voting rolls. That same year, he was a delegate to an African Methodist Episcopal convention and to a Georgia Educational Convention, and he represented his county at the Republican State Convention in Atlanta on July 4. In November, he was elected (in an election boycotted by whites) to represent McIntosh County at the state's constitutional convention. In the spring of

*Black labor remained the mainstay on Southern
plantations after the Civil War.*

1868, he became one of only three blacks elected to serve in the Georgia Senate.

His first challenge came from a white senator who argued that the state constitution did not grant blacks the right to hold office. Campbell lost that battle, and, along with his fellow black electees, was expelled from office. (Among those turned out was Campbell's son, who had been elected to serve in the Georgia House.)

By 1868 Campbell had settled his family in Darien, where local white planters perceived his presence as a threat. Fan Butler recounted: "He . . . very soon became a leader of the negroes, over whom he acquired the most absolute control, and managed exactly as he pleased." Indeed, in her private letter to Meade dated March 1867, Fan Butler had lodged a complaint against Campbell, accusing him of coercion and threatening her workers. Meade had responded: "If you will send me evidence and names and witnesses in Mr. Campbell's case, I will attend to that gentleman." Campbell's interest in promoting black autonomy was seen as a fearsome challenge even to white Republicans and Union authorities.

Thwarted in statewide politics, Campbell decided to concentrate his efforts in McIntosh County. Butler complained: "He had no difficulty in having himself elected a magistrate and for several years administered justice with a high hand and happy disregard of law, there being no one to oppose him." The harder authorities tried to counter Campbell's influence, the greater his sway. At one point local planters wanted to bribe him; Fan refused to join in the plan. She claimed to be opposed on principle, but conceded a practical motive: "If we bought him one day he would sell us the next." Her agent complained, whenever she asked him to be firm with the workers, to enforce her will: "It's of no use, Miss B——, I should only get myself into trouble and have the negro sheriff sent over by Campbell to arrest me."

Planter unrest over the intractability of black labor was compounded by economic woes. Harvest after harvest was plagued by natural disaster. Drought came in 1867 and floods in 1868, damaging crops severely. The 125 acres of cotton on St. Simon's also suffered from an infestation of armyworms, moth larvae that move through fields en masse, eating as they go. When they destroyed Fan's cotton crop in the fall of 1869, she reported miserably: "This gave the deathblow to the Sea Island cotton, as least as far as I was concerned, for I had not capital enough to plant again after losing three crops."

Reluctantly, she disbanded her model St. Simon's force and rented out her lands (cotton fields, $2 to $3 per acre; rice, $10 an acre) to local blacks to till, with the ultimate goal of turning the place into a stock farm. In 1868, looking to expand beyond Sea Island cotton, Butler discovered oranges to be a profitable cash crop. That year she sold 16,000 fruit.

Rice was becoming harder to cultivate, largely because the workforce was increasingly recalcitrant. Fan was forced to "have a gang of

Irishmen doing the banking and ditching which the negroes utterly refuse to do any more at all." (The building and upkeep of extensive drainage systems was hard and unhealthful labor.)

The freedpeople began to abandon the last vestiges of deference so long required by white masters. First came the practice of calling former owners by their last names, without a title. When Butler went from "Mistress" to "Miss Fanny," she found the behavior impertinent but passably tolerable. However, any black who spoke to her with his hat on was instantly rebuked. Determined to exert her authority, she explained: "One or two who seemed rather more inclined to be insolent than the rest, I dismissed, always saying, 'You are free to leave the place, but not to stay here and behave as you please, for I am free too, and moreover own the place, and so have a right to give my orders on it, and have them obeyed.'" Fearing that her authority was "touch and go," Butler struggled to retain the "upper hand" against these ill-mannered workers, who took to toting guns on their shoulders.

By the winter of 1868–69, Butler feared the subtle signs of resistance might be leading into full-scale rebellion. "The negroes this year and the following seemed to reach the climax of lawless independence, and I never slept without a loaded pistol by my bed." Following the completion of the transcontinental railroad in May 1869, labor agents hoped to transplant their imported Chinese workers. They swarmed the South, soliciting orders for "coolie labor." To some planters, this was an attractive alternative to the escalating difficulties of dealing with former slaves. Butler did not give the prospect serious consideration.

The plantation business was abbreviating Fan's annual escapes to the North, too, severely testing her endurance. But the political climate in the spring of 1869 so worried her that she decided remaining South was imperative. She sought relief from both her labor troubles and the malarial climate at Butler Island. In July, she visited her friends the Pringles in South Carolina.

The Pringles were part of a colony of Carolina rice planters who had been economically devastated by the war. These once wealthy families, no longer able to summer in Newport or Saratoga, created settlements in the Carolina pine woods. Few had the Northern resources Fan Butler could command. She sympathetically described her young female counterparts, "girls well-educated and brought up with every luxury turned adrift as dressmakers, schoolteachers and even shop-girls, in order to keep themselves and their families from starvation."

She was surprised at the roughness of the log houses, with their unplastered interiors, and moonlight streaming through cracks in the roof. Fan claimed the chintz-covered easy chairs and plush sofas were comfortable enough, but she also observed: "There was an amusing incongruity between a grand piano and fine embroidered sheets and pillow cases, relics of past days of wealth and luxury, and our bare floors and walls." In their attempts to keep the area malaria free, each night residents built pine fires on mounds of sand in front of their cabins. Fan found the blazing tableaux most picturesque.

She was able to journey north just once that fall, long enough to meet a visiting English cleric—the Reverend James Leigh, son of Lord Leigh of Stoneleigh Abbey, Warwickshire—at a friend's in New York. Upon her return to Georgia, she found the situation had grown dire. Her workers were "almost in a state of mutiny" and she was forced to fire her manager. Butler believed that the proper manager of African American labor was "born and bred a gentleman," and he must be a Southerner. So she hired a neighbor's son, who fit both these requirements.

As 1870 dawned, Butler despaired that her heart, once full of pity for the workers she supervised, was growing "weary and disgusted." Her family found her emotional hardening predictable; as early as 1867, Sarah had written: "I am sorry that Fanny is destined to encounter opposition & disappointment in her plans, whatever they are, but it could hardly be otherwise." The next year, Fanny Kemble wrote of her daughter's decision to remain in Georgia until June: "Such a determination on her part worries me. She has taken upon herself (very rashly

& unwisely I fear) the whole management & responsibility of the plantation."

Before the Confederate surrender, Fanny Kemble had written enthusiastically to Charles Greville about the South, and included her predictions in her epilogue to the 1863 edition of *Journal of a Residence on a Georgian Plantation:*

> The land offers no spontaneous produce that will sustain life without labor. The negroes, therefore, must work to eat; they are used to the soil and climate, and accustomed to the agriculture, and there is no reason at all to apprehend—as has been suggested—that a race of people singularly attached to the place of their birth and residence would abandon in any large numbers their own country. . . . The future ownership of land by negroes, as well as their admission to those rights of citizenship which every where in America such ownership involves, would necessarily be future subjects of legislation. . . . These and other modifications of the state of the black population of the South, would require great wisdom to deal with, but their immediate transformation from bondsmen to free might, I think, be accomplished with little danger or difficulty, and with certain increase of prosperity to the Southern states.

But by 1869, Kemble's idealism was gone. She confided to a friend: "I have no hope whatever that as long as one man, once a planter, and one man, once a slave survives, any successful cultivation of the southern estates will be achieved." She argued that the legacy of slavery would have to be "grubbed out of the soil," not wrought by some miracle. She had always been opposed to her daughter's Georgian adventures, but even more so as the impossibility of her goals became increasingly apparent.

Fan Butler had set out to Georgia in 1867 with ideals nearly as lofty

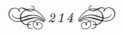

as her mother's, though opposed in intention. While Fanny Kemble believed liberty might lead to independence for blacks, Fan despaired: "From the first, the fixed notion in their minds has been that liberty meant idleness and they must be forced to work until they become intelligent enough to know the value of labour." The white community, she maintained, must stand united in this belief, and she berated neighbors who treated freedpeople and white workers equally, because "they [blacks] must be kept in leading strings until they are able to stand alone."

Over time, Butler abandoned such notions of racial uplift in favor of the racism and vitriol so common among former Confederates who tried to reclaim their prewar dominance. Fan Butler wrote in 1869: "I confess I am utterly unable to understand them, and what God's will is concerning them, unless He intended they should be slaves. This may shock you; but why in their own country have they no past history, no monuments, no literature, never advance or improve and here, now that they are free, are going steadily backwards, morally, intellectually, and physically?"

In her frustration, Fan failed to see that she was arguing both sides of the same point. On the one hand, she pointed to blacks' profound lack of ambition. You "couldn't starve a negro," she insisted, because the land provided too much bounty. Why should they sign contracts, she railed, when freedmen hung about the plantation anyway, "rais[ing] a little corn and sweet potatoes, and with their facilities for catching fish and oysters and shooting wild game, they have as much to eat as they want, and now are quite satisfied with that, not yet having learned to want things that money alone can give."

At the same time Butler found blacks overly ambitious—the prime examples being Tunis Campbell and her workers, with their continual demands. January 10, 1870, proved to be the nadir of her waning hope. Restored to his seat in the Georgia Senate by a military commander, Tunis Campbell redoubled his efforts to guarantee blacks their rights under Reconstruction laws.

But Frances Butler's personal fortunes were unexpectedly improved by a visit three Englishmen made to her plantation. Included in the party was Reverend James Leigh, whom she had met in New York the autumn before. Leigh's description of his arrival at Darien reads like a fairy tale: "I found some negroes, who took me across to Butler's Island about three miles across the river. Here a fair queen resided amongst her sable subjects and entertained strangers with royal grace." Leigh was invited to preach to the local blacks, and generally made himself an agreeable companion to his hostess. Clearly, by the time he returned to England, Fan Butler was aware of his romantic feelings, which she reciprocated.

Kemble had seen her daughter infrequently during these years, which she spent touring the Great Lakes giving readings, and making trips back to England. Kemble was well acquainted with the Leighs through British friends, and was very happy, at long last, to see her younger daughter interested in a man—even better, an English clergyman from a wealthy family.

Chaperoned by her sister Sarah, Fan Butler visited England in the spring of 1870, staying first at Stoneleigh Abbey, then at the home of James Leigh's twin sister. During this visit, Leigh asked Fan Butler to marry him. She accepted his proposal, but—mirroring what her mother had asked of Pierce Butler so many years before—said she would need time to settle her plantation business before she could quit America and settle in England.

Fan Butler entertained grandiose hopes that her success as an absentee planter would rival that of Major Butler himself. But she arrived in Georgia in December 1870 to find that her current agent had made a mess of things. By the end of January, she had enlisted a nearby failed planter to handle her accounts, and entrusted the management of the fields to "negro captains," wanting to "excite their ambition and pride by telling them that everything depended upon them now, and I expected them to show me how well they could manage."

In March 1871, the end of what she hoped would be her last winter

Fanny Kemble's son-in-law James Leigh eventually
became a vicar of the Church of England.

in residence, Butler wrote to a friend: "The negroes are behaving like angels, so that my heart is very sad at the thought of leaving." Fan rewarded this diligence with a week's holiday, and organized boat races between her workers and those at the nearby Couper plantation. It reminded her of her father's tales of the era before the war, and of the festivities sponsored by her grandfather and members of the St. Clair Club. These final Georgian days constituted Fan's elegy to the bygone days of the Old South.

Fanny Kemble celebrated her younger daughter's match in part by lavishing praise upon her betrothed: "He has admirable common sense, excellent moral sense, great liberality of thought and sensibility of feeling and true sympathy with the poor and hardworking folk of this country." She also noted, "I hardly know anyone who has a keener relish for all the luxuries of the highest civilization." But Kemble hardly regarded epicureanism as a shortcoming.

Although Fan's betrothed received very high marks from his future mother-in-law, Owen Wister, Jr., offered a rather different opinion in his preface to James Leigh's memoir: "Intellectual and theoretic matters did not concern him much." During his Cambridge days, Leigh—known to friends as Jimbo—performed on stage in blackface. He was a devoted huntsman and cricketer. Henry James offered perhaps the most brutal assessment of Leigh: "J.L. is an excellent liberal, hardworking parson, but with the intellect and manners of a boy of seven." But, at the age of thirty-three, Fan Butler married for love.

The fashionable ceremony took place at St. Thomas's at Portman Square in London in June 1871. The bride was dressed in exquisite Brussels lace, chosen by her mother. A Leigh relation performed the service, and the composer Arthur Sullivan (who first collaborated with W. S. Gilbert that same year) played the organ. The privileged young couple was afforded a prolonged and leisurely honeymoon, which, like her mother's, began in the company of a brother and sister-in-law. The Leighs stayed at his sister's country estate, Titsey Place.

The Wisters had been living in England for over a year before the wedding, and afterward they stayed on. Their happiness had been only recently renewed. In the late 1860s, Owen Wister had become incapacitated by illness, succumbing, by the summer of 1869, to "neuralgia & nervous weakness from overwork, cannot exert his brain *at all,* not even to read, & has given up his practice *entirely* for the present." Wister tried rest cures at Saratoga and in Newport, mountain cures in the Adirondacks, all to no avail.

Wister continued to work intermittently, but in May 1870, when the couple came into an inheritance, they sold their Germantown home to embark, along with their nine-year-old son, on a prolonged period of leisure and European travel. For Sarah Wister, it was a radical—and welcome—break with the past. She wrote that for years her life in Philadelphia had seemed "'the lane that had no turning,' wh[ich] had opened with bright promise of wh. no doubt there had been some fulfillment, but in wh. we had dropped youth, health, illusions and hope."

Fanny Kemble saw to the Wisters' every comfort and pleasure. Once in England, Sarah's "apathy changed to delight" and, she rejoiced, "I was alive again." Sarah was especially happy to renew ties with her aunt, Adelaide Sartoris, and Adelaide's two surviving children, May (who had been painted by Lord Leighton) and Algernon (who would become one of the family's black sheep, not unlike his uncle Harry Kemble).

The Wisters enrolled Dan in a boarding school near Berne, Switzerland, in time to join Fanny in Rome by January 1871. Sarah was wholly entranced by the place, marveling, "It seemed as if I had been waiting for Italy all of my life."

The family holiday culminated in Fan Butler's wedding in the summer of 1871. Fanny Kemble could hardly suppress her delight at the family's remarkable good fortune—both daughters married to men she adored, and so well off that they could congregate for prolonged holidays in Italy during the autumn of 1871. Owen was improving, Sarah was thriving, and they agreed to put Dan in a British boarding school (the Swiss facility having proved unsuitable). Young Dan settled in at Kenilworth, conveniently located near Stoneleigh.

Like many other families, Kemble and her daughters wanted to put the Civil War behind them. Even while traveling abroad, thousands of miles from the battlefields, they were haunted by the divide.

In 1895, *Scribner's* published Edith Wharton's "The Lamp of Psyche." The story offers an understated yet caustic portrait of those men who "sat out the war," and considers women's role in keeping sacrifice—and its meaning—alive. Wharton's own father did not see military service, but young Edith was voracious in her appetite for stories of wartime heroics. Perhaps this story, one of her earliest pieces of fiction, was semi-autobiographical. Wharton's family may have been offended by it; when her *Scribner's* editor, Edward Burlingame, wanted to reprint it in an 1899 collection titled *The Greater Inclination,* Wharton refused.

"The Lamp of Psyche" traces a couple, the Corbetts, who spend their time in European salons until a family emergency draws them home to Boston, where they are forced to confront the reality of the war. The fictional Corbetts represent the drifting expatriate community the Wisters and Leighs had now joined. They, too, received sad news from home—their longtime friend Sidney Fisher had died in July 1871, and in September, Ella Butler died at her Philadelphia home. But unlike the fictional Corbetts, the Wisters did not suspend their travels.

In 1872, Kemble accompanied the Wisters, including Dan, to France for a long holiday, followed by a stop in London, and finally to Rome for the Christmas holidays. By this time, Adelaide Sartoris had become a renowned society hostess, reigning queen of the expatriates; she attracted a glittering array of American artists and writers to her Italian salon.

During this period, Kemble became acquainted with the young American novelist Henry James. From the moment of their first introduction, it seems, the two were mutually smitten, and their friendship became one of the mainstays of Kemble's life over the next twenty years.

Sarah, too, immediately attracted James's attention. Writing from Rome on December 29, 1872, the twenty-nine-year-old James described to his mother his first encounter with Sarah Wister: "I went a couple of nights since to a little party. . . . There I met the famous Mrs. (Kemble) Wister who is very handsome and who nailed me for last evening, when I met everyone including the terrific Kemble herself, whose splendid handsomeness of eye, nostril and mouth were the best things in the room."

James went on to describe his flirtation with Sarah:

> Me voilà already intimate with Mrs. Wister to the point of having promised to go with her to the Villa Medici, the Academy of France; where she wishes to "shew me something she is fond of." On this mysterious object I shall repeat; also as to whether I am growing very fond of her. This I don't for see [*sic*]. I vaguely mistrust her. She is almost beautiful and has the handsomest hair in the world; but she is "intensely conscious," and diffident and lacks a certain repose comfortable to herself and others. She greatly resembles her mother; but beside her, Mrs. W. looks like the echo of Mrs. K.

Although James was much taken with Fanny Kemble, his correspondence early in his acquaintance with the family, surviving letters suggest, was mainly with Sarah. After a visit to the Colonna Gardens, James expounded upon her varied charms. "A beautiful woman who takes you to such a place and talks to you uninterruptedly learnedly and even cleverly for two whole hours is not to be disposed of in three lines."

James sent Sarah warm, chatty letters from Rome in May 1873, from Homburg in August, and in July 1874 from Baden-Baden: "I am writing a novel for the *Atlantic* next year (beginning January) and, as I go, have had frequent occasion to think of you. It all goes on in Rome (or most of it) and I have been hugging my Roman memories with extraordinary gusto." He also reported he would be sailing to America in August and was impatient to have the voyage over with, but "it has at least the merit that it will make it possible for me to see you within some calculable period."

Some have speculated about the nature of James's affection for

Sarah for whom, in chivalric tradition, he played the young knight romantically devoted to an older, married lady (Sarah was thirty-seven when they met). But his feelings seem to have been purely platonic, and much less sustaining than what he later felt for Kemble.

By spring of 1873 the Wisters had returned to Philadelphia. Owen Wister was able to resume his medical practice, while Dan was ready for preparatory school, and his parents wanted him to return to American life before they sent him off to St. Paul's, in New Hampshire.

That summer, the Leighs, who had been living at Stoneleigh, heeded a crisis call from Georgia. A fire (probably started by a disgruntled worker) had destroyed $15,000 worth of property, including the seed for the next year's rice crop.

Although Fanny Kemble never wavered in her belief that Georgia was not the place for Fan, she nonetheless joined the Leighs on the voyage back to the States, colorfully remarking to her son-in-law that "if we [the Leighs] went to the bottom, she might as well go with us." For his part, Leigh was enthusiastic at the prospect of reviving his wife's estates. Aside from his interest in the exotic climate and the rituals of plantation life, Leigh hoped to minister to African Americans in Georgia, in the tradition of such famous British divines as Wesley and Whitefield.

Leigh was also an agricultural evangelical. He wanted to resolve plantation labor problems through old-fashioned English know-how. Eight British workers were sent directly to Georgia, while the Leighs stopped over in Philadelphia in the autumn of 1873.

When the Leighs arrived at Darien in November, they delayed addressing the economic disarray to host a large "Thanksgiving" feast. President Grant had only recently declared Thanksgiving a permanent national holiday, and Fan wanted to herald the new tradition while celebrating her marriage. James Leigh sat down, along with over a hundred blacks, to a table groaning with stewed oysters, sweet potatoes, rice, rounds of beef, hominy, oranges, and coffee. Afterward, the Leighs were treated to canoe and boat races organized by the African

Fanny Kemble's younger daughter, Frances Butler
Leigh, also known as Fanny or Fan.

small house at York Farm, along with her English maid, Ellen, who had promised to stay with her for two years. Her return to Branchtown allowed her frequent visits with her great friend and former neighbor, Mary Fox. The Wisters had renovated Butler Place in anticipation of her arrival, but the results elicited mixed emotions: "I looked at S[arah] the other day as she stood on my former doorstep, superintending the unloading of cars full of furniture and household goods; it gave me something of a German 'Doppel Ganger' to look at her, like an apparition of my own youth."

Fanny Kemble, closer to seventy than to sixty, was finding life in the Philadelphia suburbs challenging. She confided to a friend: "I am bet-

*The Irish aristocrat Harriet St. Leger was Kemble's close
friend and confidante for over half a century.*

ter satisfied with my conditions of existence here than I should be any
where else but for all them am very often very lowly, very much de-
pressed and terrible, in want of some distractions besides my own
'weeping madness.'" She complained of becoming "old and fat," and
suffered from sciatic rheumatism, which brought on prolonged bouts
of pain. In addition, she found her bleak moods deepening: "The
thing that I suffer from most is depression, languour and debility,
which I attribute partly to the climate." Summer heat proved intolerable and winters difficult. At times, snow blocked her crossing to visit
Sarah at Butler Place. She told Harriet St. Leger, "My enduring this
climate is proof of my affection for my children."

Family differences resurfaced in 1874 when Algernon Sartoris became engaged to Nellie Grant, the daughter of the American president. Surprisingly, in light of her Confederate loyalties, Fan Leigh was a great supporter of this liaison. Her mother was extremely skeptical, however, derisively calling Nellie a "princess." The White House wedding, which might have brought the clan together for a grand occasion, became yet another cause for discord. Adelaide was dismayed because President Grant had made the couple's residence in the United States a prerequisite for his consent to the union, and Algernon had agreed.

Kemble's grandchildren were perhaps her greatest comfort; she doted on them. She worried over the frailty of Fan's daughter Alice, complaining in 1875: "The little L[eigh] baby is a very delicate little creature at present, but has *held on* to her life through its feeble and puny beginning with such a good *will*, that I think there is enough of that to make a constitution out of it."

Dan was, by contrast, physically robust. Kemble was growing fonder by the year of Sarah's "uncommonly clever and gifted boy." His returns to boarding school elicited great sadness: "He leaves us next week, and will carry away every ray of brightness from his mother's atmosphere. His father dotes upon him, and will miss him terribly, and so shall I." During his holiday visits with Fanny, young Dan would entertain her by playing the piano and reciting verses. She encouraged his writing talent; when he was just sixteen, the two of them collaborated on an opera.

In 1874 Fanny Kemble embarked on another important phase of her formidable career as a writer. Harriet St. Leger's worsening eyesight had prompted her to return to Kemble a trunkful of letters she had written to her good friend over the previous four decades. Rereading them absorbed Kemble, especially since she had been unable to preserve her own correspondence. She decided to take up an editor's offer to publish some of her reminiscences. Although she had made her mark with three previous journals, these memoirs, culled from her letters to Harriet and her private diaries, were to increase her fame and fortune during her later years.

Kemble worked on her memoirs for nearly two hours whenever, of an evening, she did not have a social engagement. She characterized the writing as sheer delight, even though the past, as she relived it, evoked heartache. During this busy period of reflection, she wrote to Harriet: "I go on scribbling my Reminiscences more or less. It is an occupation which amuses me, but which I put aside, of course, very frequently for other things, as I can always resume it at any time, and am not bound ever to finish it."

She turned the writings first into a series of magazine articles, entitled "An Old Woman's Gossip," the first of which appeared in the August 1875 issue of the *Atlantic Monthly*. It and nineteen subsequent installments stirred widespread interest in Kemble's early career and led to publication of multiple volumes (*Records of a Girlhood, Records of Later Life,* and *Further Records*). In 1875 Kemble was hard at work at her York Farm cottage, using a brand-new typewriter Owen Wister, Sr., had acquired for her—one of the earliest of these machines purchased for personal use.

Sarah Wister had also launched a writing career, producing poems, essays, and literary criticism for the *North American Review*. When she was called upon to assess *Roderick Hudson,* by her friend Henry James, she was not very complimentary. She compared the task to a medical student's viewing of a vivisection.

Sarah's mother liked James's writing rather better:

Mr. James does not go "deeper than the surface of things" in what he writes. His gift is neither power [n]or propensity but a very fine and refined [illeg.] & suggestive treatment of surfaces—below which I think he allows you very well to see depths of pathos and [illeg.] which a heavier [illeg.]

CHAPTER NINE

Peace and Remembrance

The lengthy lead-up to Fanny Kemble's final departure from America coincided with the nation's centennial celebration, whose elaborate pageantry dovetailed with Kemble's series of sentimental farewells, nearly stageworthy themselves.

With her brilliant reputation as an actress preceding her, Fanny Kemble had made a grand entrance to the States in 1832. Nearly half a century later, her reputation derived mainly from her writing—from her youthful *Journal of America,* to the searing social commentary of her Georgian journal, to her reminiscences recently serialized in the *Atlantic Monthly,* Kemble was a paramount memoirist, and Henry James predicted that "[her] fine memory would become the occasion of a lively literature."

In 1865, still at the height of her powers, Kemble commemorated the Civil War era, pausing to catalogue the changes she'd witnessed in her adopted country: "When I first came here thirty-four years ago, the whole country was like some remote part of England that I had never seen before, the people like English provincial or colonial folk."

As the nation moved into the future, she trusted in America's ability to withstand adversity. "[Its] activity, energy, wealth and material progress are something amazing."

Kemble felt especially qualified to characterize American society because of her peacetime renewal of her national Shakespearean reading tours (excluding the South, where she still refused to travel). Upon her happy reunion with her daughters following Pierce Butler's death in 1867, she vowed to maintain an American residence, "as long as my life lasts, and my health and strength are equal to the effort of crossing the ocean." If only Sarah and Fan returned her affections in kind. She wrote in despair to Harriet St. Leger: "I have felt you wanted me so much more than my children do."

Nonetheless, she remained near her family, buoyed by the successes of her professional commitments. In 1868, she netted nearly $8,000, a considerable sum during a time when the average family income was not more than a few hundred dollars a year. Reading for Philadelphia charities, she generated over $2,000 as well.

But by 1870 Kemble had retired and the pace of her life had slowed considerably. She worried about her ability to participate in America's "very vigorous" civilization as an "elderly Englishwoman." In nearly all of her letters from the United States to friends abroad, she inserted the phrase "should I survive" or "if I am still alive" alongside any mention of future plans.

In 1875 the Philadelphia Opera House invited the sixty-six-year-old Kemble to read before an audience of seven thousand, as part of the grand program planned for the opening of the American Centennial Celebration. Kemble was not tempted in the least. Certain that neither her voice nor her nerves could withstand the strain, she politely declined.

She, like her daughters, would be content to join in the Centennial Celebration as observers. They would enjoy the celebration when they diverted their attentions from the scandals erupting during President

Grant's second term. The sensational accounts of high-level political corruption and abuses of office seemed all the more pertinent now that Fanny Kemble's nephew was Grant's son-in-law.

Grant's administration was plagued by the collusion of distillers and government revenue collectors in the infamous tax-evading Whiskey Ring, a network traced directly to Grant's private secretary; in addition, both the wife of the attorney general and the wife of the secretary of war were guilty of accepting bribes to influence their husbands, as was the son of the interior secretary. Guilt by family connection was no laughing matter within Grant's White House. Throughout 1876, congressional investigations produced fodder for news coverage of high-level corruption.

But the tarnished presidency in no way dulled the glitter of that summer season, launched with the opening of the Philadelphia Centennial Fair. The federal government had allocated $1.5 million to fund this event, which also benefited from generous donations by citizens from across the country. Nearly five hundred acres of Fairmount Park had been set aside for the exhibition. A reporter for the *Chicago Tribune* described the bustle of the grounds on the eve of the May 10, 1876, premiere of the fair: "politicians, doctors, merchants, lawyers, thieves, farmers, bankers, gamblers, showmen, shopkeepers and every known class of man in the country."

A magnificent Women's Pavilion played host on opening day to a series of meetings sponsored by the National Woman Suffrage Association and culminating in a "Womanifesto." This document demanded equal rights for women in honor of the nation's hundredth birthday, a gift feminists believed was long overdue.

Kemble remained indifferent to organized feminism, even though she had suffered bitterly from discriminatory laws governing women's earnings, marital rights, and child custody. In her correspondence, however, she frequently waxed philosophic on women's issues. In 1874, she wrote Harriet St. Leger from America: "I have no doubt

*The older Fanny Kemble did not appear in the press
as frequently as the young actress had. But she was much
admired both in England and America.*

that women, both here and in England will eventually obtain the right
to vote, if they persist in demanding it . . . and what I covet more for
them, a better, perhaps even a tolerably good education."

Kemble's personal history shaped her idiosyncratic views. Conced-
ing that a father's control over his children limited married women's
options, and presumably their chance of equality, she declared to St.
Leger, "I think that the women who have contemplated *any* equality
between the sexes have almost all been unmarried." When Lucretia
Mott and other Kemble acquaintances launched their campaign for
equal rights in the summer of 1876, Kemble reflected, "I suppose my
own individual superabundant sense of independence, and the unfor-

tunate circumstances which have given full scope to its exercise, prevents me from sympathizing, as I ought, with the clamorous claims of the unfair sex in this particular."

Sarah Wister, apathetic toward the Centennial Fair during its planning stage, became fascinated by the exposition. She began to attend as often as she could, making a "systematic study" of the exhibits. When Dan Wister came home from boarding school for summer holiday, he frequently accompanied his mother, and the fifteen-year-old also became "enchanted with it." One leading attraction was the upper portion of the arm—including the torch and flame—of the Statue of Liberty, which would be erected in New York Harbor in 1886. Dan's special favorite was the Belmont Hill Tower, an elevator carrying people nearly two hundred feet up to an observation deck for an incredible panoramic view.

Sarah became so swept up in the spirit of the fair that she extended hospitality to three hundred centennial tourists for an afternoon at Butler Place. The visitors played croquet and enjoyed the grounds. Owen Wister cared little whether the City of Brotherly Love lived up to its name, and did not share his family's enthusiasm. Kemble observed in late June that he would not even go near the exhibition.

Fanny Kemble was generally unimpressed by the centennial's "international" aspect, with the possible exception of the tasteful goods on display from the Far East. In her view, only the Chinese and Japanese finery merited comparison with the magnificent offerings at earlier fairs in London and Paris, both of which she had attended and found far superior to this American imitation.

However, she admired the American industrial exhibits. She was most stirred by the large machinery and "triumphs of science," which, she confessed, moved her to tears. These mechanical displays were a highlight for many; the *Atlantic Monthly*'s editor, William Dean Howells, opined, "It is in these things of iron and steel that the national genius most freely speaks." In his memoir, written nearly half a century later, James Leigh vividly recalled the giant Corliss engine, surrounded by thirteen acres of revolving machinery, which caused all Americans to swell with pride over its "mighty limbs and sinews of iron and steel."

To many it seemed that all of America wished to attend the fair to partake of this sense of exhilaration. One visitor commented to a *New York Times* reporter: "An American can only see one Centennial, so we decided to make the most of it." Some industrialists sponsored tours of the exhibition. For example, the Yale Lock Company, the Baltimore Cotton Mill, and the Reading Coal and Iron Company arranged for their workers' holidays at the fair and even paid for round-trip transportation for the workers' families.

The May 10 opening ceremony attracted a crowd of nearly 100,000, and first-day admissions totaled 186,000. For Kemble, the crowds flocking to Philadelphia meant welcome visitors, such as Henry Wadsworth Longfellow, who paid a visit to York Farm. But they also proved troublesome to Kemble, who, at sixty-six, complained to friends that she found walking difficult—indeed, she had her daughter push her around the exhibition in a wheelchair.

Spring heat waves drove Kemble to the Berkshires, where she would pay some last visits before journeying to England. She stayed at Curtis's Hotel, where she thoroughly indulged herself in nostalgia. Despite her complaints of feebleness, she went on foot to look at her former cottage, the Perch, which stood a mile out of town. From a local map, Fanny discovered to her delight that the lane to the Perch had been renamed Kemble Street in her honor.

While in Lenox, Kemble learned of the death of her dear friend Harriet Martineau, whose passing prompted her to reflect on another recent literary death, that of George Sand. Although she lauded Sand as a genius, and one of the best writers of the day, she also pronounced that "she had not *clean hands,* and could hardly touch the picture of a woman without smirching it." Kemble, always a stickler for female rectitude, was becoming more prudish with advancing age.

Next Kemble visited Boston, her favorite among all American cities. She wrote to a friend, "How cordial, how kind, how very in-

The grave of Adelaide de Camp, Fanny's
beloved Aunt Dall, in Mount Auburn Cemetery,
Cambridge, Massachusetts.

dulgent and friendly Boston has shown it self to me. It would be diffi-cult for me to say, much more difficult to express how deeply I have felt all the good will that has been showered upon me in public and private." She had always felt at home in New England, as she wrote to a British friend: "No where out of my own country and away from our own early friends can I hope to regret them so little" as in New England.

Kemble paid a poignant call to Mount Auburn Cemetery, where she had buried Aunt Dall so many years before. She reminisced that on her

first trip to Boston, Mount Auburn was a deserted place to roam. Indeed, she and Pierce Butler had spent romantic hours there, wandering undisturbed amidst the scattered monuments. Nearly forty years later, "a perfect stone labyrinth" obscured the path to Dall's grave. Only by following a numbered map of the plots through elaborate terraces and rows of marble did she finally locate it.

In early September, she lingered in Boston despite the city's unbearable heat, to meet with Dan Wister on his way back to school in New Hampshire. Back in Philadelphia by month's end, she first visited Mary Fox at Champlost, then returned to York Farm to keep Fan and Alice company while James Leigh headed south to conclude unfinished business on the Sea Island plantations.

During October 1876 the country was caught up in election fever. Republican Rutherford B. Hayes of Ohio was pitted against the Democratic reform candidate, Samuel Tilden of New York. Kemble believed that the black vote would be a deciding electoral factor, which her daughter Fan doubtless dreaded.

With the close of the fair set for November 10, just weeks away, the turnstiles at the entrance to the Centennial Exhibition spun steadily; attendance would total nine million. On October 15, Kemble recorded that Sarah was still visiting the exhibition daily, and she worried how her daughter would fill her time when the centennial finally ended. A deeper concern was the void in her older daughter's life that loomed with her and Fan's impending departures. Luckily, news arrived in November that Sarah's closest friend, Jeannie Fields, who in 1870 had married Sir Anthony Musgrave and accompanied him to Australia, would soon settle in Jamaica, where her husband had recently been appointed governor.

Fraud in the presidential election was alleged, and the controversy went on long after the polls closed on November 8. By Kemble's birthday, November 27, it was clear the matter could not be amicably settled. Kemble made two incorrect predictions: that Congress would have to arbitrate, and that Tilden would prevail.

Her last Christmas in Pennsylvania was steeped in meaning and tradition. Mary Fox presented her with a flower in a cachepot that had been Butler's first gift to her after she was married. On December 23, Dan Wister arrived home from boarding school. Returning from her reunion dinner with her grandson, Kemble slipped on the icy steps but was not seriously injured. Delighting in the moment, she laughed at herself sprawled in the snow, and from her unique vantage point was bewitched by the "perfect heaps of glittering icicles" which looked "as if a thousand chandeliers had been smashed in the road."

Christmas preparations involved a whole week of activities. Kemble observed that the elaborate decorations and "the American passion for interchanging gifts" were a delight for children, but hard work for parents and elders. Noting that Alice's pile of new toys covered an entire table, she feared her granddaughter was being spoiled. For all her grumbling, however, Kemble was chagrined that the end of Yuletide meant she would have to begin in earnest preparations for her final departure. She celebrated New Year's Eve with Sarah and felt "thankful that my last hours in America will be spent in the house that was my only married home in this country, under whose roof my children were born."

Fanny and the Leighs were due to set sail on the *Britannic* the last week of January. James Leigh returned belatedly from the South, finally having made suitable arrangements for management of the sisters' plantation property. Fanny's remaining days in the United States were spent trying to press the image of friends' faces, familiar places, and all that she would miss, into her rapidly overflowing memory.

Before her departure, Fanny had told a British friend that she would resettle in London, as she felt as "a lonely old woman" it would be the best place for her. Macfarland, her British manservant, who had been with her in Philadelphia until the summer of 1876, met her at the boat when she landed in February 1877.

Kemble's first order of business was to visit Harriet in Ireland. St. Leger had become infirm, and was losing her eyesight. Their long

*May Gordon, who bore a striking resemblance to her
aunt Fanny Kemble in this portrait by Fanny's good friend,
British artist Sir Frederick Leighton.*

overdue reunion lasted until March, whereupon Kemble settled into
rented quarters in London's Portman Square. From there, she over-
saw the marriage of her beloved maid Ellen—who had stayed with her
for nearly three years in America—to Luigi Brianzoni. When the Bri-
anzonis settled in Italy, Fanny became increasingly dependent on
Macfarland, whose familiar presence comforted her. She had always
disliked interviewing and hiring domestic help, but as she grew older,

she found it more and more difficult to cope with even minor changes and abhorred the tedium of daily household management.

It was a time to revive acquaintances with family and friends. While James Leigh was preoccupied with his new clerical duties, Kemble invited Fan and Alice to spend several weeks in London during May and June. She also gave her blessing to her nephew Harry—her brother Henry's son—who aspired to take his place among the famed theatrical Kembles and embark on an acting career.

Renewed contacts with her nieces—brother John's daughter, Gertrude, who had married a concert singer named Charles Santley; and Adelaide's daughter, May Gordon, an amateur performer who sang in choirs—kept Fanny, at nearly seventy, in touch with the younger set and much involved in artistic circles in London. Even though she complained to Harriet that she saw no one and went nowhere, her letters were filled with descriptions of visits and activities. She was drawn back into enjoyment of the theater, concerts, and other entertainments.

Henry James was Fanny's favorite companion throughout the spring of 1877, and when she left in June for her annual trek to Switzerland, James told friends that he missed her company. The pair was reunited in France in September, only to be parted anew by unhappy circumstances. The deteriorating health of Harriet St. Leger brought Fanny to her friend's side for a month-long visit. In all their years of friendship, Harriet and Fanny had maintained their bond primarily by long and frequent letters. For Fanny to undertake two journeys to see her friend in the same year suggests she recognized that Harriet was rapidly failing.

At Christmastime, Kemble invited James to join her at the Leighs' home, Alverston Manor. While James was suitably charmed by his surroundings—"The picturesque old house with its big trees and its hanging of holly and mistletoe helped me through my thirty-six hours"—he was not impressed by his hostess. In a letter to his sister, James described Fan Leigh as "(except for strength of will) . . . inferior both to her mother and sister . . . detesting the English, alluding to it invidiously five times a minute, and rubbing it unmercifully into her good-natured husband." James wryly observed Kemble's fruitless efforts to convince her daughter to prefer England to Georgia, as she did. "Poor Mrs. Kemble looks on and wonders what her daughter can make of his [Leigh's] future here."

Despite his wife's refusal to find any comfort or contentment in Stratford, the Reverend Leigh was enjoying a charmed life. Within months of Leigh's arrival, the vicar of Leamington died, and Leigh was offered the post, which he readily accepted despite his wife's reluctance. Fan loathed the idea of changing households so soon, so Fanny kept her daughter company for some months while her husband commuted to his new parish.

In 1878, Fanny gave up a rented house in London's Connaught Square to attend, in a village near Lake Como, Italy, the baptism of Ellen and Luigi Brianzoni's baby, with Macfarland standing as godfather. A lifelong opponent of Catholicism, Fanny noted with pleasure that Ellen had requested a Protestant ceremony, a sure sign of her former employer's influence. Despite Kemble's abiding affection for Italy, she disdained Catholic ritual and especially scorned Anglican converts to the Roman faith.

That summer, Kemble took full advantage of England's proximity to the Continent. She spent many pleasant days touring Switzerland with Arthur and Mary Anne Malkin.

During the autumn of that year Kemble drifted, with no fixed residence. When her daughter finally moved household to Leamington, Fanny often kept her company, as the vicar's work frequently took him away from home. It was at Leamington that she learned of Harriet St. Leger's death. Though not unexpected, the loss of her lifelong friend was a terrible blow. Following a subdued excursion to Paris in November, and another Christmas with the Leigh family, Fanny set out for London alone.

By February 1879, she was living at Queen Anne's Mansions, which

Henry James, the expatriate American author,
became one of Kemble's closest friends during the last
twenty years of her life.

she described to Sally Cleveland as "comfortable & convenient," being close to St. James's Park and Westminster Abbey. She added that her fourth-floor apartment had what "the Irish call an *allevator* & the English a *Lift* so that you need not bring your wings to come to me."

Her fixed residence in London was a welcome turn of events for Henry James, who took to calling on her at least once a week. He declared to his mother: "She is certainly one of the women I know whom I like best. . . . she is like a straight deep cistern without a cover, or even sometimes a bucket into which, as a mode of intercourse, one must tumble with a splash."

Her pages seemed to have the same inviting clarity as her conversation, demonstrating her vivid talent for dialogue. Of Fanny's new memoir, *Records of a Girlhood,* published in the fall of 1878, James wrote to his sister: "Her book (it will probably amuse you to learn) has been quite an *immense* success here and has brought her considerable money; but she cares no more for it—for the book and the success— than for the sole of her shoe. She hasn't read a single notice of it." Kemble might have been indifferent to reviews, but James knew her well enough to know she was *not* indifferent to the financial gains such enthusiasm afforded.

In 1879, before her usual summer journey to Switzerland, Kemble joined Adelaide on a family seaside holiday in England. Although Adelaide was loyal to Fanny in public, in private their quarrels could not be contained. Kemble made much in her journal over Adelaide's disapproval of her separation from her children, and the lengths to which Fanny felt her sister had gone to prevent the Butlers' divorce. Further, they maintained a bitter rivalry, intensified by proximity.

Dozens of family intimates commented on the warmth between the sisters, but the more astute Henry James observed, "These two ladies don't love each other and I may possibly have some fresh sensations as a peace-maker." That holiday, however, he found both sisters in fine form, declaring: "One might have worse fortune than to sit and talk with Mrs. Kemble and her [Adelaide] together, for the talk of each is first rate and each is such a distinguished 'personality': Mrs. S. has not the magnificent integrity of my sublime Fanny—but she plays round her sister's rugged mefiance like a musical thunderstorm."

As it happened, the presence of Nellie and Algernon Sartoris— whose marriage Fanny had opposed—cast a pall over the festivities. Nellie Grant Sartoris, according to James, was "as sweet and amiable (and almost as pretty) as she is uncultivated—which is saying an immense deal." Adelaide, he said, charitably blamed her daughter-in-law's shortcomings on Nellie's mother, who had left "such excellent soil so perfectly untilled." In a deliciously conspiratorial aside, James added: "(She speaks of course only privately of this—*please repeat it to no one.*)" He felt freer to disclose the details of less closely held gossip: that Algernon had become a hopeless drunk, an embarrassment to the family, that care for Nellie and her children was shouldered by her in-laws.

James found himself so smitten by Kemble that he rose to her defense against any criticism. "You mustn't judge her by her indifferent book [*Records of a Girlhood*]," he chided his mother. Her memoir, he proclaimed, "is no more about her than a pudding she might make." He was clearly trying to placate his mother, at the expense of his enormous regard for Fanny.

James's constant championing of Kemble's cause inadvertently produced a rivalry with another of his confidantes, Grace Norton of Boston, to whom he wrote, "I have a sort of notion you don't like her; but you would if you knew her better. She is to my mind the first woman in London, and is more over one of the consolations of my life." In a flourish of diplomacy, James suggested that Kemble reigned supreme only in England—implying that Norton could claim the land across the Atlantic.

In June 1879, Kemble traveled to Switzerland, as she did every summer. While still abroad, she learned sorrowfully of her sister's sudden and unexpected death on August 4. She was doubtless grateful that the two had recently spent such a long and pleasant time together on holiday. The loss of both her closest friend and her younger sister within the same twelve months weighed heavily on Fanny as her seventieth birthday approached.

Kemble returned to England dejected. Adding to her melancholy were worries over Fan's diminished state. In mid-September Fanny dashed off an apologetic note to Sally Cleveland: she would be away from London during Cleveland's upcoming visit, because "[Fan's] condition just now makes me cruelly anxious about her for she is again expecting her confinement and has written to me to go to her & I do."

Memories of her infant son's harrowing birth and his subsequent burial in Georgia haunted Fan Butler Leigh. Kemble spent several weeks in Leamington, ministering to her fretful daughter, calming her son-in-law, and doting on granddaughter Alice. On November 2, a healthy baby boy was born. Fanny confided to her friend Sally that much of the anxiety in the weeks leading up to the birth was due to the fact that the child's arrival had been miscalculated by a month.

Fan and James planned to christen the child Pierce Butler Leigh despite the loss of their first son, to whom they had given the same name. When they refused Kemble's entreaties to name the child William Shakespeare Leigh, Fanny complained bitterly: "I cannot be present to hear the child so baptized & can only pray God to avert from it the evil omen of such a name."

Kemble dwelt on the fact that not only Fan but also her husband's mother and brother had buried sons named for Major Pierce Butler. Her superstitious foreboding provoked in Fan an inconsolable rage, and her refusal to attend the christening precipitated a breach between mother and daughter that perhaps never completely healed.

Tragically, young Pierce contracted a skin disorder and died in 1880, months before his first birthday. Fan Butler Leigh couldn't bear the possibility that her mother's warnings might not have been pure nonsense. Nevertheless, Fanny loyally spent Christmas in 1880 with her grief-stricken daughter while James Leigh was abroad. She had arrived to find Fan ill and wan, suffering from a persistent cough. Equally worrisome were Alice's "pale cheeks & hollow eyes."

Fan's mental health was deteriorating, too, alarming Sarah Wister—perhaps all the more because Fan's crumbling spirits mirrored her own increasing malaise. James Leigh's presence in America strengthened Sarah's resolve to speak her mind to her sister. In December 1880 she confessed to Fan: "For over a year I have thought yr. letters hardly those of a person in their right mind; even before the little boy's birth, before your pregnancy." Fan's "sense of universal grievance," Sarah wrote, showed that her "mind was off its balance." Sarah sternly warned Fan: "if any such terrible consequence shd overtake you there will be nobody to blame but yr.self." She ended her letter with an apology: "If I have been so unfortunate as to wound or offend you in this letter it is most unintentional."

This was written at a time when Sarah herself felt she was slipping from ennui into mental disorder; in 1881 she entered a two-year depression. She later referred to this episode as a breakdown followed by a long period of recovery.

In 1881 Fan's fragile mental state was further shaken by the news that her mother planned yet another installment of her memoir. In her first book to be published by Richard Bentley, *Records of a Girlhood* (1879), she was reluctant to extend the material beyond her decision to go onstage. But at Bentley's gentle and persuasive urging, Kemble included journal entries and commentary covering the period up until her marriage. She discreetly closed with the line, "I was married in Philadelphia on the 7th of June 1834 to Mr. Pierce Butler, of that city."

When it came time for a second installment, covering her marriage and subsequent difficulties, Kemble was reluctant to publish and several times balked. In March 1881, Kemble was firm in her plans to publish a next volume, to the point of bickering with Bentley over the title. She wanted the book to be called "Old Woman's Gossip," after her first magazine series, while he preferred "Records of Womanhood," to capitalize on the success of *Records of a Girlhood*. Kemble imperiously dismissed this suggestion: "There is no record of my womanhood in what you are about to publish or anything that I shall ever publish."

Fan was adamant that her mother's literary reminiscences not move beyond her wedding day, so much so that she decided to take any indication otherwise as an open declaration of war. Since her father was unable to defend himself from the grave, it would be up to Fan to take up his cause, which she did on May 1, 1881, in the form of a stinging rebuke:

My dearest Mother

You have said over & over again that you thought people most unjustified in writing personal reminiscences of others which would be painful to their relations and friends. Then how come you think of writing about a person no longer alive whose memory is sacred & honored by his children & whom what you wrote would give the greatest pain and those children yours too! Does being their mother give you the right to wound and distress them? You have also said several times that you would not publish your memoirs after your marriage. . . . Why have you changed your mind about our right to express an opinion as to whether or not we should like it published[?] . . . I have never lost in the least degree by the feeling of bitterness I have always felt about the publication of your first Southern book wh. nothing would ever induce me to have it in the house. . . . I never can forgive it . . . any mention you make of him or your life in America which treats the time you were living with him as his wife must be intensely painful to me. I implore you not to alienate my affection from you entirely by doing it.

Your loving daughter
F.

Kemble responded tersely: "My dear Fanny, I can only acknowledge your letter, I cannot answer it otherwise than by saying that I must myself be the judge of what I think to write and publish and of course accept the consequences of doing so."

For Fanny it must have been all too galling to return to this familiar standoff. After she had endured so many years of her husband's attempts at censorship, her headstrong daughter was doing the same in

his stead. Fan solicited her sister's support in this campaign against their mother, complaining: "If she repeats her Southern experiences or in any way alludes to her married relations I do not think I can ever see or speak to her again." She sniped uncharitably that "the success of her first book [*sic*; Fan meant *Records of a Girlhood*] has so aroused her vanity and love of notoriety that the desire to keep herself before the public is irresistible."

In fact, Kemble was convinced that published accounts of her private doings were inevitable, as much because of the long public life of the Kemble family as because of her own celebrity. She felt it was her right and responsibility to personally edit and annotate her journal entries and letters, declaring that "only such portions as I thought would give less pains and offence to everyone" would find their way into print. However, surviving correspondence indicates that Kemble did not ignore her daughter's pleas entirely. Fanny keenly felt her responsibility to the living persons discussed in her published writings. When Bentley requested that she restore names where she had used initials and dashes to disguise identity, she refused: "I do not wish my friend Miss St. Leger's *name* inserted—it is clearly indicated by the place of her residence etc. I thought at first there would be no objection to the filling in of all the initials, but I think I would rather not have them indiscriminently [*sic*] filled in."

Certainly Kemble's defense of her actions is somewhat disingenuous. After all, she had burnt letters between herself and Harriet St. Leger dealing with the most painful aspects of her marriage and divorce. She had already expunged the record in many ways. Was it not possible to have simply kept all personal and family material out of print? If Kemble had so desired, it would have been done, as Fan well knew.

As a young woman, Kemble offered judgmental, even snide assessments dashed off in haste and regretted at length. Ever conscious of her youthful missteps, she indicated to Henry James that the editing "nauseated" her, and that it was difficult going: the book was "coming

Tombstone of James Hamilton Couper on St. Simon's Island.

through the Press like glue." She was extremely worried about her family's and the public's responses to this memoir.

In 1881, Henry James wrote encouragingly from France, "I am afraid you have been having a foggy life, but I trust that is the worst. You will soon be out of your tunnel—." She missed him as she endured the painful interlace of domestic discord and professional toil. That same year, Fanny had to move out of Queen Anne's Mansions because of the building's poor management. She was lucky enough to be able to lease a house in Hereford Square, a lovely place owned by Mary Lloyd, the companion of her great friend Frances Cobbe, the writer and feminist.

To have an inexpensive rental in Hereford Square was a comfort and a godsend. Appalled by Kemble's wanderings, James commented, "The incongruity of this hotel life for a person of her ripe habits is almost grotesque." But he recognized that economizing as much as wanderlust dictated his dear friend's living conditions.

In January 1882 Kemble consulted with Bentley on the possibility of withdrawing the manuscript for her next book: "it was not written for publication & contains entirely private matter relating not only to my own affairs but to those of Mr. Butler, of my father and of my sister." (Her daughters are notably omitted from the formula.) But once again, even though prudent cutting followed, Bentley's will prevailed.

Her daughter's strenuous objections notwithstanding, Fanny Kemble published *Records of Later Life* in 1882. She had removed as many personal references as she could, even masking identities, perhaps to mollify Fan; and perhaps Fan recognized and appreciated these minor concessions, for despite her threats, contact did not cease between the two. Fanny still spent a good deal of time in Leamington with the Leighs; she was especially fond of her granddaughter. In May 1882, she commented on the enjoyable sights of the spring and her daughter in bloom.

This installment of her memoirs brought Kemble even greater fame and recognition, especially with a younger generation of readers and fans. Reviewers commented on her contact with famous persons on both sides of the Atlantic; on her brilliant insight into matters literary and political; on the way in which her voice—approaching legendary status—recalled a bygone era. Kemble was naturally flattered. Although she claimed not to read reviews, she did correspond with admiring new readers.

But Fan had not forgotten her father's trampled memory, and planned what she thought a fitting revenge. She hoped to overshadow her mother's memoir with a book of her own, a testimonial to her father's life and legacy.

Fan's provocative text, *Ten Years on a Georgian Plantation Since the*

War (1883), was intended as a literary and historical counterpoint to her mother's Georgian journal, an alternative vision of life in the Sea Islands. Fan emphasized that her mother's fleeting visit to the place lasted just a few months, while her own accumulated knowledge was gained from a decade's labors on the plantation. Leigh disregarded the fact that her own book dealt with Georgia during Reconstruction, decades after the period her mother had described.

Ten Years overflowed with formulaic sentimental scenes of a type common among plantation memoirs written during this period. Leigh described the funeral of James Couper (who had been a favorite of Fanny Kemble's):

> The steps of the church were broken down, so we had to walk up a plank to get in; the roof was fallen in so that the sun streamed down on our heads; while the seats were all cut up and marked with the names of Northern soldiers who had been quartered there during the war. The graveyard was so overgrown with weeds and bushes, and tangled with cobweb like grey moss, that we had difficulty in making our way through to the freshly dug grave.

Equally familiar was Fan's didactic take on the politics of the region. "Standing there I said to myself, 'Some day justice will be done, and the Truth shall be heard above the political din of slander and lies and the Northern people shall see things as they are, and not through the dark veil of envy, hatred and malice.'"

Particularly in her "Addenda," daughter took direct aim at mother: "The question whether slavery is or is not a moral wrong I do not wish or intend to discuss. . . . I doubt our slaves being willing to change places with the free English labourer of those days [the 1820s] had the change been offered him. . . . they [slaves] did not suffer under the system [slavery] or regard it with the horror they were supposed to do by all the advocates of abolition."

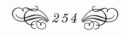

Leigh described in detail how under the care of slavemasters African Americans were able to eschew the free laborer's struggle for subsistence, and she offered pointed and repeated claims of white racial superiority. She concluded her book with a familiar neo-Confederate refrain: emancipation freed the owners from the "terrible load of responsibility which slavery entailed."

Fan believed that her eyewitness account of life on her St. Simon's plantations, supported by antebellum letters and other documentation, could undermine her mother's resonant portrait of two races straining to coexist. But both volumes were extremely partisan. One intimate of the two women complained that Fanny Kemble thought all the South's problems stemmed from slavery, while Fan Leigh believed all the problems of the South were created by African Americans. Regardless, Fan Leigh's book did little damage to Kemble's reputation. A later critic commented that to contrast Fan's book with her mother's was to compare *The Swiss Family Robinson* to *Wuthering Heights*.

Perhaps it was this "inferiority" and the poor response to Leigh's volume that allowed Fanny Kemble to ignore her daughter's attack. If she felt wounded, she never indicated it in any extant correspondence or commentary. In any case, Fanny's proud adamancy that writing was an individual's right to free expression offered her little latitude to ask her daughter to modify her manuscript.

Perhaps Kemble was additionally motivated by the benevolence that comes from personal good fortune. In 1882 she had finally published her *Notes on Some of Shakespeare's Plays,* a compilation of essays and reviews she had undertaken over the years. Bentley also brought out a new edition of her collected poems (they included many unambiguous expressions of her marital discord, appearing in print for the first time).

But this seemingly boundless productivity came at a high cost. In February 1884, Henry James reported to his sister that he found Fanny "more broken" than he had ever seen her, robbed of her characteristic vigor by age and infirmity. By her November birthday, she complained: "If one will persist in living to seventy five, one surely will find one's *intimacy* is with death, not life."

Yet Kemble's indomitable spirit renewed itself and her health improved as she made her annual pilgrimage to Switzerland. Henry James reported jubilantly in 1885, "Mrs. Kemble is wonderfully well this year, and (in conversation) full of action and passion. She sings, spouts, dances (almost), gives imitations and says fifty good things a minute."

In February 1887, James complained from Venice to Sarah Wister that it had been three months since he had seen her mother. He noted that during their last visit—an autumn week in London—"she was in a very quiet, comfortable frame." James reiterated his special fondness for Kemble: "I am so attached to her and my periodical visits to her, of an evening, have become after so many years, so much a part of my life—that the interruption of them really operates as a drawback and loss to me, whenever I come abroad."

Later in the summer of 1887, James was reunited with Kemble in Italy, where the two spent a week on Lago Maggiore. He commented to Grace Norton that Kemble now resembled an "extinct volcano," because she was so "very easy and delightful to dwell with."

Later in the summer, Kemble went mountain climbing in the Alps with Sarah. At seven thousand feet up Mount Eggishorn, she found herself unable to breathe, and had to return to the base. And although it was Sarah's ill health, rather than her seventy-seven-year-old mother's, that sent them to a Swiss spa, where they both took the waters in August, Kemble knew this trip to Switzerland might be her last. If she could no longer be the woman who "sang in the mountains," she did not want to remain silently behind in the valleys. In fact, she made her last visit to Switzerland two years later, in the summer of 1889, and it was with sadness that she returned to England that fall.

All through 1889 Kemble was being pressed by Bentley to produce yet more volumes of memoir, as the public's appetite seemed insatiable. Despite the income and acclaim it would afford her, plowing through her remaining correspondence to carve out another volume of reminiscences seemed a dreary prospect. Kemble consented to consider the project only on condition that Bentley survey the raw material and find it to his liking; otherwise it would be "very tiresome" to continue. According to their agreement, Kemble turned over stacks of her collected letters, telling Bentley, "pray believe once and for all that your entire rejection of the Mss. will not cause me the slightest annoyance."

The material must have satisfied Bentley, for by early the following year he had received a manuscript from Kemble. However, it was too short to publish. She gave him some additional letters—her correspondence with Arthur Malkin—and told him to print them "where you please and how you please." By early 1890, she had little interest in the outcome and told him he could do whatever he wanted short of "adding to them any thing not written by me." She had washed her hands of the project; Bentley was unable to convince her even to offer clues concerning undated material. As a result, these last two volumes of memoir, entitled *Further Records* (1890), are a disappointing hodgepodge, clearly inferior to previous installments. Indeed, many of the dates are wrong, so that the work is unreliable even as a record of Kemble's activities.

Yet it was not advancing age that had soured Kemble's interest in her memoirs. She had not abandoned literary ambition but rather had turned her limited energies toward a different kind of writing. In 1889, she published *The Adventures of Mr. John Timothy Homespun in Switzerland,* a labor of love in honor of her beloved Alps. She claimed this light, cheerful piece was a kind of adult fairy tale, "stolen from the French." But Kemble added the American heroine Miss Scattergold and many other delightful transatlantic touches.

Scattergold, hotly pursued by British suitors, shows the worst traits of the nouveau riche on the Grand Tour. In many ways this lighthearted treatment of European tourism was Kemble's tribute to her past. She cherished the bygone era of Swiss travel, with its emphasis on taste and refinement, and mourned its replacement by brassy commercialism, by trends and vogue, which bore no relation to the love of nature Kemble and her Alpine circle shared. Retired from climbing, she turned to satire to ease her loss. Kemble's parody demonstrated her flair for comedy, inherited, she believed, from her Swiss forebears, most notably her mother.

When Kemble's health finally began to deteriorate, she moved in permanently with Fan. Sarah commented sympathetically during an 1889 visit to England: "I found a change for wh. her letters had not in the least prepared me. I found a childish old woman . . . No longer a rational being. Yet I pity her so much that I feel it easier to get on with her than ever before."

Socializing became increasingly difficult, for Kemble grew deafer year by year and had to use an ear trumpet. As early as 1874 she had confessed that she tried not to read at night, "afraid of using up my remains of eyesight." Even though her vision was worsening, fifteen years later Kemble still had not given up on writing. Indeed, in her late seventies, she began working on a full-length novel.

She published *Far Away and Long Ago* in 1889. As Henry James remarked, "To write one's first novel at the age of eighty is a thing which could have happened only to a woman who has done everything, all her life, just exactly as others *don't*." This achievement was indeed amazing, regardless of the book's critical shortcomings.

Like most of Kemble's writing, *Far Away and Long Ago* is full of rich, descriptive prose. The story is set in the Berkshires during the early nineteenth century. The plot is melodramatic: a woman loves her sister's husband-to-be, and this forbidden love, once confessed, leads to guilt, remorse, and tragic death.

In many ways the story is reminiscent of *The Scarlet Letter;* coincidentally, Nathaniel Hawthorne had been Fanny's tenant in Lenox. Her plot is extremely contrived and the protagonists are not even as fully drawn as her stage characters. Nevertheless, as James suggested, she was a remarkable woman, having tried her hand at a novel before deciding to lay down her pen once and for all.

After the age of eighty, Kemble felt unable to fulfill her responsibilities as a correspondent, much less pursue her literary career. Fanny was attended in her infirmity by her granddaughter Alice, who was a devoted companion. But as her strength declined and she became housebound, confined to a wheelchair or sofa, Kemble required more constant supervision.

In 1891 Ellen Brianzoni, who had never lost touch with her former mistress, returned to England to care for Kemble. Ellen managed all of Kemble's personal affairs, took dictation, and handled Fanny's correspondence. Henry James was still a faithful visitor, enjoying outdoor excursions with Fanny and her Scottish terrier, Romp. But increasingly Kemble was able to move only between couch and bed. This invalid's migration was quite a diminishment for a woman who had once made annual hikes up the Alps.

Kemble felt trapped in her daughter's house, challenged by her confinement. James wrote to Sarah Wister that Kemble told him "it is rather a melancholy mistake in this uncertain life of ours to have founded oneself on so many rigidities and rules." She had detested sickness and dreaded this predicament, being nursed as an invalid, but Ellen's steady care eased her dismay.

In 1880 James had observed, "She always talks as if she were going to die the next month, but fortunately her previsions are not realized, and every now and then she has explosions of vitality." Now, over a decade later, vitality was a fading memory for Kemble. Her mind remained clear, even as her vision was clouding and her hearing faded. Communication, for this great communicator, became more and more difficult, making Kemble an unhappy prisoner within her slowly wasting body. She became incapable of meeting any social obligations, and by 1892 finally made her peace with the inevitability of death.

In the 1860s, she had written emphatically to Harriet St. Leger that she did not wish her children to be present at her deathbed. Perhaps this was because she remembered caring for her aunt Dall during Dall's final illness. Dall had steadfastly looked after Fanny throughout her youth, and she was grateful to be of comfort in her aunt's last days; at the same time, nursing a dying loved one had been a cruel psychological ordeal, and she wanted her daughters "spared the useless pain of seeing me die."

Kemble was granted her wish. Fan was abroad visiting Sarah Wister when Fanny died, on January 15, 1893.

Ellen Brianzoni, present at the end, lovingly described Kemble's last moments:

> My dear mistress . . . passed away peacefully on Sunday night as I was putting her to bed about half past eleven. . . . She was tired of life and longed to go, even I cannot wish for her back, but oh, and it was so sudden, she could not have suffered.

James Leigh and Alice made funeral arrangements, assisted by the solicitous Henry James. On January 20, Fanny Kemble was buried in Kensal Green Cemetery. James conveyed his emotions to Sarah Wister:

> I stood by your mother's grave this morning—a soft, kind, balmy day, with your brother-in-law and tall pale handsome Alice, and a few of those of her friends who have survived her, and were in town—and were not ill—as all the world lately has been. The number is inevitably small—for of her generation she is the last. . . . She was laid in the same earth as her father—and buried under a mountain of flowers. . . . it seemed quite like the end of some reign or the fall of some empire. . . . She was very touching in her infirmity all these last months—and yet with her wonderful air of smoldering embers under ashes.

. . .

Although Kemble's fame had grown out of her theatrical debut more than sixty years before, many formed their primary memories of her from the lavish eulogies that poured forth after her passing. James himself composed perhaps one of the most memorable tributes, a forty-page essay in *Temple Bar:* "Her endowment was so rich, her spirit so proud, her temper so high that, as she was an immense success, they made her indifference and her eccentricity magnificent."

Whether costumed in a full-scale stage production, or reading aloud in a drawing room with her voice as her only prop, Kemble never failed to mesmerize her audience. James celebrated her luxurious habit of writing just as she talked, providing a vibrant, compelling record of she who "reanimated the old drawing rooms, relighted the old lamps, re-tuned the old pianos." His sincerest hope was that her literary talents would receive more recognition over time. He recalled her *Journal of America,* published in 1835, as "still one of the freshest pictures of what is called a 'brilliant girl' that our literature possesses." The memories of that brilliance would inspire future generations of performers, writers, readers, and thinkers, daring them to emulate her wit and courage.

Nearly a decade later, still mourning the memory of his departed friend, James wrote forlornly to Sarah Wister: "I sit *alone* in the evenings with the lamp and the fire and the ticking of the clock think-ing of nothing less than of your mother."

EPILOGUE

On a lonely stretch of Georgia highway just north of Darien, a huge brick tower—the vine-choked chimney of an abandoned rice mill—rises up from the wetlands hundreds of feet. An impressive totem, this large silent beacon beckons the imagination of all who pass by. Just off the roadside, by the river crossing, a brass plaque proclaims the historical significance of this forsaken place: "FAMOUS BUTLER AUTHORS: Pierce Butler and his daughter Frances, who shared his interest in the South, returned to Butler Island in 1867. . . . She wrote a book, 'Ten Years on a Georgian Plantation.'" The sign goes on to identify her nephew, Owen Wister, as the author of *The Virginian*. Fanny Kemble's name is conspicuously absent.

Henry James had suggested that Kemble's death in 1893 marked the end of an era, ushering in the debates over what heritage her tumultuous life and times had left. Her daughters, Sarah Butler Wister and Fan Butler Leigh, were the first to grapple with this question. Sarah tried to know her mother better by reading, for the first time, the marital exposé privately published by her father two years after the couple's infamous divorce. For her part, Fan seemed unlikely to ever forgive her mother for the intimate contents of her published works, whatever their literary value.

Her daughters' grief was complicated by a pressing legal and finan-

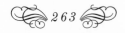

DINNER

for

MARGARET DAVIS CATE

Whose Pen has made her Famous

Oglethorpe Hotel

Nov. 24, 1930.

Oglethorpe Celery   Cannon's Point Olives

Gualquini Oyster Cocktail

Zapala Quail on Toast

Neptune Small's Yams   St Clair Lima Beans

U.S.S. Constitution Hot Rolls

Fanny Kemble Salad

Orange Sherbert Brunswick

Ebo Coffee

A 1930 dinner menu featuring "Fanny Kemble Salad," prepared for a banquet in honor of Margaret Davis Cate.

cial concern: the fate of the Butler plantations. By the end of the 1890s, the properties were in woeful disrepair, largely owing to hurricane damage sustained in 1898. Although by 1901 the sisters were in agreement that the time was right to sell, they were unable to find a buyer willing to offer a suitable price. As a result, they maintained ownership, charging former Butler slaves nominal rents to work the land. A thriving black society revolved around the church, St. Cyprian's, built by the Leighs during their residence in Georgia. Descendants of Butler slaves taught at the local black school and were prominent members of the African American coastal community.

Since the sisters' ongoing contact with these "former Butler" blacks was well known, the minister at St. Cyprian's sent a telegram on August 31, 1899, to Sarah Wister, begging for help during an outbreak of racially motivated violence. The last week of August a lynching had been planned, in retaliation for the alleged rape by a black man of a white woman—who made her accusations eight months after the alleged attack. With the allegations came threats of vigilante retribution, and a riot ensued, landing several former "Butler people" in jail. The Reverend F. W. Mann urgently asked Sarah Wister to intervene on behalf of his parishioners. She immediately contacted Georgia authorities and solicited donations from wealthy Philadelphians to pay for a legal defense, which ultimately secured acquittal for the accused rapist. Several others were convicted of rioting and served up to a year on the infamous Georgia chain gangs. But thanks to Wister's rapid intervention, no black corpses hung from trees, though this was an all too common blight on the Southern rural landscape at the turn of the century.

An appropriate buyer for the Butler lands finally came forward in 1908, the very year Sarah Wister died at Butler Place, where she had been born. Fan Butler Leigh died at home in England two years later, in 1910. Her husband had accepted the deanship of Hereford Cathedral in 1894, putting an end to her latent hope of returning to America. In her final years, however, Fan had made annual visits to

FANNY KEMBLE'S CIVIL WARS

Philadelphia; her daughter Alice was to make a pilgrimage to St. Simon's as well, in the 1920s.

Dan Wister studied music at a Paris conservatory until his health gave out in 1885. After taking a summer rest cure in Wyoming, he entered Harvard Law School, graduating in 1888. His decision to become a writer rather than practice law was supported by Sarah Wister and Fanny Kemble, but was a great disappointment to his father. Wister went on to publish an acclaimed novel, *The Virginian*, in 1902. Married to a distant cousin, Mary Channing Wister, he raised a large family, and spent the rest of his days at Butler Place, or at the family's summer home in Rhode Island, writing and living off his royalties and inheritance.

Fanny Kemble did not live to see her daughter Sarah's activism on behalf of African Americans, nor to see her grandson claim the reputation for literary fame that she had once so proudly held. In the first decades following her death, the memory of Fanny Kemble was seldom evoked outside her extended family, although she became the subject of several popular biographies between the two world wars.

The question of her historical legacy first emerged following World War II, when Georgia enacted a statewide plan to furnish markers for sites of historic importance. During the debate over how best to commemorate the former Butler plantations, it became clear that Kemble was remembered as a villain by many white Southerners. Most notable among these was the historian Margaret Davis Cate, the legendary keeper of the flame of Georgia's coastal history. In 1960, Cate contended to a visiting researcher: "The plantation people of St. Simon's need no defense. Their lives stand for what they were and there was no culture anywhere in the South that was superior."

In support of her statement, Cate dissected specific passages of *Journal of a Residence on a Georgian Plantation*, vilifying Kemble in the process. Particularly outraged over Kemble's claim that a pregnant slave woman had been whipped on a Butler plantation, Cate coun-

Fanny Kemble's grandson Owen Wister, who wrote the best-selling novel The Virginian *(1902).*

tered that the indisputable value of an unborn slave child proved this brutal scene was a fabrication—"one of Fanny's 'acts' in the drama she wrote, and based on nothing." Further, as "proof" that the Butler slaves were well treated by their masters, Cate recalled that in the 1920s, when Lady Alice Leigh (Fanny's granddaughter, who had married a distant cousin, Sir Richard Butler Leigh) returned to visit the ancestral lands, crowds of "Butler Negroes" gathered around, eager to greet her.

Cate amassed a collection of primary material and solicited letters she hoped would prove damning to Kemble's reputation. One elderly woman wrote that when she visited Fanny Kemble in London near the end of her life, Kemble confessed that she had been a "fanatic" and was lucky her husband didn't strangle her. Kemble allegedly admitted to a visitor from Georgia in 1890 that she "bitterly regretted many things I said in that book! I was a young and passionate woman."

The vigor of Cate's campaign shows that even in the middle of the twentieth century—nearly seventy-five years after Kemble's death, nearly a hundred since the publication of her Georgian journal—Kemble's writings were still generating considerable controversy. But also by the 1950s, there was a shift in the academic community in Kemble's favor, as a new generation of slavery scholars—most notably Kenneth Stampp, author of *The Peculiar Institution* (1956)—began to cite Kemble as an authority. It was the vivid intensity of her prose that attracted scholars' attention and won her a new audience. What seemed brash and even vulgar to some nineteenth-century readers appears compelling and fresh to modern eyes.

Over a century has passed since the death of Fanny Kemble, who, as the abolitionist Catharine Sedgwick recalled, was "steeped to the very lips in genius." Her life reflected quixotic and absorbing dramas, as she struggled against the boundaries drawn on both sides of the Atlantic to allow her unique voice to be heard. The passage of time has shown how the struggles of Fanny Kemble's life—between blacks and whites, Northerners and Southerners, husbands and wives, parents and children—reflect the most compelling elements of nineteenth-century history and also resonate with our own struggles, as a people and a nation, as we move into the twenty-first century.

NOTES

Preface

10   "imperative duty, knowing what I know": FAK to Harriet St. Leger, 186?, Kemble Collection, Folger Shakespeare Library.

10   "from his grave": Armstrong, *Fanny Kemble*, p. 334.

10   "make her what I call historic": James, *Essays*, p. 86.

CHAPTER ONE   Enter Fanny Kemble

19   "At last comes the moment": Kelly, *The Kemble Era*, p. 20.

19   "Nothing ever was": ibid., jacket copy.

19   "whatever qualities of mind": FAK, *Records of a Girlhood*, p. 2.

21   "The great actors": ibid., p. 7.

25   "The fame of my brother": Williamson, *Charles Kemble*, p. 37.

27   "a hopelessly ruined concern": FAK, *Records of a Girlhood*, p. 59.

30   "the sifting, examining": ibid., p. 140.

30   "exacting taste": ibid., p. 311.

31   "a clever performance": ibid., p. 135.

32   "to earn hard money": ibid., p. 137.

32   "should not have been thrown away": ibid., p. 123.

35   "The nearest period talked of": ibid., p. 193.

37   "Upon the whole": Bobbe, *Fanny Kemble*, p. 40.

37   "For our part": ibid., p. 41.

39   "I have almost a Father's interest": Marshall, *Fanny Kemble*, p. 49.

40   "From an insignificant school-girl": FAK, *Records of a Girlhood*, p. 226.

41   "a dinner party on Monday": ibid., p. 363.

41   "a bodyguard of about": ibid., p. 288.

41   "Fanny Kemble, you are": ibid., p. 82.

41   "next door to homely": Furnas, *Fanny Kemble*, p. 91.

41   "The nearer one gets": Bobbe, *Fanny Kemble*, p. 42.

42   "gipsy complexion": FAK, *Records of a Girlhood*, p. 442.

42   "strong head not to be so": ibid., p. 227.

42   "without a shrinking": ibid., p. 221.

42   "My life in London": ibid., p. 267.

43   "luxurious refinement": ibid., pp. 301–302.

43   "extremely kind to me": ibid., p. 301.

43   "It is incumbent": ibid., pp. 289–90.

46   with her beloved "Mr. C.": ibid., p. 415.

46   "While you remain single": ibid., pp. 436–37.

47   her words haunted Fanny: ibid., p. 423.

47   "Somehow I don't think": ibid., p. 397.

47   "ephemeral love": ibid., p. 374.

47   "And so I am to act Lady Macbeth!": ibid., p. 417.

47   "The house was good": ibid., p. 412.

47   "You have done it better": ibid., p. 361.

48   Meanwhile, older brother John: ibid., p. 356.

48   "lounging about the streets": ibid., p. 295.

48   "any hope of support": ibid., p. 513.

CHAPTER TWO O Brave New World

51   "I have seen": FAK, *Journal of FAK*, vol. I, p. 18.

51   to a drunken reel: ibid., pp. 27–28.

51   "We . . . sang": ibid., p. 47.

51   "lighted shop-windows": FAK, *Records of a Girlhood*, p. 535.

52   "Your washerwoman sits": FAK, *Journal of FAK*, vol. I, p. 103.

52   "she appears deserving": Nevins, *Diary of Philip Hone*, p. 54.

52   "These democrats": FAK, *Journal of FAK*, vol. I, p. 56.

52   shoes were too tight: ibid., pp. 60, 87.

53   "Her fault appears to be": Marshall, *Fanny Kemble*, p. 80.

53   "a washed-out man": FAK, *Journal of FAK*, p. 92.

53   "My days are passed": *Records of a Girlhood*, p. 525.

53   "intensity and a truth": Furnas, *Fanny Kemble*, pp. 103–104.

53   "I have never witnessed": Nevins, *Diary of Philip Hone*, p. 77.

54   "Fanny Kemble!": Armstrong, *Fanny Kemble*, p. 155.

54   And even gardeners: Bridgeman, *The American Gardener's Assistant*, p. 84.

54   The play became so popular: Dudden, *Women in the American Theater*, p. 198.

54   "to hiss us off": FAK, *Journal of FAK*, vol. I, p. 112.

54   "a perfect shower of saliva": ibid., p. 138.

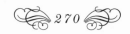

54   "bumping, thumping, jumping": ibid., p. 131.

54   "The town is perfect silence": ibid.

54   "bewitching Newfoundland puppy": ibid., p. 139.

55   "strongly drawn as Europe": Weigley, *Philadelphia*, p. 330.

56   "He is, it seems": FAK, *Journal of FAK*, vol. I, p. 153.

56   "offered to ride": ibid.

57   "a comfortless, handsome looking": FAK, *Journal of FAK*, vol. II, p. 92.

59   "He talked about South Carolina": ibid., p. 96.

59   "I have never seen": Story, *Life and Letters of Joseph Story*, p. 116.

61   "She is the most captivating": Fanny Wister, *Fanny, the American Kemble*, p. 113.

61   "Their visit to this city": ibid., p. 115.

62   "The houses are like English houses": FAK, *Journal of FAK*, vol. II, p. 153.

62   "decidedly the best company": ibid., p. 132.

62   "grow on every bush": ibid., p. 152.

62   "I scarcely ever go by": Furnas, *Fanny Kemble*, p. 126.

63   "Pierce Butler, a man": Marshall, *Fanny Kemble*, p. 99.

64   "Mr. [Trelawny] is sun burnt": FAK, *Journal of FAK*, vol. II, p. 173.

65   "What a savage": ibid., p. 178.

67   "came pouring down": ibid., p. 188.

68   "Butler is a gentlemanly man": Furnas, *Fanny Kemble*, p. 144.

69   "cautions which reached me": Fanny Wister, *Fanny, the American Kemble*, p. 140.

69   "Do let me know": Furnas, *Fanny Kemble*, p. 140.

69   "The whole world": ibid., p. 130.

69   "Her character": ibid.

70   "How happy Fanny's friends": ibid., p. 143.

70   "I did not expect": Fanny Wister, *Fanny, the American Kemble*, p. 135.

70   "I shall not return": FAK, *Records of a Girlhood*, p. 586.

71   "We cannot like those": Fanny Wister, *Fanny, the American Kemble*, p. 136.

71   "I will now tell you": FAK to Sarah Perkins, 31 May 1834. Cleveland Letters, Berg Collection, New York Public Library.

71   "I must tell you how": Fanny Wister, *Fanny, the American Kemble*, p. 139.

72   "Pierce has promised": ibid.

72   "could not consent to the separation": Furnas, *Fanny Kemble*, p. 145.

73   "I do not think": FAK, *Records of a Girlhood*, p. 135.

CHAPTER THREE Not So Somber Airs

75   "fortune and fame": FAK, *Records of a Girlhood*, pp. 436–37.

75   "a mere idler": Furnas, *Fanny Kemble*, pp. 121–22.

75   The brothers' maternal grandfather: Major Pierce Butler passed over his own son in favor of his favorite daughter's three male heirs. He offered them the

bulk of his inheritance if they would abandon their father's name (Mease) in favor of Butler.

77   John and Gabriella: Pierce had allowed his brother to split the major's estate with him although John had delayed changing his name beyond the legal deadline to share the inheritance.

77   "a sense of imagined oppression": Butler, *Mr. Butler's Statement,* p. 12.

77   "The three golden threads": Gilman, *Recollections of a Southern Matron,* p. 257.

79   "This farewell": Butler, *Mr. Butler's Statement,* p. 9.

80   "Human companionship": Marshall, *Fanny Kemble,* p. 109.

80   "Persuade your lover": FAK to Sarah Perkins, 5 May 1835. Cleveland Letters, Berg Collection, New York Public Library.

81   "We are fortunately different": Marshall, *Fanny Kemble,* p. 109.

81   "I cannot believe": FAK, *Records of Later Life,* pp. 23–25.

81   "I am myself": FAK to Sarah Perkins, 14 June 1835. Cleveland Letters, Berg Collection, New York Public Library.

81   "I was at first": FAK, *Records of Later Life,* p. 25.

81   "Every chink and cranny": ibid.

82   "a very fine strong": FAK to Sarah Perkins, n.d. (June 1835). Cleveland Letters, Berg Collection, New York Public Library.

82   "The manner in which": ibid.

82   "I am weary": Butler, *Mr. Butler's Statement,* p. 26.

83   "long and vehement treatise": FAK, *Records of Later Life,* p. 22.

83   "Northern people pursue": Furnas, *Fanny Kemble,* p. 177.

84   sold eight hundred copies: ibid., p. 162.

84   "In correctness of taste": *North American Review,* July 1835.

84   "A female, and a young one": *Southern Literary Messenger,* May 1835.

84   "accept this very mediocre": FAK, *Journal of FAK,* pp. 154–55.

84   "foolish and fearless": Furnas, *Fanny Kemble,* p. 161.

84   "The city is in an uproar": ibid., p. 162.

86   "one of the most deplorable": ibid., p. 164.

86   "very pertly": Esher, *Girlhood of Queen Victoria,* p. 126.

86   "The refined state": Bryan, *The Book of Berkshire,* p. 39.

87   "our most truthful novelist": Mellow, *Nathaniel Hawthorne,* p. 323.

88   "The cross roads": FAK, *Records of Later Life,* p. 24.

88   "her little brow": FAK to Sarah Perkins Cleveland, 20 April 1836. Cleveland Letters, Berg Collection, New York Public Library.

88   "would require": FAK to Sarah Perkins Cleveland, 26 May 1836. Cleveland Letters, Berg Collection, New York Public Library.

88   "Though people occasionally": FAK, *Records of Later Life,* pp. 3–4.

88   Her husband would not allow: FAK to Sarah Perkins Cleveland, 26 May 1836. Cleveland Letters, Berg Collection, New York Public Library.

89   "when ladies marry": Buckingham, *Slave States of America,* vol. II, p. 124.

89   "such a nuisance that": FAK, *Records of Later Life,* p. 573.

89   "Gone, dear Fanny": Furnas, *Fanny Kemble,* p. 181.

CHAPTER FOUR Transatlantic Currents

92   "dram he has taken nightly": FAK, *Records of Later Life,* p. 47.

92   "My father bore it all": ibid.

92   "brilliant society": ibid., p. 46.

93   "I have been at Ascot": FAK to Sarah Perkins Cleveland, 8 June 1837. Cleveland Letters, Berg Collection, New York Public Library.

93   "sought me": FAK, *Records of Later Life,* p. 291.

94   "the only good thing": Armstrong, *Fanny Kemble,* p. 200.

94   "I find London more": FAK, *Records of Later Life,* p. 48.

95   "The Queen's voice": ibid., p. 54.

95   "The turmoil and dissipation": ibid., p. 49.

95   "I should be": ibid., p. 81.

95   "My return": FAK to Sarah Perkins Cleveland, 8 June 1837. Cleveland Letters, Berg Collection, New York Public Library.

96   "It has led me": Butler, *Mr. Butler's Statement,* p. 11.

97   "It has been": FAK to Sarah Perkins Cleveland, 12 November 1837. Cleveland Letters, Berg Collection, New York Public Library.

98   "Spoke of Pierce Butler": Wainwright, *A Philadelphia Perspective,* p. 10.

98   "I like Pierce": Furnas, *Fanny Kemble,* p. 344.

99   "There is abundance": Butler, *Mr. Butler's Statement,* p. 27.

99   "They use a double-barreled": FAK, *Records of Later Life,* p. 82.

99   "invalid all winter": FAK to Sarah Perkins Cleveland, 24 March 1838. Cleveland Letters, Berg Collection, New York Public Library.

101   "Mr. Hone, I cannot express": Nevins, *Diary of Philip Hone,* p. 141.

101   "In part this is my own fault": Butler, *Mr. Butler's Statement,* p. 27.

106   "The steward of our ship": FAK, *Records of a Girlhood,* p. 543.

106   "several of the black women": FAK, *Journal of FAK,* vol. I, p. 66.

107   "Philadelphia appears": Weigley, *Philadelphia,* p. 353.

108   "everything southern was exalted": ibid.

108   "Our fellow citizens": FAK, *Records of Later Life,* p. 22.

110   "I am sitting on the veranda": ibid., p. 89.

112   "Whether I shall die": FAK to Sarah Perkins Cleveland, 30 October 1838. Cleveland Letters, Berg Collection, New York Public Library.

CHAPTER FIVE The War Over Slavery

115   Slaves sent: Presley, *Dr. Bullie's Notes,* p. 154.

115   "Butler cotton": "Sea Island cotton," both in this country and abroad, still signifies high quality and premium price.

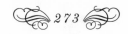

115 For his courage: This cup is on display at the Richard-Owens-Thomas House in Savannah.

117 "preferred washing to eating": Scott, *Journal of a Residence on a Georgian Plantation,* p. 24.

117 "The sight of them": ibid., p. 17.

117 "It is so very long": ibid., p. 36.

119 "the measured rush": FAK, *Journal of a Residence on a Georgian Plantation,* p. 177.

119 "thick and close": ibid., p. 184.

119 "I should like": ibid., p. 165.

119 "people on this plantation": ibid., p. 190.

119 "wash my soul": ibid., p. 193.

119 "One after another": ibid., p. 176.

119 "Sometimes at the end": ibid.

120 "Whether I be": ibid., p. 73.

120 "How horridly brutish": ibid., p. 144.

120 "there is not a girl": ibid., p. 58.

120 "A woman thinks": ibid., p. 60.

120 "Mr. [Butler] was called out": ibid., p. 79.

121 "I was observing": ibid., pp. 57–58.

121 "I can state truly": Presley, *Dr. Bullie's Notes,* p. 153.

121 "utter ignorance": ibid., p. 150.

121 "Perhaps he is afraid": FAK, *Journal of a Residence on a Georgian Plantation,* p. 171.

121 "I pity them": ibid., p. 156.

122 "perfectly consistent": ibid., p. 68.

122 "Abolition is impossible": ibid., p. 78.

123 "raised with threefold force": ibid., p. 57.

123 "this sojourn": ibid., pp. 79–80.

123 a pregnant woman tied: ibid., p. 200.

123 slaves prevented: ibid., p. 220.

123 "owners [who] have a fancy": ibid., p. 231.

123 "I do not wish": ibid., p. 199.

123 "smell any worse": ibid., p. 23.

124 "Almost every Southern planter": ibid., p. 15.

124 "A long chain": ibid., p. 104.

125 "For the last four": ibid., p. 105.

125 "I think I should die": ibid., p. 178.

126 "Fanny has had": ibid., pp. 190–91.

128 "the act of marrying": Butler, *Mr. Butler's Statement,* p. 87.

128 "'What need of intellectual": ibid., p. 31.

128 "Your mind is positively": ibid., p. 40.

129 "If I cannot have happiness": ibid., p. 46.

129 "God bless you": ibid., p. 90.

130 During the summer: FAK to Sarah Perkins Cleveland, 11 October 1840. Cleveland Letters, Berg Collection, New York Public Library.

130 "radiant with the fire": FAK, *Records of Later Life,* p. 263.

130 "Adelaide sang": Armstrong, *Fanny Kemble,* p. 257.

130 "out in search of amusement": Furnas, *Fanny Kemble,* p. 251.

130 "Now after wasting": Wilson, *Greville Diary,* vol. II, p. 547.

132 "wide and deep feeling": Stewart, *Holy Warriors,* p. 75.

132 "studied the character": Furnas, *Fanny Kemble,* p. 258.

133 "a pea jacket": Bell, *Major Butler's Legacy,* p. 300.

133 "unprepossessing": Only William McFeely suggests that Adelaide's husband may have been anything but ideal; he hints at infidelities. See William McFeely, *Grant* (New York: W. W. Norton, 1981), p. 401.

133 "Mr. Butler *thinks*": FAK to Sarah Perkins Cleveland, 2 February 1843. Cleveland Letters, Berg Collection, New York Public Library.

133 "Do not, for God's sake": *Philadelphia Public Ledger,* 4 December 1848.

133 "On my soul": Butler, *Mr. Butler's Statement,* p. 69.

133 "my heart still answers to your voice": ibid., pp. 73–74.

134 "I propose an entire separation": ibid., p. 73.

134 "I am quite satisfied": Gibbs, *Affectionately Yours,* p. 137.

134 "Anguish has come over me": FAK to Sarah Perkins Cleveland, 17 July 1843. Cleveland Letters, Berg Collection, New York Public Library.

134 "Of the discomfort": FAK, *Records of Later Life,* p. 35.

135 "On the night of Saturday": Schott, *Statement,* p. 3.

135 "never in any way": Butler, *Mr. Butler's Statement,* p. 128.

136 "There is no 'circumstance'": ibid., p. 129.

136 cease "forever" all acquaintance: ibid., p. 154.

CHAPTER SIX Fighting for Her Rights

137 "has sent me penniless": FAK to Sarah Perkins Cleveland, 10 November 1845. Cleveland Letters, Berg Collection, New York Public Library.

138 "If I want to institute": ibid

138 "Sooner than lose my children": FAK, *Year of Consolation,* vol. I, p. 118.

138 "I have a great contempt": FAK, *Records of Later Life,* p. 124.

139 "Sorrow and sin": FAK, *Year of Consolation,* vol. II, p. 6.

139 "We can hardly give": "Mrs. Butler's *Year of Consolation,*" *Living Age* (1847), p. 472.

139 "much the best account": *North American Review,* July 1847.

139 "It would be impossible": FAK, *Records of Later Life,* p. 455.

139 "I do not suppose": FAK to Sarah Perkins Cleveland, 7 April 1846. Cleveland Letters, Berg Collection, New York Public Library.

140 "This my dearest friend": FAK to Sarah Perkins Cleveland, 16 January 1847. Cleveland Letters, Berg Collection, New York Public Library.

140 "positively odious": Furnas, *Fanny Kemble*, p. 319.

140 "I hope that in spite": FAK, *Records of Later Life*, p. 486.

140 "suffered for years indeed": FAK to Sarah Perkins Cleveland, 1 June 1847. Cleveland Letters, Berg Collection, New York Public Library.

141 "chloroform as a pastime": FAK, *Records of Later Life*, p. 369.

141 "lose all self government": FAK to Sarah Perkins Cleveland, 1 June 1847. Cleveland Letters, Berg Collection, New York Public Library.

141 "mature judgement": *Illustrated London News*, 1 May 1847.

143 "left the house as quickly": FAK, *Records of Later Life*, p. 306.

143 "I have never seen": Trewin, *Journal of William Charles Macready*, p. 248.

144 "How I do loathe": FAK, *Journal of FAK*, vol. II, p. 16.

145 "The happiness of reading": FAK, *Records of a Girlhood*, p. 247.

146 "It appears to us": Grossberg, *Governing the Hearth*, p. 239.

147 "I shall be obliged": FAK to Sarah Perkins Cleveland, Lenox, 23 October 1848. Cleveland Letters, Berg Collection, New York Public Library.

147 "I really have grounds for thinking": FAK to Sarah Perkins Cleveland, November 1848. Cleveland Letters, Berg Collection, New York Public Library.

147 "I am driven half crazy": FAK to Sarah Perkins Cleveland, Lenox, 14 November 1848. Cleveland Letters, Berg Collection, New York Public Library.

148 "Upon this afternoon": FAK to Sarah Perkins Cleveland, New York City, 26 November 1848. Cleveland Letters, Berg Collection, New York Public Library.

148 "a momentary": FAK to Sarah Perkins Cleveland, London, 19 April 1848. Cleveland Letters, Berg Collection, New York Public Library.

148 "a hallucination": Marshall, *Fanny Kemble*, p. 219.

149 "Now the charge of cruelty": Presley, *Dr. Bullie's Notes*, p. 157.

149 "devotion to Miss Coleman": FAK to Sarah Perkins Cleveland, undated. Folder #33, Cleveland Letters, Berg Collection, New York Public Library.

149 "I am not without hope": FAK to Samuel Gray Ward, Saturday 11, 18??, Massachusetts Historical Society.

150 "She reads Shakespeare's plays": Furnas, *Fanny Kemble*, p. 334.

150 "I am happy to say": FAK to Sarah Perkins Cleveland, Lenox, 18 July 1849. Cleveland Letters, Berg Collection, New York Public Library.

151 "It is quite notorious": Wainwright, *A Philadelphia Perspective*, p. 210.

151 "a family which for three generations": Alderman, *Letters of James K. Paulding*, pp. 501–502.

151 "an income of fifteen hundred": FAK to Sarah Perkins Cleveland, Lenox, 18 July 1849. Cleveland Letters, Berg Collection, New York Public Library.

153 "We are not all made up": Butler, *Mr. Butler's Statement*, p. 31.

153 "She held that marriage": ibid., p. 9.

153 "It is not in the law": ibid., p. 11.

154   "was the rock that wrecked": Presley, *Dr. Bullie's Notes,* p. 157.

154   "her letters became": Butler, *Mr. Butler's Statement,* p. 187.

154   "I was intended": Furnas, *Fanny Kemble,* p. 338.

154   Joshua Fisher would continue: FAK to Joshua Fisher, London, 7 September 1850. Fanny Kemble Collection, Library of Congress.

156   "It was a hard": Marshall, *Fanny Kemble,* p. 227.

156   "to wait for the event": FAK to Joshua Fisher, 17 June 1852. Fanny Kemble Collection, Library of Congress.

156   Fisher advised her: FAK to Joshua Fisher, 20 October 1852, Fanny Kemble Collection, Library of Congress.

157   "I have had": FAK to Sarah Perkins Cleveland, Lenox, 22 June 1856. Cleveland Letters, Berg Collection, New York Public Library.

157   "My life now chiefly": ibid.

157   "Heard from Henry": Wainwright, *A Philadelphia Perspective,* p. 257.

157   "this beautiful old place": ibid., p. 277.

158   "the ruin of my girls'": FAK to Sarah Perkins Cleveland, New York, 28 December 1858. Cleveland Letters, Berg Collection, New York Public Library.

CHAPTER SEVEN Battle Cries for Freedom

159   "It is a dreadful affair": Wainwright, *A Philadelphia Perspective,* p. 317.

160   "Gang of 460 Slaves": Bell, *Major Butler's Legacy,* pp. 328–29.

161   "All the clinging ties": *New York Tribune,* March 9, 1859.

163   "They have now gas & water": Wainwright, *A Philadelphia Perspective,* p. 328.

163   "My mother was the most stimulating": Cobbs, *Owen Wister,* p. 2.

163   "blacksmith's horses": Wainwright, *A Philadelphia Perspective,* p. 356.

164   "Always liked Mrs. Kemble": ibid., p. 360.

164   "shrugged her shoulders": FAK, *Further Records,* p. 334.

164   "The southern states": ibid., p. 330.

165   "I suppose the impressions": Sarah Butler Wister to FAK, 5 February 1865. Wister Family Papers, Historical Society of Pennsylvania.

165   "of six or seven": Fanny Kemble Wister, "Sarah Butler Wister's Civil War Diary," p. 297.

165   "receive a Southerner": Frances Butler Leigh, *Ten Years,* p. 83.

165   "The country has": McPherson, *Civil War and Reconstruction,* p. 126.

165   "The United States schism": FAK, *Further Records,* pp. 330–31. Dated 8 May 1860, but more likely 1861.

167   "Butler is eager": Wainwright, *A Philadelphia Perspective,* p. 375.

167   "Odd changes": ibid., pp. 383–84.

168   "Oh how thankful I am": Fanny Kemble Wister, "Sarah Butler Wister's Civil War Diary," p. 275.

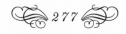

168 "standing at the window": ibid., p. 290.

168 "Practised [piano], read & drew": ibid., p. 276.

168 "even the book sellers": ibid., p. 277.

169 "still finer than any others": ibid., p. 281.

169 "Owen in a moment": ibid., pp. 288–89.

169 "I wish I could say": ibid., p. 289.

169 "Thank goodness": ibid.

170 "Half a dozen Southern": ibid., p. 290.

170 "spending two hours": ibid., p. 294.

170 "the tightness of the times": ibid.

170 "She came by Kentucky": ibid.

171 Sarah told: ibid., p. 299.

171 "Feeling that it might be": ibid., p. 302.

171 "Like mother like daughter": ibid., p. 315.

171 "would not take up arms": ibid., p. 304.

171 Owen Wister, Jr., later: Fanny Kemble Wister, *That I May Tell You*, p. 3.

172 "It is said": Wainwright, *A Philadelphia Perspective*, p. 400.

172 "Poor little thing": Fanny Kemble Wister, "Sarah Butler Wister's Civil War Diary," p. 322.

172 "The charges against": FAK, *Further Records*, p. 335.

173 "Whatever right the government": Fanny Kemble Wister, "Sarah Butler Wister's Civil War Diary," p. 324.

173 "If Fan refuses": Owen Wister to Sarah Butler Wister, 31 August 1861. Wister Family Papers, Historical Society of Pennsylvania.

173 "Perhaps if she does not": FAK, *Further Records*, p. 336.

174 "I am beginning": Owen Wister to Sarah Butler Wister, 11 August 1861. Wister Family Papers, Historical Society of Pennsylvania.

174 "Good bye my own dearest": Sarah Butler Wister to Owen Wister, 2? September 1861. Wister Family Papers, Historical Society of Pennsylvania.

174 "I long for you": Sarah Butler Wister to Owen Wister, 3 September 1861. Wister Family Papers, Historical Society of Pennsylvania.

174 "I have been haunted": Owen Wister to Sarah Butler Wister, 24 September 1861. Wister Family Papers, Historical Society of Pennsylvania.

175 "The President should": Owen Wister to Sarah Butler Wister, 13 September 1861. Wister Family Papers, Historical Society of Pennsylvania.

175 Butler "refused": Bell, *Major Butler's Legacy*, p. 350.

176 "After some bad and good": FAK, *Further Records*, p. 336.

176 "She is very enthusiastic": Wainwright, *A Philadelphia Perspective*, p. 417.

176 "We have passed the Rubicon": McPherson, *Civil War and Reconstruction*, p. 126.

176 "great satisfaction": FAK to Harriet St. Leger, n.d., 186?. Kemble Collection, Folger Shakespeare Library.

176 "Of social pleasures": Fanny Kemble Wister, *That I May Tell You,* p. 72.

177 "says little of public affairs": FAK to Harriet St. Leger, December 1862 or January 1863. Kemble Collection, Folger Shakespeare Library.

177 "last disastrous engagement": FAK to Harriet St. Leger, n.d., 186?. Kemble Collection, Folger Shakespeare Library.

177 "If there is a worse place": McPherson, *Civil War and Reconstruction,* p. 306.

177 "the hostile opinions": Wainwright, *A Philadelphia Perspective,* p. 417.

177 "I hope to God": FAK, *Further Records,* p. 336.

178 "A more startling": *Athenaeum,* 6 June 1863.

178 The Ladies' Emancipation Society: Furnas, *Fanny Kemble,* p. 403.

179 "deep, thorough and detailed": Bell, *Major Butler's Legacy,* p. 377.

179 "The book is a permanent": ibid., p. 378.

179 "Filth, squalor, cruelty": Wainwright, *A Philadelphia Perspective,* p. 456.

180 "These letters are now": ibid.

180 "I have never lost": Fanny Butler Leigh to FAK, 1 May 1881. Wister Family Papers, Historical Society of Pennsylvania.

180 "Altho her father": Wainwright, *A Philadelphia Perspective,* p. 458.

180 His sex and his name change: John Butler, like his grandfather before him, only named as his heirs male descendants willing to assume and carry on the Butler family name. Daughters and granddaughters were passed over in favor of male heirs.

181 "The marshes, or savannahs": Bell, *Major Butler's Legacy,* p. 361.

181 "encourage the escape": ibid.

181 "Select, if you can do so": ibid.

182 "my supplies": ibid., p. 363.

182 "I started from St. Simon's": ibid., p. 364.

183 "Today I rode over": ibid., p. 368.

184 "It seems to me": ibid.

185 "Generous and kind attention": Presley, *Dr. Bullie's Notes,* p. 126.

186 "He said": Wainwright, *A Philadelphia Perspective,* p. 430.

187 "charming . . . gay, graceful": ibid., p. 470.

187 "in great satisfaction": FAK to Harriet St. Leger, 186?. Kemble Collection, Folger Shakespeare Library.

187 "What I provide for Fan": FAK to Harriet St. Leger, 186?. Kemble Collection, Folger Shakespeare Library.

187 "all the heroic courage": FAK to Harriet St. Leger, 186?. Kemble Collection, Folger Shakespeare Library.

188 "I with joy": Furnas, *Fanny Kemble,* p. 406.

188 Only the intervention: Wainwright, *A Philadelphia Perspective,* p. 497.

188 "In countless thousands": FAK, *Records of Later Life,* p. 160.

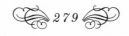

CHAPTER EIGHT Lost Causes

192   "the negroes would be removed": Frances Butler Leigh, *Ten Years,* p. 14.

192   "an unfortunate propensity": Wainwright, *A Philadelphia Perspective,* p. 507.

193   "to look after our property": Frances Butler Leigh, *Ten Years,* p. 14.

193   "The hotel": ibid., p. 7.

193   "I was glad to leave": ibid., p. 6.

193   "Street after street": ibid., p. 9.

193   "It was piteous": ibid., pp. 12–13.

194   "they received him": ibid., p. 14.

194   "I have relapsed into barbarism": ibid., pp. 16, 20.

194   "On the acre of ground": ibid., p. 20.

194   "The negroes seem": ibid., p. 21.

195   "Half a day's work": ibid., p. 26.

195   "To show what perfect confidence": ibid., pp. 36–37.

195   "often had to cook": ibid., p. 39.

196   "Three times have I settled": ibid., p. 40.

196   "I was rather nervous": ibid., p. 41.

197   "might, by a little judicious": ibid., p. 42.

197   "with no doctor": ibid., p. 41.

197   "he is obliged": Wainwright, *A Philadelphia Perspective,* p. 524.

197   "rather fanciful words of rebuke": FAK to Harriet St. Leger, 1866. Kemble Collection, Folger Shakespeare Library.

197   "It is a great pleasure": Sarah Butler Wister to Owen Wister, 30 April 1867. Wister Family Collection, Historical Society of Pennsylvania.

197   The elderly former slaves: Bell, *Major Butler's Legacy,* p. 401.

198   "stands apart": Sarah Butler Wister to Owen Wister, 30 April 1867. Wister Family Collection, Historical Society of Pennsylvania.

198   "I was sad in Savannah": ibid.

198   "I am guilty": Owen Wister to Sarah Butler Wister, 25 July 1867. Wister Family Collection, Historical Society of Pennsylvania.

198   "For several nights": Owen Wister to Sarah Butler Wister, 15 August 1867. Wister Family Collection, Historical Society of Pennsylvania.

198   "looks much better": Sarah Butler Wister to Owen Wister, 30 April 1867. Wister Family Collection, Historical Society of Pennsylvania.

199   "news of political disturbances": Frances Butler Leigh, *Ten Years,* p. 65.

199   "If they would frankly say": ibid., p. 67.

200   "forced upon us": ibid., p. 69.

200   "a man of strongly": Wainwright, *A Philadelphia Perspective,* p. 531.

201   "Mrs. Kemble has returned": ibid.

201   "From the entrance soliloquy": Furnas, *Fanny Kemble,* pp. 333–34.

201   "I had seen the flame": ibid.

201   "I w'd gladly": Fanny Kemble Wister, *That I May Tell You,* p. 75.

202 "And now this woman": Wainwright, *A Philadelphia Perspective,* p. 534.

202 "Before anything else": Frances Butler Leigh, *Ten Years,* p. 74.

203 "small shopkeepers": ibid., p. 79.

203 "a Northern man": ibid., p. 81.

203 "My agents were": ibid., p. 84.

203 "I thought sixty-two": ibid., p. 89.

204 "I had school": ibid., p. 95.

205 "the old plantation midwife": ibid., pp. 91–92.

205 "I never did succeed": ibid., p. 92.

205 her workers "much preferred": ibid., p. 96.

205 "the serpent had not": ibid., p. 64.

206 Meade replied: ibid., p. 104.

206 "You seem to think": ibid., pp. 106–107.

206 "agents belonging": ibid., p. 111.

206 "the people were working": ibid., p. 139.

208 "Everything is in confusion": Duncan, *Freedom's Shore,* p. 20.

209 he was appointed: ibid., p. 44.

210 "He . . . very soon became": Frances Butler Leigh, *Ten Years,* p. 134.

210 "If you will send": ibid., p. 105.

211 "He had no difficulty": ibid., p. 134.

211 "If we bought him": ibid., p. 136.

211 "It's of no use": ibid., p. 137.

211 "This gave the deathblow": ibid., p. 151.

211 "have a gang": ibid., pp. 127–28.

212 "One or two": ibid., p. 132.

212 "The negroes this year": ibid.

213 "girls well-educated": ibid., p. 119.

213 "There was an amusing": ibid., p. 142.

213 "weary and disgusted": ibid., pp. 147–48.

213 "I am sorry that Fanny": Sarah Butler Wister to Owen Wister, 28 November 1867. Wister Family Collection, Historical Society of Pennsylvania.

213 "Such a determination": FAK to Sarah Perkins Cleveland, Philadelphia, 1868. Cleveland Letters, Berg Collection, New York Public Library.

214 "The land offers": FAK, *Journal of a Residence on a Georgian Plantation,* pp. 332–33.

214 "I have no hope": FAK, *Further Records,* pp. 349–50.

215 "From the first": Frances Butler Leigh, *Ten Years,* pp. 124–25.

215 "they [blacks] must be kept": ibid., p. 125.

215 "I confess": ibid., p. 147.

215 "rais[ing] a little corn": ibid., pp. 124–25.

216 "I found some negroes": Bell, *Major Butler's Legacy,* p. 413.

216 "excite their ambition": Frances Butler Leigh, *Ten Years,* pp. 177–78.

217 "The negroes are behaving": ibid., p. 193.

217 "He has admirable": Marshall, *Fanny Kemble*, p. 249.

218 "Intellectual and theoretic": J. W. Leigh, *Other Days*, p. 9.

218 "J.L. is an excellent": Edel, *Henry James Letters*, vol. II, p. 148.

218 "neuralgia & nervous weakness": Wainwright, *A Philadelphia Perspective*, p. 552.

219 "'the lane that had": Fanny Kemble Wister, *That I May Tell You*, p. 179.

219 "apathy changed to delight": Bell, *Major Butler's Legacy*, p. 430.

219 "It seemed as if": Fanny Kemble Wister, *That I May Tell You*, p. 86.

219 In 1895, *Scribner's* published: Greenberg, *Civil War Women II*, preface.

220 "I went": Edel, *Henry James Letters*, vol. I, pp. 317–18.

221 "Me voilà already intimate": ibid., p. 318.

221 "A beautiful woman": ibid.

221 "I am writing a novel": ibid., p. 460.

221 "it has at least": ibid., p. 461.

222 "if we [the Leighs] went": J. W. Leigh, *Other Days*, p. 126.

222 Leigh hoped: ibid., p. 137.

223 "Our castle was": ibid., p. 128.

223 His wife proudly reported: Frances Butler Leigh, *Ten Years*, p. 211.

223 With funds solicited: Bell, *Major Butler's Legacy*, p. 418.

223 "the inhabitants consisted": J. W. Leigh, *Other Days*, p. 148.

223 "'The Freeman's Bureau'": ibid., p. 186.

224 "king of the darkies": Bell, *Major Butler's Legacy*, p. 418.

225 "I looked at S[arah]": FAK, *Further Records*, p. 35.

225 "I am better satisfied": FAK to Harriet St. Leger, York Farm, 6 March 187?. Kemble Collection, Folger Shakespeare Library.

226 "the thing that I suffer from most": Marshall, *Fanny Kemble*, p. 251.

226 "My enduring this climate": ibid., p. 250.

227 "The little L[eigh] baby": FAK, *Further Records*, p. 356.

227 "He leaves us next week": Bobbe, *Fanny Kemble*, p. 305.

228 "I go on scribbling": ibid., p. 286.

228 "Mr. James does not go": FAK to Harriet St. Leger, York Farm, 6 March 187?. Kemble Collection, Folger Shakespeare Library.

229 "there must be": FAK, *Further Records*, p. 17.

230 "The old man": Bell, *Major Butler's Legacy*, p. 419.

230 "were beaten": Duncan, *Freedom's Shore*, p. 108.

230 "We think it very doubtful": ibid., p. 109.

CHAPTER NINE Peace and Remembrance

233 "[her] fine memory": James, *Essays in London*, p. 82.

233 "When I first came here": Marshall, *Fanny Kemble*, p. 242.

234 "as long as my life": Bobbe, *Fanny Kemble*, p. 315.

234 "very vigorous": FAK, *Further Records,* p. 342.

235 "politicians, doctors, merchants": Brown, *The Year of the Century,* p. 112.

235 "I have no doubt": FAK, *Records of Later Life,* p. 472.

236 "I think that the women": ibid.

236 "I suppose my own": FAK, *Further Records,* p. 190.

237 "enchanted with it": ibid., p. 204.

237 She was most stirred: ibid., p. 181.

237 "It is in these things": Brown, *The Year of the Century,* p. 130.

238 "mighty limbs and sinews": J. W. Leigh, *Other Days,* p. 175.

238 "An American can only see": Brown, *The Year of the Century,* p. 116.

238 Some industrialists sponsored: Schlereth, *Victorian America,* p. 2.

238 "she had not *clean hands*": FAK, *Further Records,* p. 190.

238 "How cordial": FAK to ?, Sunday, 15, n.a., Kemble Collection, Huntington Library.

240 "a perfect stone": FAK, *Further Records,* p. 199.

241 "as if a thousand chandeliers": ibid., p. 211.

241 "thankful that my last hours": ibid., p. 215.

243 "The picturesque old house": Edel, *Henry James Letters,* vol. II, p. 147.

245 "the Irish call": FAK to Sarah Perkins Cleveland, Queen Anne's Manor, London, Friday 28 (February) 1879. Cleveland Letters, Berg Collection, New York Public Library.

245 "She is certainly": Edel, *Henry James Letters,* vol. II, p. 212.

246 "Her book": ibid., p. 225.

246 "These two ladies": ibid., p. 231.

246 "One might have": ibid., p. 233.

246 "as sweet and amiable": ibid.

247 "You mustn't judge": ibid., p. 212.

247 "I have a sort of notion": ibid., p. 241.

247 "[Fan's] condition": FAK to Sarah Perkins Cleveland, Queen Anne's Manor, 16 September 1879. Cleveland Letters, Berg Collection, New York Public Library.

248 "I cannot be present": FAK to Sarah Perkins Cleveland, 23 December 1879. Cleveland Letters, Berg Collection, New York Public Library.

248 "For over a year": Sarah Butler Wister to Fanny Butler Leigh, 17 December 1880. Wister Family Collection, Historical Society of Pennsylvania.

249 "There is no record": FAK to Richard Bentley, London, 1 March 1881. Kemble Collection, University of Illinois (Urbana).

250 "My dearest Mother": Fanny Butler Leigh to FAK, 1 May 1881. Wister Family Collection, Historical Society of Pennsylvania.

250 "My dear Fanny": FAK (response to letter of 1 May 1881), Box 1, Folder 8, Wister Family Collection, Historical Society of Pennsylvania.

251 "If she repeats": Bell, *Major Butler's Legacy,* p. 398.

251 "only such portions": Marshall, *Fanny Kemble,* p. 263.

251 "I do not wish": FAK to Richard Bentley, London, 5 February 1879. Kemble Collection, University of Illinois (Urbana).

251 "coming through the Press": Marshall, *Fanny Kemble,* p. 263.

252 "I am afraid": Edel, *Henry James Letters,* vol. II, pp. 343–44.

253 "The incongruity": Edel, *Henry James Letters,* vol. III, p. 21.

253 "it was not written": FAK to Richard Bentley, 4 January 1882. Kemble Collection, University of Illinois (Urbana).

254 "The steps of the church": Frances Butler Leigh, *Ten Years,* p. 47.

254 "The question whether slavery": ibid., pp. 230–37.

255 A later critic: Armstrong, *Fanny Kemble,* p. 354.

256 "If one will persist": FAK to Harriet St. Leger, n.d., n.a. Kemble Collection, Folger Shakespeare Library.

256 "Mrs. Kemble is wonderfully": Edel, *Henry James Letters,* vol. III, p. 106.

256 "she was in a very quiet": ibid., p. 171.

256 "extinct volcano": ibid., p. 197.

257 "pray believe once": FAK to Richard Bentley, 15 October 1889. Kemble Collection, University of Illinois (Urbana).

257 "adding to them any thing": FAK to Richard Bentley, 28 March 1890. Kemble Collection, University of Illinois (Urbana).

258 "I found a change": Bell, *Major Butler's Legacy,* p. 447.

258 "afraid of using": FAK, *Further Records,* p. 24.

258 "To write one's first novel": Edel, *Henry James Letters,* vol. III, p. 213.

259 "it is rather a melancholy": ibid., p. 197.

259 "She always talks as if": Edel, *Henry James Letters,* vol. II, p. 311.

260 "spared the useless pain": FAK to Harriet St. Leger, n.d., n.a. Kemble Collection, Folger Shakespeare Library.

260 "My dear mistress": Ellen Brianzoni to Fanny Cobbe, 19 January 1893. Kemble Collection, Folger Shakespeare Library.

260 "I stood by your mother's grave": Edel, *Henry James Letters,* vol. III, pp. 399–400.

261 "Her endowment was so rich": James, *Essays in London and Elsewhere,* pp. 102–103.

261 "reanimated the old": ibid., p. 114.

261 "still one of the": ibid., p. 89.

261 "I sit *alone*": Edel, *Henry James Letters,* vol. IV, p. 258.

Epilogue

266 "The plantation people": Margaret Davis Cate to John Anthony Scott, 2 April 1960. Cate Collection, Georgia Historical Society.

266 In support of her statement: Margaret Davis Cate, "Mistakes in Fanny Kemble's Georgia Journal," *Georgia Historical Quarterly,* vol. 44 (1960).

267   "one of Fanny's 'acts'": Margaret Davis Cate to Dr. Black, 13 December 1960. Cate Collection, Georgia Historical Society.

268   Kemble confessed: Rebecca Wylly to Caroline ?, 28 August 1912. Cate Collection, Georgia Historical Society. See also Mary Ellen Hare to Margaret Davis Cate, n.d., n.a. Cate Collection, Georgia Historical Society.

268   "bitterly regretted": J. T. Dent, n.d., n.a., "copied 4 February 1960 by Margaret Davis Cate, 'exactly as written.'" Cate Collection, Georgia Historical Society.

BIBLIOGRAPHY

Certainly one of the best ways to enjoy learning more about Fanny Kemble is to read her own writing—memoirs, poems, plays, essays . . . A list of her major publications (in chronological order) will follow. Only a few of her books are still in print.

I am partial to my own *Fanny Kemble's Journals,* selections from her eleven volumes of autobiographical writings, as a starting point. John Anthony Scott's edition of *Journal of a Residence on a Georgian Plantation* remains an excellent source book. Further, Dana Nelson's *Principles and Privilege: Two Women's Lives on a Georgia Plantation* (Ann Arbor: University of Michigan Press, 1995) is an intriguing volume, with Fanny's and her daughter's portraits of Georgia presented in tandem. I would caution readers to avoid Monica Gough's *Journal of a Young Actress* (New York: Columbia University Press, 1990).

I am greatly indebted to J. C. Furnas, whose theatrical biography of Kemble is an indispensable guide to her acting career, and to Malcolm Bell's magnificent volume covering five generations of the Butler family.

Quite useful primary records and papers are to be found at the Lenox (Mass.) Library Association; the Library of Congress; the Folger Shakespeare Library (Washington, D.C.), Houghton Library (Harvard University), and the Theatre Collection at Harvard University; the Historical Society of Pennsylvania (Philadelphia); the Massachusetts Historical Society; the Berg Collection at the New York Public Library; and the Georgia Historical Society (Savannah). All have extensive holdings pertaining to Kemble. Of limited usefulness are collections at the Huntington Library (Pasadena, California), the University of Illinois (Urbana), and the Coastal Historical Society at St. Simon's Island—but this last repository is certainly one of the loveliest spots I've ever worked in, and I would recommend it to anyone who wants to understand Fanny Kemble's sojourn in the Sea Islands.

The bibliography that follows mainly supplies titles referred to in the notes, as

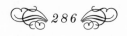

well as some additional titles to place Kemble within her transatlantic world. Abbreviated titles (in parentheses) are those used in the notes.

Fanny Kemble's Publications
(In Chronological Order)

Francis the First, An Historical Drama. London: John Murray, 1832.

Francis the First, A Tragedy in Five Acts. New York: Peabody & Co., 1832.

Journal of Frances Anne Kemble (*Journal of FAK*; 2 vols.). Philadelphia: Carey, Lea & Blanchard, 1835.

Journal of Residence in America (2 vols.). London: John Murray, 1835.

The Star of Seville. London: Saunders & Otley, 1835; New York: Saunders & Otley, 1837.

Poems. Philadelphia: John Pennington, 1844; London: H. Washbourne, 1844.

A Year of Consolation (2 vols.). London: Edward Moxon, 1847; New York: Wiley & Putnam, 1847.

The Christmas Tree and Other Tales. London: John W. Parker & Son, 1856.

Poems. Boston: Ticknor & Fields, 1859.

Plays. London: Longman, Green, Longman, Roberts & Green, 1863.

Journal of a Residence on a Georgian Plantation. London: Longman, Green, Longman, Roberts & Green, 1863; New York: Harper & Bros., 1863.

Records of a Girlhood (3 vols.). London: Richard Bentley & Son, 1878; New York: Henry Holt & Co., 1879.

Records of Later Life. London: Richard Bentley & Son, 1881; New York: Henry Holt & Co., 1882.

Notes on Some of Shakespeare's Plays. London: Richard Bentley & Son, 1882.

Poems. London: Richard Bentley & Son, 1883.

Far Away and Long Ago. London: Richard Bentley & Son, 1889; New York: Henry Holt & Co., 1889.

The Adventures of Mr. John Timothy Homespun in Switzerland. London: Richard Bentley & Son, 1889.

Further Records (2 vols.). London: Richard Bentley, 1890; New York: Henry Holt & Co., 1891.

Additional Sources

Alderman, Ralph, ed. *Letters of James K. Paulding*. Madison: University of Wisconsin, 1962.

Armstrong, Margaret. *Fanny Kemble: A Passionate Victorian*. New York: Macmillan, 1930.

———. *Trelawny*. New York: Macmillan, 1940.

Baker, Herschel. *John Philip Kemble: The Actor in His Theater*. Cambridge, Mass.: Harvard University Press.

Bell, Malcolm, Jr. *Major Butler's Legacy: Five Generations of a Slaveholding Family*. Athens, Ga.: University of Georgia Press, 1987.

Bobbe, Dorothie. *Fanny Kemble*. New York: Minton, Balch & Co., 1931.

Bridgeman, Thomas. *The American Gardener's Assistant*. Philadelphia: Porter & Coates, 1866.

Brown, Dee. *The Year of the Century: 1876*. New York: Scribners, 1966.

Bryan, Clark W. *The Book of Berkshire*. 1886; reprint ed., North Egremont, Mass.: Past Perfect Books, 1993.

Buckingham, J. S. *Slave States of America*. London: Fisher, Son & Co., 1842. 2 vols.

Butler, Pierce. *Mr. Butler's Statement*. Philadelphia: J. C. Clark, 1851.

Clinton, Catherine. *Civil War Stories*. Athens, Ga.: University of Georgia Press, 1998.

———. *Fanny Kemble's Journals*. Cambridge, Mass.: Harvard University Press, 2000.

———. *Tara Revisited: Women, War and the Plantation Legend*. New York: Abbeville Press, 1995.

Cobb, John L. *Owen Wister*. Boston: Twayne Publishers, 1984.

Driver, Leota S. *Fanny Kemble*. Chapel Hill: University of North Carolina Press, 1933.

Dudden, Faye. *Women in the American Theater*. New Haven: Yale University Press, 1994.

Duncan, Russell. *Freedom's Shore: Tunis Campbell and the Georgia Freedman*. Athens: University of Georgia Press, 1986.

Dusinberre, William. *Them Dark Days: Slavery in the American Rice Swamps*. New York: Oxford University Press, 1996.

Edel, Leon, ed. *Henry James Letters*. 4 vols. Cambridge, Mass.: Harvard University Press, 1974, 1975, 1980, 1984.

Esher, Viscount, ed. *Girlhood of Queen Victoria: A Selection From Her Majesty's Diaries Between the Years 1832 and 1840*. New York: Longmans, Green & Co., 1912.

Furnas, J. C. *Fanny Kemble: Leading Lady of the Nineteenth Century*. New York: Dial Press, 1982.

Gibbs, Henry, ed. *Affectionately Yours, Fanny: Fanny Kemble and the Theatre*. London: Jarrolds, 1947.

Gilman, Caroline. *Recollections of a Southern Matron*. New York: G. P. Putnam's, 1852.

Greenberg, Martin, Charles Waugh, and Frank D. McSherry, eds. *Civil War Women II*. Little Rock, Ark.: August House, 1997.

Grossberg, Michael. *Governing the Hearth: Law and Family in Nineteenth Century America*. Chapel Hill: University of North Carolina Press, 1985.

James, Henry. *Essays in London and Elsewhere*. New York: Harper & Brothers, 1893.

Kelly, Linda. *The Kemble Era: John Philip Kemble, Sarah Siddons and the London Stage*. New York: Random House, 1980.

Leigh, Frances Butler. *Ten Years on a Georgia Plantation Since the War*. London: Richard Bentley & Son, 1883.

Leigh, J. W. *Other Days*. London: T. Fisher Unwin, Ltd., 1921.

Marshall, Dorothy. *Fanny Kemble*. London: Weidenfeld & Nicolson, 1977.

McPherson, James. *Civil War and Reconstruction*. New York: Knopf, 1982.

Mellow, James R. *Nathaniel Hawthorne in His Times*. Boston: Houghton Mifflin, 1980.

Nevins, Allan, ed. *The Diary of Philip Hone*. New York: Dodd, Mead & Co., 1936.

Pickett, LaSalle Courbell *Across My Path*. New York: Brentano's, 1916.

Pollock, Sir Frederick. *Macready's Reminiscences & Selections from His Diaries and Letters*. New York: Harper & Brothers, 1875.

Presley, Delma E., ed. *Dr. Bullie's Notes: Reminiscences of Early Georgia and of Philadelphia and New Haven in the 1800s*. Atlanta: Cherokee Publishing Co., 1976.

Ransome, Eleanor, ed. *The Terrific Kemble: A Victorian Self-Portrait from the Writings of Fanny Kemble*. London: Hamish Hamilton, 1978.

Rushmore, Robert. *Fanny Kemble*. New York: Crowell-Collier Press, 1970.

Schlereth, Thomas J. *Victorian America: Transformations in Everyday Life, 1876–1915*. New York: HarperCollins, 1991.

Schott, James, Jr. *Statement by James Schott, Jr.: July 29, 1844*. Philadelphia, privately published, 1844.

Scott, John Anthony, ed. *Journal of Residence on a Georgian Plantation in 1838–39*. New York: Alfred A. Knopf, 1961.

Stewart, James B. *Holy Warriors: The Abolitionists and American Slavery*. New York: Hill & Wang, 1996.

Story, William, ed. *Life and Letters of Joseph Story*. Boston: Charles C. Little, 1851.

Trewin, J. C., ed. *The Journal of William Charles Macready*. London: Longmans, Green & Co., 1967.

Wainwright, Nicholas B., ed. *A Philadelphia Perspective: The Diary of Sidney George Fisher Covering the Years 1834–1871*. Philadelphia: Historical Society of Pennsylvania, 1967.

Weigley, Russell, ed. *Philadelphia: A 300 Year History*. New York: Norton, 1982.

Williamson, Jane. *Charles Kemble, Man of the Theatre*. Lincoln: University of Nebraska Press, 1964.

Wilson, Philip Whitwell, ed. *The Greville Diary*. New York: Doubleday, Page & Co., 1927.

Wister, Fanny Kemble. "Sarah Butler Wister's Civil War Diary," *Pennsylvania Magazine of History and Biography*, vol. 52 (July 1978).

BIBLIOGRAPHY

———. *That I May Tell You.* Wayne, Pa., 1979.

———, ed. *Fanny, the American Kemble: Her Journals and Unpublished Letters.* Tallahassee: South Press, 1972.

Wister, Jones. *Jones Wister's Reminiscences.* Philadelphia: Lippincott, 1920.

Wright, Constance. *Fanny Kemble and the Lovely Land.* New York: Dodd, Mead & Co., 1972.

ACKNOWLEDGMENTS

Having spent more than half my life puzzling over Fanny Kemble, I have incurred enormous debts that can never be repaid. I fear too many kindnesses and assistances will be inadvertently omitted from the following lists, and I apologize for my failings in this regard.

Most of all, I owe a debt to Kemble, who has proven a topic of endless and sustaining fascination. She has been a challenge and delight to explore. Shortly after the birth of her first child, she confessed in despair: "I do not think nature intended mothers to be authors of anything but their babies, because, as I told you, though a baby is not an 'occupation' it is an absolute hindrance to everything else that can be called so. I cannot read a book through quietly for mine; judge, therefore how little likely I am to write one." She went on to publish nearly a dozen books, and to produce another child as well.

Her appeal to generations of women has created a cottage industry for Kemble fans: the twentieth century has been filled with one-woman theatrical shows, such as *The Invincible Miss Kemble: A Monodrama in Three Acts* and, more recently, *The Emancipation of Fanny Kemble*. The Georgia writer Eugenia Price stocked her popular novels with Kemble and her contemporaries, and documentaries (*Africans in America: Judgment Day*) and commercial projects have followed.

I want to begin by thanking those who knew me when I first began my Kemble adventures. Your friendship over the years has been important to me: Robert H. Chapman; Zeph and Diana Stewart; and the gang from Sussex, including Douglas and Jill Tallack, Craig and Fran D'Ooge, Richard Crockatt, Anne Bacon, and the late Marcus Cunliffe.

Librarians and archivists have been extraordinarily generous; for their efforts on my behalf, I want to thank: Linda Stanley (formerly of the Historical Society of Pennsylvania); Dennis Lesieur of the Lenox (Mass.) Library Association; Frederic Woodbridge Wilson and the staff of the Harvard Theatre Collection; the Brandon

ACKNOWLEDGMENTS

Matthews Collection at Columbia University; Jo Wallace of the Victoria and Albert Picture Library, the Theater Museum Study Room (London); Leslie Morris of the Houghton Library of Harvard University; W. Todd Groce of the Georgia Historical Society; Bob Wyllie of the Coastal Georgia Historical Society; and the extraordinary staff of the Folger Shakespeare Library.

Again, it would be impossible to thank all those who have extended a hand during my many years of research and writing, but the following list is a partial account of those whose assistance was critical along the way. First and foremost is Aida Donald. Much help also came from Malcolm Bell, Jr., Jessie Betts, James Butler, Lisa Cody, Robert Forbes, Virginia Gould, Heather Hathaway, John Inscoe, Jane Levey, Phil and Frances Racine, Mason and Mary Robertson, Janet Schulte, Mr. and Mrs. John Stokes, Buddy Sullivan, Pilar Viladas, and Lauren Winner.

I wish to acknowledge the extremely supportive scholars who have been essential to my personal and professional learning, and to thank them for their consistent generosity and indulgences: Jean Baker, Carol Berkin, Carol Bleser, David Donald, Ellen Fitzpatrick, Jacquelyn Hall, Christine Heyrman, and Jacqueline Jones.

I would be remiss if I did not single out two historians in particular for their distinctive influence: Drew Gilpin Faust and James M. McPherson.

Eric Foner has been more than a role model. An important mentor and friend, for the past quarter-century he has made me want to continue this quixotic balancing act between writing and teaching, parenthood and scholarship; between the beguiling past and the relentless present.

I thank my terrific agent, Kris Dahl, for her input and invaluable insights.

From Eric Rayman, who first put me in touch with my editor; to Tara Parsons, who helped me sort out the illustrations; to Lydia Buechler and Jolanta Benal, copyeditors extraordinaire; to Victoria Meyer and Aileen Boyle, who have lent their special enthusiasm, I have been treated royally by Simon & Schuster.

But above all, my editor, Denise Roy, deserves special praise for her heroic role in bringing this manuscript to fruition. She brought so much to the project, including her penchant for perfectionism. Once she sent me material on Fanny Kemble that, in over twenty years of research, I had not yet encountered: an excerpt from a book entitled *Bright, Particular Star*. It struck me then and has struck me since that Denise was the bright, particular star whose light led the way on my journey to completing this book, a wonder for which I remain extraordinarily grateful.

I have dedicated this volume to Michele Gillespie, with profound gratitude. Kevin, Michael, and Matthew Pittard are important to me as well.

Counting my blessings, I must include my husband, Daniel Colbert, and my sons, Drew and Ned Colbert. They won't be sad to see Fanny go—a contentious, competing, and engulfing force in my life. I have taken advantage of their deep and abiding love, which buoys me ever onward even as it gently tugs me homeward.

Catherine Clinton
Riverside, Connecticut

INDEX

(Page numbers in *italic* refer to illustrations.)

INDEX

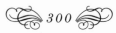